Architectures of Embodiment

M000290453

Architectures of Embodiment

Disclosing New Intelligibilities

Edited by Alex Arteaga

DIAPHANES

THINK ART Series of the Institute for Critical Theory (ith)—
Zurich University of the Arts and the Centre for Arts and
Cultural Theory (ZKK)—University of Zurich.

ISBN 978-3-0358-0199-6

Design: TheGreenEyl, Gunnar Green with Jens Rudolph
Printed in Germany

www.diaphanes.com

Introduction

Alex Arteaga

This book was originated within the research environment *Architecture of Embodiment,* which I started in November 2013.[1] I conceived of this research environment following the intuition that a methodic inquiry into architecture from an enactivist perspective could bring forth new insights in both fields—principally in architecture, but also in enactivism. My way to activate the enactive approach to cognition as a conceptual framework for researching architecture is based on my understanding of the material modification of surroundings through design-based construction as a condition in the process of the emergence of sense. Accordingly, when I initiated this research environment, I posed the question: how does architecture condition the emergence of sense?[2]

I thought that an efficient way of realizing this investigation would be through practices that enable immediate and unmediated relationships between researchers—acting as highly sensitive bodies due to the intensification of their perceptive and emotional skills through these practices—and the inquired architecturally conditioned environments. Aesthetic research practices, as systematized sets of aesthetic actions, can realize this variety of relationships. These practices increase researchers' receptive and connective capabilities. In doing so, they enable researchers to operate not only with their own agencies, but also in deep interaction with the agencies of the architectural surroundings to be inquired. Researching in the resulting field of *shared agencies*—that is, researching aesthetically—enables an intimate touch between the researchers and their main object of inquiry: the process of the emergence of sense.[3]

Aesthetic research practices and other practices of research that build on their results are systemically organized here as hybrid methods conceived specifically for and with each inquired issue. These sets of practices are structured as research cells.[4] This term designates units of inquiry designed to investigate particular topics within certain spatiotemporal frames and social contexts through specific methods realized by a determined set of researchers.

By inquiring into architecture in and through this research environment, my aim has been primarily not to formulate answers to the aforementioned research question and related ones but, firstly, to provide adequate conceptual, methodical, and communicative conditions for researching architecture in the framework of the enactive approach and through aesthetic practices. Furthermore, my intention is to destabilize each specific object of research as well as the concept of an architecture of embodiment in order to allow myself and other researchers to disclose new intelligibilities for the issues confronting us. In this sense, *Architecture of Embodiment* aims at fulfilling what I consider to be a fundamental cognitive function[5] of processes of research through aesthetic practices. My attempt to identify the specificities of aesthetic research as an autonomous variety of inquiry leads me to address the following question: What is the goal of aesthetic research practices? Or, more precisely: What do they intend to achieve in relation to the issues they inquire into? Aesthetic research offers an alternative to the production of knowledge—that is, the compilation of artifacts relating to the object of research by way of explanation, description or modeling. By destabilizing—both perceptually and conceptually—the researched objects and, on this basis, disclosing new intelligibilities—new potentialities for addressing the objects' phenomenal co-constitution—aesthetic research contributes to the general field of research, and beyond, as an unavoidable ultimate goal, to the transformation of society. Accordingly, I conceive of aesthetic research as a form of fundamental research capable of disrupting the stability of the inquired phenomena. It is a way to subvert sedimented phenomenal manifestations endowed with unquestioned meanings and forms. This destabilization is accomplished fundamentally through the generation and organization of conditions for new forms of sensuous interaction. Aesthetic research practices generate aesthetic apparatuses *dispositifs* that dispose the objects of research and the bodies that investigate them in ways able to disturb their habituated reciprocal relationships. These dispositions of the researched objects and the researching bodies lead to specific forms of mutual exposition that induce discontinuities in the stream of sense emerging out of their dynamic connection. Consequently, the phenomenal manifestation of the researched issues—and thus, unavoidably, of the researcher—enter a state of crisis, a liminal order of no-longer-and-not-yet. Inhabiting the uncertainty of these uninhabited, meaningless, diffuse presences, driven by the ineluctable power of intentionality—that is, of making sense and beyond, fixing meaning—unforeseen and unforeseeable possibilities of understanding can emerge: new intelligibilities of the inquired objects and of the inquiring bodies can be disclosed.

Aesthetic research processes end up at this point. Other research procedures realized through practices oriented towards the stabilization of new meanings—towards the closure of uncertainties—can begin there where aesthetic research ends. In order to enable this continuity between different forms of research, aesthetic research processes should include the kinds of apparatuses that I briefly described and should invite researchers operating with other research practices to participate in the processes of destabilization and disclosure that these apparatuses enable. This will allow researchers to continue their investigations autonomously, through their own practices, with their own methods, but on the fruitful soil of fertile uncertainties—of the disruption of the given.[6]

This was the function of the research cell with which I concluded the first phase of *Architecture of Embodiment.* This cell, entitled *Architecture of Embodiment: An Aesthetic Research Dispositive,* took place in October 2016 at the Aedes Network Campus Berlin. It included a lecture on some of the insights that emerged out of three years of research, an exhibition of some artifacts produced throughout this first phase and some new ones realized specifically for this apparatus, and a workshop with the authors of the present book.[7] I did not invite my colleagues to reflect upon my work but to think through and with it—to think by being exposed to it. I did not present the traces of my research in order to be their objects of inquiry. Instead, I disposed the artifacts resulting out of my aesthetic research practices in order to achieve media agency, i.e. to constitute a medium for systemic thinking—a research medium.

The idea of this book was born in this context. Towards the end of the workshop, we decided to continue our open-ended dialogue within the horizon of making a book together and so we met twice again: first at the Zurich University of the Arts and then at La Virreina Centre de la Imatge in Barcelona. We decided that the structure of the book should not only mirror our process of dialogue, but should be another moment of this conversational procedure. This is the reason why the book you are reading is a constellation of coexisting autonomous artifacts:[8] the texts of each author in dialogue with other authors expressed as comments and comments to the comments.[9] This book, thus, is another research cell of *Architecture of Embodiment*—a hybrid cell, a cell reshaping its membrane (to continue with the biological metaphor). A cell in which the contact between aesthetic research practices and other practices of inquiry takes place. A cell in which the destabilizing agency generated through aesthetic practice potentiates other authors' ongoing processes of inquiry, enabling them—us, collectively—to participate in the disclosure of new intelligibilities and—eventually, through other practices, in other research cells of an organically growing tissue—actualize them, that is, realize their potentialities as new and stable descriptions and/or explanations.

This was the process that enabled the complex singularity of *Architecture of Embodiment* to acquire the explicit plural form that gives this book its title: *Architectures of Embodiment.* The singular term "architecture" refers here to those material modifications of surroundings endowed with the agency of intervening in and thereby transforming the coupling between subjects and their environments—this is my succinct outline of an architecture of embodiment, that is, of architectural design processes capable of conditioning the emergence of sense. However, the pluralized word "architectures" refers here, in an extended sense, to conceptual rather than material constructions; more precisely, it refers to "structions." Mika Elo outlines the concept of "struction" coined by Jean-Luc Nancy with the following formulations: "non-coordinated and contingent simultaneity of forces, forms, pulsions, projects, elans, etc."; "[Struction] only puts into play the simple contiguity and its contingence. […] It is the pure and simple juxtaposition that doesn't make any sense."[10] Freely embedding Nancy's line of thought as presented by Elo in the enactivist framework, I would say that the coexistence of the texts that configure this book does not "make" sense—does not produce it, does not manufacture it according to a common "end" that might be fixed in advance, referring again to Elo's exposition. Instead, it puts at the disposal of the readers a field of contingent conditions for the emergence of open trajectories of sense through reading—another enabling, contingent, and necessary constraint. In this sense, this book is understood as a dialogic research dispositive: an invitation to participate in a common, diverse, and open-ended process of research in the framework of a growing ecology of research practices.[11]

This book is the result of the confluence of the excellent work of wonderful people. This is the moment to express my sincere gratitude. First of all, I would like to thank Ana García Varas, Dieter Mersch, Gerard Vilar, Jonathan Hale, Lidia Gasperoni, Mika Elo, and Susanne Hauser for their generous engagement and outstanding intellectual work throughout the process of realizing this book; additionally, I thank heartily Dieter Mersch and Gerard Vilar and their institutional frameworks for ensuring the financial viability of this endeavor; I would like to thank as well Gunnar Green for his patient observation of this process and his ability to find a graphic form for our dialogues and Jens Rudolph for making the design of this book tangible. I would like to express my gratitude to Dunya Bouchi and Hans-Jürgen Commerell (AEDES / ANCB) for trusting my research and providing the conditions for sharing it publicly. Finally, going back to the beginning, I would like to thank the Einstein Foundation Berlin for supporting the first phase of Architecture of Embodiment with an Einstein Junior Fellowship and the whole teams of Sound Studies (now Sound Studies and Sonic Arts), the Institute of History and Theory of Design, and the Berlin Career College—all of them part of the Berlin University of the Arts—for hosting and supporting my research.

1   www.architecture-embodiment.org [accessed Oct 28, 2020].

2   The term "sense" is understood here according to its enactivist meaning. Although there is not an explicit enactivist definition of this term, "sense" refers in this context to the way in which environments appear to the subjects that inhabit them due to the specific way in which this process of inhabiting—technically speaking: the structural coupling between bodies and surroundings—occurs. For a clarification of these processes see Evan Thompson, Mind in Life: Biology, Phenomenology and the Sciences of Mind (Cambridge, MA: Harvard University Press, 2007), especially part two: Life in Mind.

3   For an outline of my incipient concepts of aesthetic action, aesthetic practice, aesthetic cognition, and aesthetic research, see: Alex Arteaga, "Embodied and Situated Aesthetics: An enactive approach to a cognitive notion of aesthetics," Artnodes 20 (2017), http://doi.org/10.7238/a.v0i20.3155 [accessed Oct 28, 2020], and Alex Arteaga, "Aesthetic practices of very slow observation as phenomenological practices: steps to an ecology of cognitive practices," RUUKKU – Studies in Artistic Research 14 (2020), https://doi.org/10.22501/ruu.740194 [accessed Oct 28, 2020].

4   I coined the term "research cell" as one of the key operative ideas of the Architecture of Embodiment. I am happy to see that this concept has been fruitful in the field of artistic research. See, e.g. its use in the Research Pavilion #3: www.researchpavilion.fi/ [accessed Oct 28, 2020].

5   The term "cognition" here is not limited to designating the performance of rational skills. In contrast, it is used according to the extension of its meaning realized by Humberto Maturana and Francisco Varela, who equate the concept of cognition to the concept of life. Accordingly, the autopoietic and, furthermore, enactivist concepts of "sense" and "cognition" are intimately connected. See Humberto R. Maturana and Francisco J. Varela, Autopoiesis and Cognition: The Realization of the Living (Dordrecht and Boston: D. Reidel Publishing, 1980).

6   This expression shows once again the phenomenological orientation of my thinking. Accordingly, the processes of destabilization and disclosure that I briefly described can be properly understood as forms of aesthetic epoché and, maybe, reduction—or better, transduction. For my incipient ideas on an aesthetic phenomenology, see Alex Arteaga, "Aesthetic practices of very slow observation as phenomenological practices: steps to an ecology of cognitive practices," RUUKKU – Studies in Artistic Research 14 (2020), https://doi.org/10.22501/ruu.740194 [accessed Oct 28, 2020].

7   A documentation of this research cell, including the full text of the lecture, can be found here: https://www.architecture-embodiment.org/architecture-of-embodiment-an-aesthetic-research-dispositive [accessed Oct 28, 2020].

8   The autonomy of each text manifests not only in the free selection of the addressed issues and the practices of writing but also, formally, in the diverse use of sections and forms of citations.

9   In order to lighten the process, after the Barcelona meeting where each text was presented and discussed, I assigned two main commentators to each text, although every author was free to comment on all texts.

10 Mika Elo, "What calls for thinking?," RUUKKU (2014), https://www.researchcatalogue.net/view/59435/59436 [accessed Oct 28, 2020]. In reference to Jean-Luc Nancy, "De la Struction," in Dans quels mondes vivons-nous?, ed. Aurélien Barrau and Jean-Luc Nancy (Paris: Galilée, 2011), 79–104.

11 On the concept of ecology of (research) practices see: Mika Elo, Tero Heikkinen, Henk Slager, ed., Ecologies of Practices. Special Issue of RUUKKU – Studies in Artistic Research 14 (2020), http://ruukku-journal.fi/ [accessed Oct 28, 2020].

Agencies in Architecture: Intention and Improvised Action in the Building Process

Ana García Varas

1. INTENTION, PLAN AND CONSTRUCTION

Tim Ingold describes the construction of medieval cathedrals in his book *Making: Anthropology, Archaeology, Art and Architecture* as a process not subject to a prior design; in other words, as a process for which there were no (or at least, not necessarily) plans that clearly defined and controlled each of the steps to be taken during construction. Ingold contrasts this way of building with the modern notion of architectonic design which, he claims, is a mere transcription of an intellectual idea in the form of a drawing: the architect captures intentions and ideas in a design that describes all aspects of the construction process, making the result, the final building, nothing more than the crystallization of the original design concept. He cites Giorgio Vasari's 1568 statement that design "is nothing but a visual expression and clarification of that concept which one has in the intellect, and that which one imagines in the mind and builds up the idea."[1]

Against Vasari's approach to construction, Ingold insists that when it comes to medieval buildings, there were no prior plans and drawings as such. Thus, the work of architects and masons primarily revolved around problem-solving during the construction process. It was an eminently practical task, in which their skills and their experience, learnt in long periods of apprenticeship, were fundamental resources for action and did not conform to strict rules that prescribed every step. Given the diverging opinions among experts as to whether there were project drawings of these medieval cathedrals, Ingold has no problem in accepting that medieval builders drew. But he emphasizes that these drawings cannot "be understood as plans, in the strict sense of a full geometrical pre-specification of the intended work"[2] and, referencing the ideas of the architectural design theorist Lars Spuybroek, considers this drawing practice more *descriptive* than *prescriptive.* Thus, these working drawings would form part of the arsenal of tools with which masons confronted construction on the go, since their job was to "solve problems as they went along, through the manipulation of the instruments and materials at their disposal and drawing on a fund of 'tricks of the trade' picked up along the way."[3]

In their respective studies on the Gothic cathedral of Chartres, medievalist John James and sociologist of science David Turnbull both agree that medieval builders approached their work in such an *ad hoc* fashion. James contends that the rebuilding of Chartres between 1194 and 1230 after it was decimated by a fire happened under the direction of at least nine master masons in about thirty different campaigns; thus, it could not possibly have been executed under a single plan or design (the consequence is that the harmonic structure we see is actually the result of a patchwork of irregularly disposed architectural elements).[4] For his part, Turnbull compares the construction of the cathedral to the work of a modern large-scale research laboratory: in the laboratory, teams of researchers work more or less independently under the direction of a research leader, communicating with each other

and exchanging results and new ideas.[5] All of this creates a body of knowledge, but this is not the result of a master plan; rather, it is a composite of many imperfectly integrated parts that Turnbull understands as a "contingent assemblage," by which he means "the amalgam of places, bodies, voices, skills, practices, technical devices, theories, social strategies and collective work" that constitute "knowledge [A] spaces."[6]

Ingold's approach to modern design in his account of medieval building has been rightfully criticized as too simplistic and reductionist[7], since, as Jonathan Hale points out, his description of it as "the representation of a preconceived idea" and intention fails to do justice to the complexity of the creation process that takes place in design practices (a complexity that Ingold, on the other hand, does appear to acknowledge in later chapters of his book). Opposing this account, authors like Robin Evans or Marco Frascari have long emphasized the importance of drawing as a process of exploration, discovery, and the generation of ideas, considering it a key tool for architectonic thought and highlighting its cognitive power. They show how drawing can create new insights and, in that sense, constitute a productive form of thinking. These works present, therefore, a criticism of a simplistic model of the building process in which the architect's intention, captured and represented directly in a design, determines and controls the realization of a building. That is, they challenge a simplistic intentionalist approach to the complex action that building is, where the already defined intention of the architect would be first represented directly in a drawing and then copied or instantiated on a building.

Now, a parallel and complementary strategy for opposing an intentionalist approach to architecture as a closed plan—this view where the intention of the architect defines and ultimately controls all the action—and for developing an alternative perspective on building is to concentrate on construction processes where no prior plan is available or where plans or designs are not intended to cover or control the

[A]   AA Perhaps the term "knowledge," especially if we understand it as Dieter does in his text, cannot encompass all aspects listed in the preceding quotation.

     AGV I see the differentiation, but as mentioned, I am here following Turnbull's use of the term, who conceives it in a very broad way to include all these elements.

whole construction process. [B] In this chapter, I elaborate on these forms of construction in which the building, or at least part of it, takes place "on the go." My aim is to reduce the relevance of the architect's intention and to explore what happens in construction when the architect (at least partially) loses control over the action. This perspective necessarily emphasizes building as a *process,* making it possible to better understand and acknowledge the multitude of interactions that play a role in construction.[8] Moreover, this enables researchers to recognize the myriad forms of agency that might intervene and collaborate in this process.

The example of the Chartres cathedral shows that the construction of a complex building is possible without a previously defined and decided master plan that would control all stages of the construction, and highlights two important consequences: on the one hand, this process creates its own "knowledge space," [C] which is much more complex than what can be expressed in the action plan representing the entire configuration of the building. Following Turnbull, this knowledge space could be understood as an "assemblage" or as a laboratory of cognitive practices in the broadest sense: it is an epistemic context where the role of concrete tools, social practices, and exemplary technical devices is emphasized over comprehensive theories, representations and worldviews. On the other hand, an approach that analyses instances where the construction process was not entirely fixed in advance can bring to light the multiple forms of agency involved in the construction and their very diverse mechanisms for creation, collaboration and co-determination within the construction process.

The simple model of architecture in which someone develops an idea which, directly captured in a design, is realized in a building corresponds to a very specific view on the type of action involved in construction. It assumes that construction is an act in which the individual controls all elements of their output, whether in the form of material products (the built environment they create) or in the form

[B] AA This is of course a good approach, but it would be possible as well to define as object of research the architectural processes that strive for complete control over the design and construction process, in order to show how this control is hindered by other agencies which are immanent to these processes. This would probably be a fruitful approach to take in a second paper based on the findings of this one.

> AGV Yes, I agree. But there are two reasons why that second approach is, at least right now, less attractive to me: first, that has already been done several times, showing that complete control over construction processes is more an ideal than a common reality. Secondly, and more importantly, that strategy does not challenge the control or planned action model but only its strongest version: the full or complete control in planning over building. Showing then the limits of the model, it could still leave room for a slightly modified version where the intentionalist approach and planned action are the main elements that direct the process, but where also partial modifications and negotiations with other agents are considered in the course of action. What I am here interested in is observing alternative views to the intentionalist and planned action perspectives, to try to develop other conceptual tools, that are not fundamentally based on a plan, in order to understand how different agents collaborate and create together.

[C] AA Following on my earlier comment on this issue, I would suggest the concept of "domain of significance" coined by Maturana in the framework of his theory of autopoiesis, as a more extended and potentially inclusive concept. A domain of significance includes everything that becomes relevant or significant in the process of interaction between selves and their environments.

> AGV Although in this specific context I prefer the idea of "knowledge space" because it highlights its epistemic character, I think that could be a useful suggestion in order to connect this approach to others in this book, so thank you, Alex.

of the actions that take place during that process. This kind of view is presented in philosophical action theory in the form of planning-based approaches[9], that understand action as the definition and execution of plans, and is founded ultimately on a radically intentionalistic view of action. Here, intention is supposed to not only govern the course of construction and its results, but also the criteria for their evaluation: the value both of the process and of the products would be determined by how they correspond to the initial intention or plans. Thus, creativity or any form of truly generative agency would only be present in the definition of the intention at the beginning of the process. Beth Preston calls this position the "centralised control model," which, in her view, has been the core of theories of action since Aristotle.[10]

However, this approach misses much. Doing justice to the actual construction process demands accounting for the numerous forms of negotiation involved, the multitude of people involved, and the vast diversity of material elements that intervene in the process. Different forms of collaboration and co-determination are generated over the course of construction, while a multitude of agencies, constraints and possibilities shape the building process. Now, the question here is: if we don't have a plan that directs action, how does that action take place? What form does an unplanned process take? And, in particular, how can unplanned collective action, one that is carried out in collaboration with others but which does not follow an imposed or agreed plan, take place? My proposal is to draw upon a model developed within artistic practices, [D] where those who intervene coordinate and intertwine their inputs without resorting to a pre-established plan: improvisation.

The model of improvisation firstly allows us to understand creativity in action as being distributed throughout the whole process of construction, without restricting it to a unique and prior moment—the determination of the plan. Viewing construction from the perspective of improvisation makes it possible to genuinely attribute creativity to

[D] | ^{AA} I would suggest using here the term "aesthetic practices" instead of "artistic practice." Especially regarding the process of architectural design and construction, it is evident that a lot of different practices related to a specific use of the senses that I would consider as "aesthetic" (see my comments on Gerard's text), but that do not fit under the category of "artistic" are constitutively involved.

> ^{AGV} Regarding architectural practices, I completely agree. Here I was actually referring to the tradition of contexts where improvisational strategies have been explicitly developed and encouraged in the past, as in the case of artistic musical or plastic practices. But since improvisation, as shown below, is much wider than its presence in art, I can gladly accept the suggestion.

actions throughout the development of the construction. Secondly, completely planned organization imposes a hierarchical structure of action in terms of control, because fundamental decisions are made in the planning phase by a select few before any action takes place. In contrast, an approach from the perspective of improvisation makes a horizontal structure possible, where at least certain parts of the construction are determined during the process by the different agents that intervene in the action. In this sense, and crucially, the perspective of improvisation likewise facilitates a distribution of the forms of agency in construction, focusing not only on the creator of the plan, but extending the attention to all those agents that intervene in the action. In this way, the different forms of agency in the action of construction can, in the context of improvisation, both be acknowledged and be the object of a closer analysis within action theory.

In the following pages, I will first address different forms of agency involved in building along with some of their most relevant analysis in recent theory. Secondly, I will focus on the relationship between improvisation and built space: here, I will first introduce the main aspects of improvised action that are relevant for an analysis of building activity and then I will outline a series of construction actions that can be more specifically and precisely understood with the aid of different improvising strategies.

2. AGENCIES AND ARCHITECTURE

Agency has been a recurring topic in architecture research over the last decade, producing a series of theoretical positions developed and debated in conferences, journals and edited volumes. In 2009 alone at least four major architecture journal issues were dedicated to the discussion of agency: *Agency in Architecture, Footprint* (4); *Agency and the Praxis of Activism, Field Journal* 3 (1); *Architectural Research Quarterly* 13 (2); and *Perspecta: Agency* 45.[11] A main point of reference in this debate was the *Agency* conference, organized in 2008 by

the research group "The Agency" of the University of Sheffield as the fifth AHRA (Architectural Humanities Research Association) congress. The same research group also went on to publish the collective work *Agency: Working with Uncertain Architectures*[12] in 2010 and, in 2011, Jeremy Till, Tatjana Schneider and Nishat Awan edited *Spatial Agency: Other Ways of Doing Architecture.*[13] Since then, they have developed an online resource under the same name where they reflect on the research in this field and give voice to the numerous construction processes carried out in accordance with these ideas about agency: www.spatialagency.net.

However, the meanings attributed to the concept of agency in the debate are diverse: Schneider and Till, for example, think that the idea of agency in architecture can make reference to conservative points such as the architect acting "on behalf of" a constructor, a client, a developer, etc.[14] Both they and Ana Paula Baltazar and Silke Kapp directly reject using this concept of agency to analyze architecture insofar as it "implies agents totally determined by 'others,' and thus politically annulled."[15] In other words, opposing a heteronomous determination of an action, the emphasis on the idea of agency intends, on the contrary, to open building action to the participation of a much higher number of actors, with a special focus on their political and social roles. Their goal is, therefore, to effect a kind of social change, stressing that the architect is nothing more than one among many, and emphasizing the participation of those who are not taken into account in the simple vision of an architect as being "someone who has ideas, acts as an author of those ideas, and runs projects to deliver those ideas."[16]

In this way, the discourse about agency in architecture aims to, on the one hand, highlight the complexity of the multitude of actions that converge in construction beyond the architect's ideas: from the demands of the client to budgeting, from legal and city planning constraints to the different interventions of communities of neighbors, preservationists, representatives of the government and city

authorities.[17] And here not only a large number of people with different interests and objectives intervene, but also a significant array of
norms, standards and regulations—as recently highlighted by Faulconbridge,[18] Imrie and Street[19] and Kraftl[20]—and decisive material
conditions, as indicated by the authors inspired by actor network theory. But on the other hand, a large number of agency theories have a
clear activist focus, expressly acknowledged in many of these works,
that seeks to cultivate construction practices in which users, or those
with less initial control and influence in the process, are empowered
and their own forms of agency receive more attention in the development of collective action.

In both cases, the emphasis on the notions of agency and co-determination of construction reject the idea that construction is based
solely on the architect's *intentions,* in which the architect, as *author,*
had all the authority and *control* over the process and over those that
participate in it through a hierarchical structure. In line with this position, Colin Lorne asks himself whether the cultural idea of the professional architect isn't shaped by an ideology of control in which a group,
whose shared identity is defined through educational training, "seeks
to fix and defend its claims to a territory of knowledge production" in a
capitalist economy.[21] Control, hierarchy and authority are key aspects
of the professionalist take on building that, while guarding privileged
societal status, establishes a specific "normative expert knowledge
base." Jeremy Till expands on this assessment and considers that the
insistence on the architect's forms of control and the subsequent rejection of contingency in construction must be understood as part of
the imposition of order in modernity; an imposition that is based on
a process of social control. He quotes the work of Zygmunt Bauman
to show how order is a basic element for understanding the development of modern culture, and within this, architecture as it is understood today: "Orderly space is rule-governed space" and "the rule is
a rule in as far as it forbids and excludes."[22] Accordingly, "it becomes

clear that this rejection of contingency is not a trait of architecture alone, but of modernity as a whole."[23] Consequently, indeterminacy is generally perceived as a risk or a weakness in a project that should be controlled by the architect.[24] And this idea of the architect, or rather, this mythology of the architect has manifested itself over decades in a privileged manner in the notion of the hero-author, which defines the work of starchitects such as Rem Koolhaas, Zaha Hadid, and Norman Foster.[25]

Opposing this myth of control, which does not describe real architecture but a fictional account of it,[26] agency theories intend to offer a more accurate picture of what actually takes place in construction processes. At the same time, they explore and open new channels of participation and collaboration in those processes. They seek to highlight the contributions of a larger number of agents while making the architect into "an anti-hero, someone who co-authors from the beginning, someone who actively and knowingly gives up authority."[27] Clearly, some of these concerns are not new,[28] but it is evident that for many of these authors, they have become central again since the 2008 economic crisis,[29] which provided an occasion for rethinking how construction takes place. From a political standpoint, therefore, they examine the forms of participation, negotiation, and collaborative transformation of the many actors involved in the construction of buildings and the ways in which unexpected inhabitations can reconfigure or subvert intended uses or functions.

In order to address these forms of action, the researchers of the Agency group at the University of Sheffield present three main different models for understanding agency, in which the contributors to their book organize their own proposals:[30] intervene, sustain, and mediate, all of which are defined from an activist perspective. "Intervention" has "a political and ethical meaning" and takes place through negotiation and deliberation to "bring about the empowerment of those involved."[31] However, the focus here is not necessarily on the interventions of all

users, but rather on the forms of agency of architects that question what they can do in order to empower others. "Sustaining" refers to ethically responsible engagement with the environment and, again, although it opens up the idea of collective responsibilities for sustainability, it focuses mostly on the actions and forms of agency of architects and their responses to current environmental challenges. Finally, "mediation" points to a kind of action that facilitates the development and formation of different agencies. This idea of mediation has an important connection with Jeremy Till's conception of the architect as a citizen *sense-maker,* where the goal of architectural action is not to gather all opinions and offer solutions to gain consensus, but rather to open up and negotiate *design processes* informed and transformed by the future desires of inhabitants: "Where problem-solving, predicated as it is on positivist thinking, tends to either abstract or exclude the social and the political, sense-making inevitably engages with them and, in so doing, accords with a model of architectural agency in which social and political issues are brought to the fore and then negotiated through spatial discussions."[32] [E]

However, Till mainly focuses on the design process: "In order to gain the full force of making sense, one has to address the complete range of conditions with which design, as the application of architectural intelligence, might be involved."[33] Till follows many contributions both in the book edited by The Agency and many agency theories in thinking about the collaboration and participation of a broader community on the planning side of the construction. In a good part of the projects that he refers to as examples of a perspective open to new kinds of agencies, the intervention and participation of different actors is addressed and opened only within the development of the construction plan: sometimes the possible users themselves begin the process and seek the collaboration of an architect to shape the idea into a working plan, while on other occasions, it is architects who seek the participation of potential users. But in both cases, the input of the new actors is

[E]   ᴬᴬ The shift from "problem-solving" to "sense-making" for understanding architectural processes and, more concretely, the role of the architect, mirrors exactly the shift expressed in the same terms undertaken in the framework of the enactive approach to cognition in order to define "intelligence"—and consequently the agents able to bring it about (interestingly the term "intelligence" appears in the next quote). A possible way to link both new defined terms (architecture and intelligence) could be to conceive of architecture—as I do—as a field of practice that thinks the environment (in the terms expressed in Lidia's text) or, more specifically, the relationships between selves and their environments.

undertaken within the planning process and very frequently limited to that, with the construction being developed thereafter in the traditional manner following the instructions and indications in the plan. In this sense, Tomohiro Sugeta writes that "in the current debates, there is a tendency to see users mainly as potential actors who may take some roles in projects driven by the architect" and "their emphasis is often on a participatory idea of users in design."[34] Where this is the case, therefore, the risk is to simply exchange an individual form of planning (in which only the architect plans the entire process) for a broader group and community planning, but in which the construction action would have the same structure and would continue to be shaped by the same ideas of intention and control defined by a plan. [F]

On the other hand, as identified above in the descriptions of the three models of agency proposed in *Agency: Working with Uncertain Architectures,* the emphasis continues to be on the forms of action of the architect, even if the models inquire into how they can foster the participation of other agencies, but distinctly concentrating on their own role in this move. The models of intervention and sustainability both seek ways in which the architect can concede authority and make possible the empowerment of others and how they can better engage with the environment responsibly. The model of mediation, too, once again takes the perspective of the architect, since they are the key mediator between the different forms of agency present, and they are the ones who facilitate their development and consistency. Till's notion of the sense-maker also takes this approach, insofar as making sense implies giving shape and coherence to the actions of others. Thus, it, too, ultimately re-enthrones the architect's own agency in a privileged position. [G] Till himself admits as much by quoting planning theorist John Forester: "sense-making (…) is a matter of altering, respecting, acknowledging, and shaping people's lived worlds."[35] In conclusion, therefore, from this perspective other people's views and actions are respected and included, but it has widely been a question

[F] | AA This limitation could also affect the kind of practices performed to develop the design: are they affected by the collectivization of the design process?

AGV I would say yes, the collectivization of design processes necessarily changes design practices and, certainly, makes them more participatory, even if that does not alter their planned structure of action.

[G] | AA Although the formulation "sense-making" is broadly accepted, even in the framework of the enactive approach to cognition, the use of an alternative formulation—"emergence of sense"—could contribute to overcoming the limitations implied in the term "making": if there is "making" there must be a "maker" or "makers." The concept of emergence or, to be more precise, of emerging systems—or even better, of co-emerging systems—allows for a more radical reduction of hierarchies by describing all agents—all "contingent agents" as I like to term them—as enabling conditions for the emergent artifacts and qualities.

AGV Fully agreed. That formulation would present an alternative perspective where hierarchies are leveled and the role of architects is not necessarily the only central one.

of, in Schneider and Till's words, "what part the architect might and can play"[36] to open this space for others.[37]

Thus, oftentimes the study of agency in architecture is not actually focused on other forms of agency, how they take place, how they develop, or how they shape their particular collaborative process, but instead concentrates on the architect's action.

However, a different perspective is taken by research on agency in architecture inspired by actor network theory (ANT). Works by authors such as Bruno Latour,[38] Albena Yaneva[39] and Thomas Gieryn[40] describe agency as being distributed and possessed in relational networks of people and things, without a priori attributing any primacy to a human actor, whether individual or collective. In line with this, Latour states that intentionality and will are not necessary conditions of action and that what we call actors or agents, both human and non-human, are actually products or effects of networks. Thus, they are better characterized as *actants,* as something *made* to act.[41] From this perspective, "architecture is not the work of architects," since it is actually "a co-production of the social and the formal, of humans and non-humans, of meaning and matter"[42] and creation therefore corresponds to a more complex process in which different chains of associations participate. In this context, Yaneva studies Rem Koolhaas's Office for Metropolitan Architecture (OMA) in *The Making of a Building*[43] with a similar method to that used by Latour and Woolgar in *Laboratory Life: The Social Construction of Scientific Facts,*[44] which talks about science and technology by observing and analyzing scientists at work. She looks into the everyday behavior of architects, examining their relationships, habits, models and regulated and common practices in order to understand "'architecture in the making' versus 'architecture made,'"[45] and to show that a large number of heterogeneous actors were engaged and re-connected differently in the process: "community groups, gravitation laws, historical buildings, architects, zoning requirements, street walls, museum philosophy, preservationists and neighbors."[46] [H]

Now, the end result of this approach is the opposite to that of the works of The Agency or Till and Schneider discussed above. Instead of focusing on the position of the architect, here the symmetry in agency between humans and non-humans and their understanding as actants in a network leaves no real room for the intentions of the people involved, thus eliminating in practice critical human intentionality and politicized practice.[47] [I] As Lambros Malafouris points out, in ANT "power, intentionality, and agency are not properties of the isolated person or the isolated thing: they are properties of a chain of associations"[48] and so the particular and individual forms of action are subsumed under the perspective of the network.

Therefore we have, on the one hand, research on agency like that by The Agency or Tatjana Schneider and Jeremy Till, which insists on drastically de-emphasizing the intentions and forms of control of architects in our conception of building action. While these approaches open new ways of empowering all agents involved in construction, they are clearly focused on profiling new roles for architects, who are the ones that would allow the development of such forms of empowerment. Therefore this prevents this approach from engaging in an in-depth analysis of the specific performance of these other new agencies, one that could illuminate their own routes of action and interrelation. On the other hand, the analysis of agencies from ANT's perspective offers very specific studies of all those agents—human and non-human—that intervene in the different phases or parts of construction. But, by taking up the perspective of the network and its associations, it blurs all forms of intention. As a consequence, it detracts relevance from political intervention and any form of authorship as truly important factors in construction.[J]

In contrast to these positions, addressing construction from the point of view of the model of improvisational action and collaboration offers compelling advantages for exploring processes in construction that are not necessarily controlled and determined in a pre-defined

[I] ᴬᴬ Do you really think that approaching this issue from a persepctive of network of actants leaves no place to consider different forms of intentionality? Could intentionality, as suggested in your following lines, be considered as one constitutive aspect of some of the contingent actants and/or
as embodied traits of some actants but emerging out of and distributed
through the network? I think that the work of Ezequiel di Paolo or Hanne
De Jaegher supports this hypothesis.

    ᴬᴳⱽ Possibly the formulation is too strong: by "no real room for the
intention" of those involved I mean that these intentions are not radically decisive on their own. They are, of course, part of the network
and one of its elements, but they are not properties of the individual
and their relevance is fundamentally reduced in front of that of the
associations. That is why the political significance of individual actions is also drastically reduced in this approach. The possibly more
appropriate expression of this is described later in the paragraph:
"the particular and individual forms of action are subsumed beneath
the perspective of the network."

[J] ᴶᴴ But perhaps this dichotomy is exaggerated—it suggests a distinction
between human agents (who can act politically) and non-human agents/
actants who cannot. I would argue that political action necessarily blurs
this boundary: for example, human agents can achieve nothing in the (political) world without the assistance of embodied/material media, and also
that political consequences also emerge unexpectedly from networks of
material actors—both human and non-human.

    ᴬᴳⱽ I don't think the intention of ANT theorists is to suggest that
human agents can act politically while non-human agents cannot,
and that is also not the position of the criticism I support here. I agree
with the blurring of the dichotomy in this respect exactly because of
the reasons you mention. It is not erasing the distinction between
human and non-human agents that makes ANT's approach de-
emphasize the ideas of individual intentionality, political intervention
or authorship, but rather it is its emphasis on the chain of associations, on the structural perspective, that necessarily relegates the
individual roles to a secondary space.

plan—thus investigating alternatives to a radical intentional view of the action. It provides a way for understanding how forms of agency different from that of the architect function, including what strategies they employ, how they collaborate, their constraints, etc. On the one hand, collective improvisation describes a common path in which no single person necessarily choreographs the entire composition: the task of mediating or making sense could be in the hands of one of the participants, but it could easily pass from one to another, be shared, or not exist at all. In that sense, and unlike the positions in which the architect conforms the center of attention, the emphasis on an improvisation process allows to understand some of the basic mechanisms of collaboration and to focus on the effective functioning of other forms of agents without necessarily always concentrating on a single central figure. On the other hand, this perspective does not necessarily commit us to the kind of radically anti-intentionalist view characteristic of action network theory. Thus, the partial intentions of those participating in the construction process can also be taken into account and play a partial role. Similar to improvised performances in music or theater, forms of co-authorship can be acknowledged in architecture, without making the notion of author completely disappear (as occurs with ANT) and without, on the other hand, having it solely characterising the person shaping or directing the plan.

3. IMPROVISATION AND BUILDING

Improvisation in architecture is not a new idea. However, taking it seriously might be. Richard Rogers, one of the designers of the *Pompidou Centre* in Paris, declared in 1991: "we are looking for an architecture rather like some music and poetry which can actually be changed by the users, an architecture of improvisation."[49] But, as Jeremy Till points out, the building's architects seem not to have valued improvisation as much as they initially claimed. When Gae Aulenti placed a set of solid-looking boxes in the *Pompidou Centre* in 1994, the original

architects expressed disappointment, clearly suggesting that their building was not as open to interventions and to other agencies as they had indicated.

In order to address this relationship between improvisation and the construction process, I am going to focus on three basic aspects of improvised activity that are particularly relevant for improving our understanding of not-fully-planned forms of construction: the emphasis of improvisation on the *process;* its radical openness to different forms of *agency* in a horizontal and non-hierarchical distribution; and the dialectics in improvisation between spontaneity and conditioning factors or between contingency and structure, which allow us to understand the particular forms of coordination of improvised action in certain *strategies,* and thus to consider a more specific approach to concrete, unplanned construction processes.

The first consequence of treating construction as improvisation is that it allows us to focus our attention on its entire course, and not only on part of it and certainly not only on the final result. This does justice to the processual nature of construction and its performative elements, viewing creativity as being distributed throughout the trajectory rather than being exclusively determined as a single meaningful moment in time. Thus, it decouples creation from the concepts of vision, inspiration or innovation, which all occur at an abstract moment in time and without movement, whether it be an initial instant of insight or the final results of the process.[50] These perspectives on creation generally fail to account for the process itself beyond its deviations from the plan. In contrast, improvisation as a model associates creativity [K], with the action of process and the setting into motion of spontaneity, skills, strategies, and forms of reciprocity.

Accordingly, creation within improvisation is radically temporal: not only because it takes place in time, but also because within improvisation, as Alessandro Bertinetto writes, "every situational moment acquires its meaning and, reciprocally, contributes to the meaning

[K] | ^{AA} What concept of "creativity" are you using in this text? And in which relationship does it stand to your concept of agency?

^{AGV} I conceive of creativity along the lines described in the text, without necessarily committing to a more restricted concept: it is the bringing about of something new that takes place unavoidably in a process and mobilizes a complex chain of associations between "spontaneity, skills, strategies and forms of reciprocity." And I would certainly detach it from the ideas of individual inspiration or enlightenment and connect it, rather, with what emerges from the coupling and interaction of different forms of agency.

of the whole process."[51] Therefore, in improvisation every moment is loaded with the recollection of what has just happened and the expectation of what is about to happen. In this respect, improvisation is necessarily always situated and embodied, since it requires a constant "moment-by-moment engagement of the agent with their environment."[52] Further, the meaning and the value of the performance depends on the stance taken in each of the points of this process by each of the agents involved, and consequently its characteristic form of normativity is a kind of "*live*-normativity":[53] it is not just a normativity of what happens *live,* but a normativity that transforms itself in every one of its moments (I come back to this below).

Not only is creativity distributed in improvised action throughout the process. Agency is, too. As Tim Ingold highlights in *Creativity and Cultural Improvisation,*[54] improvisation has a fundamentally relational character. It is radically open to collaboration, interaction and co-determination. Thus, action in improvisation is developed in a responsive and reciprocal manner,[55] where agents necessarily acknowledge or somehow react to the actions of others and include it in their own intervention. In improvised activity, the social, moral and political dispositions of each of its actors are clearly manifested. However, improvisation is not only relational insofar as different people participate in it, but also because, no matter how disruptive or transformative it may be, it has to make sense in a social context, or within a "widely inhabited universe of meaning," and it has to "accord to its communicative conventions."[56] Drawing on such conventions is crucial for the success of a performance.[57] Elaborating on this idea, Ingold uses the metaphor of pedestrians walking on a busy street and Michael de Certeau's concept of "tactical maneuverings," which he defines as "those improvisational adjustments of posture, pace and bearing by which one's own movement is attuned on the one hand to that of companions (…) and on the other to strangers coming from different directions with whom one does not wish to collide."[58] The

strangers' entangled and mutually responsive paths are not determined by predefined and a priori agencies. Rather, they unfold out of
"the dynamic potential of an entire field of relationships to bring forth
the persons situated in it."[59] These are not previously structured individual actions which, when crossing paths, negotiate and produce
collaboration. Rather, they develop out of mutual co-determination.
Beth Preston calls the relationship between agents that occurs prior
to the definition of their actions, and not the reverse, "sociogenerisms"
in action, as opposed to what she calls "suigenerism." The view that
the individual is formed by society in important ways is certainly not
new, but it has been typically ignored by traditional Anglo-American
action theory, which "starts with an essentially independent individual
agent and tries to build up collaborative and social agency on this
basis."[60] In her analysis of improvisation, Preston shows that "sociality
actually precedes multiple-agent action" and distinguishes between
sociality and collaboration, accounting for non-cooperative types
of action.

Alessandro Bertinetto highlights another consequence of the
relational nature of improvisation: its capacity for political and social
mobilization. In his opinion, this capacity for mobilization is not just
about bringing together those who intervene directly in the improvisation, but about all those who are in one way or another affected by the
process. After all, they can co-determine the improvisation in certain
ways, thus blurring the difference between the inside and the outside.
In this context, Bertinetto recalls a law passed in Austria at the end of
the eighteenth century that forbade improvisation in theaters for political reasons: "The then political rulers understood improvised theater
not as an expression of aesthetic art, that builds imaginary worlds in
the fictional space of the stage, but as an illegal practice that directly
intervenes in the real life of the audience, addressed as co-performers
and invited to act to transform the socio-historical situations in which
they lived."[61] [L]

[L] | JH This is a nice example of the dangers implied by the threat of loss of
control, and the tendency to try to legislate against this in the medium of
written language. i.e., the approved script must not be departed from in
order to avoid an undesirable (for some) outcome, much like the architect's
construction documents (drawings and written specifications) which take
on a quasi-legal status in protecting the client from any over-spending or
deviation from the approved design.

    AGV I very much agree.

In line with this, one of the main reasons that Charles Jencks offers in support of *adhocism* in architecture and of his emphasis on improvisation is that they "favour political pluralism."[62] In their book *Adhocisms,* Jencks and co-author Nathan Silver insist on the idea that architecture needs to open spaces for improvisation, both by "using contingent situations as opportunities for resourcefulness" and "using opportunities to produce contingent open-ended results."[63] Nevertheless, their work, once again, fundamentally concentrates on what the architect must do in order to act in an *ad hoc* way: how they can use available systems or situations to solve problems in construction or how they can deliver open-ended built products. But the authors do not say much more about how collaborative improvised action might happen in these open and contingent contexts, how it could take place and develop, what kind of structure it could have, or in which way other agents could also intervene and be an integral part of improvisation.

A further essential attribute of improvisation—and possibly the most fundamental one—is its radical contingency. This makes improvisation the ideal context for spontaneity. However, claiming that improvisation is simply identical to spontaneity would fail to capture the nature of improvised activity: on the one hand, creativity and action in improvisation do not take place ex nihilo, but are rooted in the past, in ideas, structures, and rules that they transform and reinterpret. On the other hand, another important characteristic of these improvised actions is not only that they are spontaneous, but also that they are connected to other actions. Thus, the question is understanding how this happens with no advanced plan at hand. [M]

Therefore, improvisation originates from the past. It is based on previous models and proposals that are appropriated and reformulated. [N] This doesn't mean that improvised creation can be reduced to a mere combination of prior elements in which the components are simply recomposed in a new format. On the contrary, improvisation

[M]   ᴬᴬ The connection you propose between contingency and spontaneity is, among other reasons, interesting because it questions fundamentally the apparently solipsistic nature of spontaneity. The spontaneity of one improviser is not the manifestation of the free unfolding of her embodied skills but the expression (in Merleau-Pontyan terms—see Jonathan's text) of the actualization of these skills in coupling with the current state of the whole system in and with which the improviser acts. There are two possible formulations of this idea, taking respectively two different points of observation: it is either the spontaneity of the whole system specified in and by the improviser or it is the spontaneity of the improviser as part of the whole system.

    ᴬᴳⱽ Yes, I could agree with this description.

[N]   ᴬᴬ Of course this cannot be wrong, according to the premise that any present action must be grounded in past actions simply because they are linked by an irreversible time sequence. And I would also agree in considering that any present action is enabled by the embodiment of past actions. Nevertheless, I would not consider the past as the "origin" of an improvised action. In the same way Bachelard in his Poetics of Space considers that the poetic image has no past—it is originated as a radical discontinuity in the here and now of the poetic action—I propose that the origin of the improvised action is the actuality of the situation out of which it emerges. I think that your following lines and Mead's quote support this idea.

    ᴬᴳⱽ Yes: "originate from" here means "is rooted in," not that the past is the sole (or even necessarily the main) source of the action (that would eliminate creativity and spontaneity), but rather that it is one of the elements that conform the "actuality of the situation."

is an *emerging* phenomenon, which can't be explained solely by the relation of its parts and by reference to that past. This point was made in 1932 by G.H. Mead in his pragmatist theory of emergence. Commenting on the contingency of improvisational action, he wrote: "the emergent when it appears, is always found to follow from the past, but before it appears, it does not, by definition, follow from the past."[64] Although in a subsequent revision, what is improvised shows its internal coherence and multiple connections to past ideas, it is never a simple consequence of them. In that sense, Sawyer notes that an improvised action is *emergent* both in the classic sense of the term coined in the nineteenth century by Georges Henry Lewes and in the contemporary sense associated with distributed cognition.[65] These ideas are relevant within built space since they show and highlight how, from the perspective of improvisation, sense is an emerging element in the process of construction action that undoubtedly goes beyond the mere sum of its constituent parts.

Thus, there is no contradiction within improvisation between spontaneity on the one hand and conditioning factors and the forms in which the action is previously determined on the other:[66] On the contrary, they are the conditions of possibility of improvisation. Improvised actions assimilate systems, models, rules, conventions, standards, customs, etc. These are not its only preconditions, but rather they are going to be brought to the present, repositioned and thus transformed and redirected. "Models, standards and customs (the past) come up as conditions of possibility of improvisation, precisely through the potential change that is produced in and through improvisation."[67] Accordingly, that improvisation is not a *creatio ex nihilo* means that within improvisation, the unforeseen, the processual and the inventive stand in a dialectical relationship with structure and preparation.[68]

Improvised actions can be prepared: the first and most evident form of preparation is through the development of skills. The degree of

precision in the coordination of perception and action that is achieved through practice is, more than knowledge of the rules, what distinguishes a capable improvising performer.[69] David Sudnow shows in his book *Ways of the Hand: The Organization of Improvised Conduct* how the kind of embodied learning developed by the skilled hands of a jazz pianist is the starting point and the condition of their capacity for improvising. In his own case, rather than by learning some explicit, context-free, musical knowledge, it was by repeatedly performing a small number of simple scales and chord sequences characteristic of the jazz sound he wanted to perform "that the sounds seemed to creep up into [his] fingers."[70] Likewise, the training in the repetition of specific behaviors and gestures is one of the main resources improvisers have at their disposal to use indeterminacy as a resource for creativity. In building processes, the development and implementation of construction skills is a fundamental element of construction, and this becomes a particularly key feature of the activity in contexts where no full, centralized plan is available (as Turnbull shows in the case of the construction of the Chartres cathedral).

Therefore, improvisation does not eliminate habits, rules or structures but actually integrates them into the creative process. In some genres, "performers are expected to direct their improvisations along more rigid tracks than in other genres (…). For example, in Bebop musical improvisations the general harmonic structure is more fixed than in Free Jazz."[71] [O] Additionally, Bertinetto highlights that improvisers develop "explicit and implicit perceptual and conceptual schemes in virtue of which they can understand what is going on and, consequently, they are able to evaluate what they themselves and their fellow performers are doing."[72] These schemes allow them to establish certain focal points that become common referents in the course of their movement and enable each actor to anticipate the interventions of others. Thus, expectations converge on these points, facilitating their distribution and helping performers to understand the rules

[O] JH This is an interesting aspect of structure in the sense that it may be this that provides the rules that allow a particular genre to be recognized as such—and thus provide a platform from which an audience can begin to engage in the sense-making process—at various scales of engagement. I.e., there is a certain following of rules involved in the making of sounds that allow them to be recognized as music, as such, and not simply random noise. And then a further set of rules that identify the music as belonging—however tenuously—to that style or genre we call jazz improvisation, which as we now know, also involves a certain element of not-following-rules in order to continue to qualify as a member of that specific category of creative musicianship.

> AGV I see the point and I agree it is an interesting aspect of the dialectics between structure and contingency in improvisation.

of selection in the improvisational process. "Focal points—which can be both discovered and created—should make performers able to disambiguate the rules of selection according to their artistic competence and to establish successive identities and stable points in the performance stream."[73] The rules of selection are those that shape the evaluation of the improvisation. First, this evaluation has performative power, since "it guides the decisions that are taken and re-taken (often unconsciously) and drives the performance forward." And secondly, these rules are only defined by the trajectory of the improvisation itself; they are not predefined or only built on former models.

This captures the particular kind of normativity exhibited by improvisation, a normativity that Georg W. Bertram defines as "normativity without norms."[74] This type of normativity cannot be based on pre-established rules, as the relevant aspect of improvisation has to do with the here and now, and not with how it corresponds to previous models. [P] But that doesn't mean that improvisation doesn't have rules or a normative dimension: "The normative and the unpredictable are not, as usually assumed, contradictory; they are systematically interrelated."[75] Therefore, both Bertram and Bertinetto[76] write that the norms and standards of the improvised action are constituted by and in the praxis that they determine, and that within this praxis, they can be transformed and changed. Whether improvisation works or not, is successful or not, does not depend on it conforming to previously established criteria. Rather, improvisation includes and assumes mutual recognition and self-assessment practices that are defined during the course of the action. As a consequence, it continuously develops new criteria for assessing the process and how it should move forward. In this sense, it is true that "we make up the rules as we go along."[77] This is the same reason why, as indicated above, Bertinetto calls this form of normativity *live-normativity,* because it changes and takes different shapes at every given moment of the improvisation.[78]

[P] ᴶᴴ This idea perhaps echoes the framework set up by Terry Eagleton in
The Ideology of the Aesthetic, where he contrasts moral behavior as that
which can be written down and regulated, and ethical or virtuous behavior which must be cultivated as a set of bodily (aesthetic) skills. His main
reference point is the eighteenth century emergence of aesthetics as a
philosophical specialism, which he suggests is somewhat self-contra-
dictory in intention, being based on sensibility and judgment rather than
intelligibility and logical categories.

For these reasons, indeterminacy, contingency and spontaneity within improvisation do not stand in opposition to rules, standards, the past, or conditioning factors. Different agents in improvisation make use of specific strategies to coordinate their actions. As mentioned previously, improvised actions are connected to other actions; understanding how those connections occur is the key question for a more in-depth approach to the different agencies that intervene in improvised activity. In order to specify how this articulation and coordination of actions takes place, Beth Preston proposes a study of the different *strategies* that improvisers adopt for carrying out their creations. These core strategies, discussed below, are central for understanding and describing more specifically the forms of action that take place in construction processes that are not controlled by a plan.

First, Preston analyses the different *resources* of action that help organize the development of the activity.[79] In planned action, the basic resources are plans, which coordinate both intrapersonal and interpersonal conducts over time, achieving this in a dual way: on the one hand, plans ground our expectations about future actions and, on the other hand, they provide support for practical reasoning about further actions. They ground our expectations because they are "conduct-controlling pro-attitudes": while a simple desire indicates a goal of the action, [Q] a plan commits someone to pursuing that goal through a particular course of action. Moreover, plans are stable: they help planning agents to resist reconsidering their future actions unless they encounter a significant obstacle. Secondly, plans provide support for practical reasoning about future actions, something that is the consequence both of the inherent demands of consistency in planning and its means-end coherence. "A plan can function as a set of constraints on reasoning about further actions that it does not explicitly specify,"[80] since further actions must be consistent with the ones described in the plan and since they also must uphold the overall means-end coherence of the plan. However, these basic elements for coordinating

[Q] AA I think that this is a reduction of the role of "desire," already indicated by its qualification as "simple." I do not agree with the equation between desire and goal. Although there is an undeniable component of intentionality, in a phenomenological sense, in desire—a desire is always a desire for something—there are other components at stake like motivation, qualitative (re)constitution of the object of desire, (re)constitution of the subject of desire.

> AGV I don't mean that a desire just consists in pointing to a goal (it is certainly a much more complex phenomenon): I mean that a desire, as opposed to a plan, does not include a commitment to the action.

action can also be accomplished by other means and with other resources. Plans are, as Preston puts it, "pre-existing action structures," but there are other "prescriptive" action structures as well, including laws and policies that "set out a template to which we are supposed to conform our actions"; usually, such laws are explicitly formulated. But there are also "descriptive pre-existing action structures" that present existing patterns of activity, such as habits or practices, which tend not to be explicitly articulated and are generally applied non-reflectively. While contemporary action theory has typically focused on prescriptive pre-existing action structures, Preston concentrates on the descriptive pre-existing action structures that she calls *strategies* in order to better understand improvised action.

These strategies are typical resources of improvised activity, which does not need a pre-defined plan to be organized or coordinated. Improvisation is always situated, tied to a specific situation, in two ways: it always takes place in a specific time and space, in a specific material culture, etc., and on the other hand, as the action develops, the situation is more and more defined, forging a set of con-straints that determine what can or cannot be done. [R] The net effect of these constraints and the development of the particular situation, together with the goals of the agents, help and support practical reasoning about further action, thus producing "consistency and means-end coherence constraints as surely as a plan does,"[81] even if with less stringency. Also, the developing situation grounds expectations about further action in improvisation. Since situations are as stable as plans, they guide conduct through the constraints on future actions they create, even if they do not control conduct through prescriptions. [S] To better understand how these situational constraints—which both help to ground expectations and to support practical reasoning about further activity—work and how actions develop in their context, Preston names and describes the three main strategies used to advance improvised activity: (1) the appropriate-and-extend strategy; (2) the

[R] AA "Constraints" are certainly relevant in this context but I would not over-estimate their role. In this sense, I would not talk about "determining" but rather of "conditioning." This is coherent with the idea of improvisation as system of emergence. Relating the concept of "constraints" to the concept of "rules," as you have outlined earlier, in both cases I would think in terms of conditioning, influencing, containing or framing.

> AGV Actually the point I am trying to make (and I think Preston is, too) is that these constraints are in fact stronger than we usually take them to be and they shape the action in very important ways. But as to the difference between "determining" and "conditioning," I think you and I mean the same with both expressions: that a constraint "determines what can be done" only means that it defines the range of possibilities of the result, which is just the same, in my view, as saying that a constraint "conditions what can be done." This idea of determination of course can also be understood, depending on the context, as wide and flexible, in terms of "influencing" or "framing."

[S] AA Although I agree with the idea that situations are "conducting-guiding" I disagree with the consideration that "situations are as stable as plans." I think that situations are by definition unstable. They are constitutively dynamic, varying constantly, although in different degrees. It is exactly this that makes situations an interesting alternative to plans as a conducting-guiding entity.

> AGV I don't agree with the idea that situations are always and unavoidably unstable, but I see that they might not be as stable in every single case as pre-defined plans.

proliferate-and-select strategy; and (3) the turn-taking strategy. These strategies show the functioning and the organization of improvisation and its specific form of coordination of actions without resorting to centralized control methods as occurs in planned actions.

On the basis of this description of improvised action, how can we go into greater depth and better understand unplanned construction processes? All these different elements of improvised action are useful for an enhanced understanding of unplanned construction in three main aspects: first, from the point of view of improvisation, building activity can be considered as a continuous generation process, where creativity is distributed throughout the course of the action and not reduced to a moment prior to the construction itself. Secondly, it can be viewed as a process in which agency itself is distributed horizontally, where each of the agents can intervene without being (at least completely) subordinated to an external guideline. And thirdly, the three main strategies for the development of improvised action just mentioned allow us to better understand the kind of activities that take place in indeterminate building spaces and, in particular, to explain how the different forms of agency relate to each other and how they are coordinated without necessarily responding to a supervisory set of instructions. In this way, these strategies provide insight into how improvised action can develop in the context of building.

The first of these improvised action strategies is the most basic of all: the appropriate-and-extend strategy.[82] In this kind of action, someone appropriates something that has already been made and develops and extends it creatively. If it happens in a collaborative context, such as the one we are interested in, the already made item will be the work of another person. [T] Pursuing this strategy collaboratively has different advantages, such as the possibility of acknowledging valuable aspects in unintentional elements—accepting as something valuable actions, products or facets of the work of others that were not intended as contributions to the project—or being able to take

[T] | ᴬᴬ Or, accepting non-human agency, something that happened—or was made—by any other agent.
      ᴬᴳⱽ Yes.

advantage of different forms of expertise from the different agents.[83] Further, the action must be creative—it must add something relevant— without being inconsistent with the previous activity and thus not violating the expectations or the constraints of the situation. Accordingly, actions that block, obstruct or neutralize that which preceded them would not be acceptable, since then the action would no longer be collective and collaborative. Such blockage can take place in different ways, such as cancelling, shelving—accepting the former action but keeping it for a later stage without integrating it into the course of the activity—or ignoring.[84] This strategy shows how action unfolds in a large number of improvisations: in this manner, under the principle "Yes, and…" it is the core of improvised theater activity,[85] in which, after accepting someone else's action, a new (and creative) "offer" is presented.[U] Likewise, Georg W. Bertram writes that the basic structure of improvisation consists in a process of acknowledgement *(Anerkennung)* and connected action *(Anschlussaktion)*.[86] However, Preston highlights that the "Yes, and…" rule proposed by Sawyer corresponds to a "beads-on-a-string" conception of improvisation: "take a string as it exists so far, add a suitable bead, repeat the operation until the string can be regarded as complete."[87] This conception could be adequate for a performance in improvising theater, but it misses relevant and even fundamental aspects of improvisation in general, since improvising agents do not just accept previous contributions, but make them their own by interpreting them or revising them. Interpreting the actions of others and appropriating them in one way or another are thus major elements in this strategy.[V]

Construction processes such as the one employed in *Quinta Monroy,* in the city of Iquique in the Chilean desert, are based on this strategy. In this project, future inhabitants were given a structure with the basic elements of a dwelling. It was intended as a starting point for the users themselves to continue the construction process and develop the structure according to their needs, means, number of

[U] | AA Why do you restrict the "creative" actions in terms of consistency with past actions and with expectations? Does this not limit unnecessarily the power of creativity and the potential reach of the "extension"? I think that it is possible to interpret the term "blockage" in a neutral way: it must not be a negative operation for the architectural process—beyond making it certainly slower—and it must not be opposite to collective or collaborative actions but instead one variety in their realization. As a metaphor, a wall—without doors and windows—can be the most productive, enriching and empowering element in architecture. In this sense I would accept "Yes, but …" but also "No, and …" and "No, but …" as equally valid forms of the "appropriate-and-extend" strategy. I think that the following comment on Preston goes in the same direction.

AGV I don't think I am restricting creativity here: on the one hand, and as discussed above in connection to the relational character of improvisation, the action has to make sense in a context, and in order to do that, no matter how disruptive it might be, it needs to be somehow—even in a very remote way—coherent or consistent with those past actions and expectations (again, in improvisation conditioning and creativity are not in contradiction). On the other hand, a complete blockage of previous actions (something that cancels for example the improvised activity) could not be considered in my view collaborative behavior and that is why "in a large number of improvisations," as happens commonly in improvised theater, the rule is often the "Yes and …" principle. But I agree that a partial blockage as described in the expressions "Yes, but …", "No, and …" or "No, but …" could be integrated in the chain of the improvisation: the "acknowledgement" moment (the *Anerkennung*) does not always have to be positive, it can also be a movement of denial and still be a step of appropriation and interpretation that allows the activity to continue.

[V] JH I agree this is an important aspect of both drama and architecture—while previous actions cannot be completely erased and undone, their meanings can of course be changed—distorted or redirected by the way that subsequent actions create new contexts for the interpretation of previous ones.

occupants, etc. Thus, from an initially constructed space, designed according to a clear prior plan, the project opened up a second indeterminate space where those intervening in the dwelling first appropriated the received territory and construction in order to, secondly, extend, configure and accommodate them in successive interventions, in a continuous building *process* in which each extension arises from the appropriation of the former and is carried out collectively by different *agents*. The majority of interventions are carried out collectively by different members of the community, the family, etc.

The initial project was designed by the Elemental Team, led by the architect Alejandro Aravena: they were asked to house 100 squatter families that over the last thirty years had illegally occupied a plot measuring half a hectare in the center of the city. However, resources were very limited (300 UF or $ 7500 per family) and had to pay for the land, associated infrastructure and construction costs. Therefore, the options were to either move the families to the outskirts of the city where land was much cheaper, or to drastically reduce the costs of construction by creating "an architectural complex capable of shaping a quality neighborhood, sustainable over time and that would make efficient use of the land (…) without producing overcrowding, with units that could grow easily and that were structurally safe."[88] Thus, they decided to build a "porous" building that allowed the first-floor dwellings to grow horizontally over the land and those located on the second floor to grow vertically.

The central idea of this project thus went beyond the construction of the first basic space. It was rooted in an "unfinished and unprogrammed" space, in which the inhabitants necessarily became active agents and co-determined a continuous process of appropriation-and-extension of their own built spaces. This kind of approach connects not only with what Jeremy Till calls "amateur building practices"—"the myriad of practices of self-building that occur across the world without the input of an architect"[89]—but also with self-building

projects and ideas that have been developed since the 1960s and the 1970s by architects like Walter Segal and Sérgio Ferro. Segal designed an iconic self-build modular housing system based on a timber frame construction—eliminating the need for specialist wet trades—that made it possible for people with no previous experience in construction to build their own house. Empowering the builder to take control of their action, Segal's system is flexible and open to interpretation and adaptation, both in the building process and in the final use. For his part, the Brazilian Sérgio Ferro criticized architectural design as a field of exclusive expertise alienated from the production process and called for more focus on the actual construction of buildings and the actual builders, because "it was through identification with building, not design, that a radical architecture could be achieved."[90] [W] In fact, the action model that Ferro defends, which rejects a hierarchical structure, is precisely that of improvisation in jazz: "our main metaphor was jazz: a common piece, some obligatory passages (for us, where there is the inevitable overlap of competences) and nothing else: creative freedom for all."[91] Like in jazz, where everything is subordinate to the musicians' individuality, in the new construction, "operators abandon the position of mere reproducers of a ready-made composition, and instead *improvise* autonomously and reinvent, each in their own way, like jazz soloists."[92]

Alejandro Aravena has been controversial in recent years, especially since 2016 when he received the Pritzker Prize. Some critics have highlighted his ambiguous position on social projects, and some have even considered the social housing projects by Elemental to be weak architectural proposals,[93] precisely because they do not offer full "complete designs." But this sort of "incremental housing" is not something new: the term was already being used in the 1980s by Edwin Haramoto[94] and there are numerous other examples of this kind of construction, both in Latin America and elsewhere. One of the most noteworthy examples in Chile is the *Comunidad Andalucía,* initiated

[W] ^{AA} I think that the tension between building and designing is also implicitly present throughout your text. Instead of these two terms you only use one term: "construction." Does this term in your text include both? It is a strong decision in regard to the thematic you are treating here to consider the whole architectural process as a unit or to distinguish between two categorically different sections: design and building.

> ^{AGV} The idea of design mentioned in this context is that of Ferro's, for whom design was clearly separated and removed from real building processes and was based on a fundamentally hierarchical structure. Construction for me refers mainly to the process of building, but I don't commit here to a closed idea of design and certainly not to Ferro's concept: I am leaving design aside here if it is understood only as previous planning and as a form of hierarchical control, but I would say that there are also design practices involved in construction processes that have not been fully planned in advance. From this point of view, then, construction could integrate both building and design activities (understanding these in a broad way).

in the city of Santiago in 1992 by Fernando Castillo Velasco and designed as an enclosed urban block with 178 housing units, each of them with the potential to grow up to two or three floors. Over the years, in a series of interventions in stages and with the collaboration of family members, friends and neighbors, different elements have been added to the basic dwellings that the occupants found upon arrival. Once again, in an accumulative process of creative appropriation, each one of these spaces was developed uniquely through collective action that was not previously defined or controlled. In 2010, Manuela Morales Delano recorded a video[95] in which the "jefas de familia" (the female heads of the households) residing in some of the dwellings described the construction process over the nineteen years since their arrival. When they received the houses, the parts that were not common basic areas (such as the kitchen or bathroom) had large open spaces without walls or separators. Each of the families would then distribute the space, accommodating and adjusting what they had received in their own way and progressively adding elements in a collective manner. Thus, "each home is built from elements that are in a constant state of movement," not as a finished and final object, but rather as a construction *process.* Each is the clear result of the coordinated action of numerous agencies that do not necessarily stand in a hierarchical relation to one another. Furthermore, the idea of interpretation in appropriation, which Preston highlighted within this kind of improvisation strategy, is one of the core elements that accounts for the diverse shapes and structures of each of the dwellings, their particular functions and their characteristic reading and assimilation of the space, since, as these women point out, the first fundamental step was to integrate the space received in their own way to later develop their own building processes.

The appropriate-and-extend strategy is not only used in spaces deliberately open to indeterminacy, as is the case of incremental housing, but also works in cases of re-appropriation and reconstruction of

spaces not directed by a closed plan or design and where the freedom of the builders is what guides the process. An example can be found in the successive re-appropriation of the Bauhäusle student apartments in Stuttgart, a housing project developed and built between 1981 and 1983 with the participation of 440 students of Architecture and Urban Planning on the campus of the Technical University of Stuttgart. The idea was to "learn through self-building" and was started by professors Peter Sulzer and Peter Hübner. Following (and adapting) the Segal method, the students planned, built and finally thirty of them inhabited the building, which is still functioning as student housing today. Describing the process as a clear example of participatory self-building, Sulzer nevertheless denies that the project was a "complete improvisation on site,"[96] since the students did an important amount of construction drawings and planning before actually constructing the building itself; still, in the end, much had to be improvised on site. Sulzer also describes how the new students now living in the hostel have appropriated the space they live in, changing certain functions and adding new elements. This form of appropriation, reinterpretation and extension is very common in all kinds of built spaces, independently of whether those spaces were initially designed or not, and without necessarily being subjected to a (new) and explicit prior plan.

The second strategy of improvised action mentioned above is the proliferate-and-select strategy. Here, agents generate multiple options for what to do next and then select one from among them: they do not simply imagine these options, but actually try out different ways of proceeding before choosing one of them.[97] Like with the appropriate-and-extend strategy, situational constraints provide a framework that helps participants narrow down the range of options. Therefore, one side of the action has to do with its situatedness and the other with the creativity of the agent(s). [X] There are also limiting cases of proliferation, where it is only possible to generate a single option that necessarily has to be selected due to a limiting situation, as

[X] | ^AA^ And I would add a third one: the reflection on the different possibilities underpinning the operation of selection. The possibility to reflect, that is to come back to what happened, shows a fundamental difference between this strategy and the prior one, regarding their time structure. While in the first, time is conceived and performed as a succession—as a line or an arrow, we could say—time here takes a tree-form. For me this opens the possibility of questioning this strategy as genuinely improvisational. Your following example of choosing one option while driving, that is, without interrupting the flow of successive actions—without "coming back"—is different, since here the improviser is not generating different options but considering "in real-time" different possibilities.

> ^AGV^ I don't think reflection invalidates improvisation and I believe there are different kinds of reflection in each of these strategies, including the first one. About driving, we could describe the situation as one where those different possibilities were generated as different mental "possible worlds" by the driver, that is, he creates different (mental) options among which he selects.

for example when there is pressure to do something quickly (such as while driving). When that is not the case and a choice has to be made among multiple options, doing so is often a complex process: it may develop over an extended period of time, may involve multiple criteria and different types of practices (engaging with several kinds of material cultures or with different social relationships and social skills), and may have distinct individual and collaborative phases. Nevertheless, and despite this complexity, agents involved in these selections—especially in collaborative conditions—insist on the benefits of the process since it allows for better (collective) judgements. [Y]

Further, as emphasized by Preston, this strategy brings out the characteristic prolificness of human activity, which philosophical action theory has largely ignored. But proliferation is actually "an aspect of the creativity of everyday action":[98] "we fiddle with stuff constantly, half of the time not with any particular purpose in mind" and in doing so, we learn a lot, unintentionally producing actions or things that can be later appropriated. All of this is of course valuable and relevant for planning, but it is pertinent for improvisation because improvised action depends so heavily on the environment and on the resources available to those involved.

Proliferation in the context of building activity seems, in principle, more complicated than in other fields simply for budgetary reasons: it would certainly be an expensive and arduous endeavor to construct different buildings just in order to be able to select among them. By comparison, in improvisation in song writing—the area of research chosen by Preston—it is much more straightforward to put this strategy into practice and generate different songs in order to later select from among them. This also happens in everyday situations such as when a baker bakes several cakes and then picks one or when somebody chooses what to wear by trying on different outfits. But within building activity, too, there are multiple actions and processes that make use of this strategy. Consider the process of selecting a color for

[Y] ᴶᴴ I think this collective dimension is also really important in relation to G. H. Mead's idea of the emerging sense of self, i. e. the notion that the individual self (or the sense of oneself as a distinct individual) might be something that emerges from a prior immersion in a collective social identity. In other words, perhaps we emerge (onto-genetically) as individuals out of a primary sense of continuity with the people and objects around us; and, further, that we reinvent ourselves constantly as individual members of various collectives. For example, as successful architects, or football players, on the basis of the necessary networks of collaborators (human and non-human) who make these activities possible.

ᴬᴳⱽ Yes, I agree, and that would also be very much in accordance with the socio-generism approach mentioned above.

a wall by applying different colors of paint to the wall to be able to try them out and compare them. Or when placing something in different locations in a room to choose where to finally put it (such as with a sink or a radiator, within a usually limited range of options, or with a piece of furniture, such as a big dining table that is going to define the space around it). And it is also the case in the many instances of trial-and-error problem-solving that take place during the building process.

Furthermore, this strategy is present in construction processes in which full-scale modelling is used for collective decision-making about the distribution or configuration of the space. Full-scale models have been used, for example, by URBED (Urbanism, Environment and Design), a group that seeks to "empower residents to make informed decisions about their homes and neighborhoods"[99] by carrying out training courses for tenants and devising urban interventions. In one of their projects, *Homes by Design,* developed together with the group The Glass-House, they used full-scale models made out of cardboard in order to help participants understand different spatial configurations by actually trying them out and moving around in the space and experiencing it, and with it, help them to select among them. During the construction project *2Up2Down,* both an arts project and a community-led development that was started in Liverpool in 2011, they contributed to the construction of *Home Baked,* a space that would both house several people from the community and function on the lower floor as a bakery. Here, again, the use of full-scale modelling helped people gain a greater understanding "of how someone actually inhabits the spaces."[100] Evidently, full-scale modelling can be a step in a design process that helps decision-making for the plan that will guide the construction. But it can also form part of a construction process that doesn't first go through a planning stage and is not based on a design. In this context, full-scale models facilitate the proliferation of options which, if they were to be made in brick or wood, would be much more difficult to execute. This kind of modelling, as shown in the

example of URBED, serves primarily not just to project, but fundamentally to *try out* the different possibilities, kinds of actions and practices that each option opens; thus, it clearly corresponds to a kind of activity organized and coordinated by the proliferation-and-select strategy.

Finally, the third kind of strategy common in improvised action mentioned before is the turn-taking strategy. This is a basic way of organizing and coordinating different agents that sometimes can take the form of easily recognizable "chunks" of action where rules directing the turn-taking are often explicitly formulated. But it can also be a much more complex phenomenon, with different kinds of possible transitions and a set of implicit rules or practices governing how long a turn can last, how to indicate the imminent end of a turn, etc. This is the case, for example, with the turn-taking practices of one clearly improvisational collaborative activity that has extensively been studied: conversation. Here, the detailed descriptions that research on turn-taking strategies in conversation has produced show how "action that is not preplanned is nevertheless organized on the spot by agents in coherent, extended sequences of action that provide for intrapersonal and interpersonal coordination over time."[101]

One of the main features of turn-taking is that it is an orderly process, but not a mechanical or deterministic one: even when the rules for transition are explicit, the transitions have to be actively established and/or decided upon.[102] Also, the turns might be simultaneous, not just sequential. And, as mentioned, practices themselves can substitute for explicit rules, such as when jazz musicians improvise solos during a group performance. Both the length and the order of the solos may be settled in advance, but if not, the players must indicate when the solo is ending and who will take the next one, and these elements are for the most part determined by local habits and constrained by practices well known to jazz musicians. Usually, however, since practices and local habits are not definitive hard rules, agents have here a wider range for deciding about their process of turn-taking

than in the context of explicit rules. Finally, turn-taking practices often occur when division of labor is required because they can facilitate the intervention of agents with different skills that don't necessarily follow a plan.

Within building activity, the strategy of turn-taking is common in works carried out by different people collectively and in tasks that require a division of labor. The building of the Bauhäusle again offers a classic example: instead of covering the walls directly with the tiles they had received (they received most of their materials from the building trade), the students broke them into small pieces that they used to make beautiful mosaics, taking turns in the process. In this way, the final pattern exhibited on the wall was the graphic result of this turn-taking improvised collaboration. Another example might be the construction of a wall where the agents take turns erecting it or in setting up the floor of a room in different turns of work; these activities can be directed by a plan, but they can also be carried out without one in an improvised manner. This strategy also facilitates collaboration when different skills are required and they are not pre-established in a schedule: in this way, wall builders can work together with plumbers or electricians, combining their abilities and expertise in turns.

The turn-taking strategy also has limiting cases, as occurred with the proliferation-and-select strategy. Here, the limiting case would be where only one turn is taken, but the action could possibly continue further in turns. The work of the project *Adaptive Actions,* initiated by Jean-François Prost in 2007, follows this idea: the project shows an archive of "urban alterations" that are understood as instigating tactics to transform the perception of the environment and, through this, to motivate others to become agents as well, responding in their turn to the action. "By observing, revealing and sharing residents' adaptive actions, this project aims at encouraging others to act and engage with their environment."[103] The first move here is understood as the first turn that is supposed to prompt others to take further action in an ensuing

chain of turns. With this goal, the platform is open to any alterations that challenge planned space and the actions controlled by it. [Z]

An instance of this is the Liverpool project *PLA: Public Loitering Area,* where benches were installed on top of fences that had been put up around public land, thus leading to the space becoming disused. Local residents were given the opportunity to place a bench on site or select where to place it, and after the first launch of the intervention, many others joined in and the action continued for several months. In this way, the turn-taking strategy developed from one single turn into a process of improvised and collaborative space transformation.

Furthermore, the turn-taking strategy does not only take place in sequences in time, but also simultaneously in contiguous spaces. This is true of the collective construction of a garden, in which each agent takes an area to configure and develop in their own way, and where turns have thus a spatial, rather than temporal, configuration. Here, too, the rules of separation between turns can be explicitly established or decided through common practice and use. The final pattern of the garden would also be the result and the graphic expression of the turn-taking strategy and not of a previously defined design, thus presenting a patchwork-like arrangement that is the end result of improvised collaborative effort.

Several gardens created by the Guerrilla Gardening movement are prime examples. The idea of guerrilla gardening dates back to the 1970s and the work of Liz Christy, an artist who initiated a community garden on a vacant plot in Manhattan by (illicitly) taking over some unused and abandoned public space. With the invitation to start community gardens elsewhere, they would soon become the Green Guerrillas, and today guerrilla gardening is a worldwide phenomenon in a community of cells connected over the internet. As Richard Reynolds, webpage founder and activist in London, notes, "there is neglected orphaned land all over the place,"[104] so the goal of the guerrilla gardeners is to "fight back to reclaim this precious resource and cultivate it."

[Z] AA I think that this case as well as the following one do not really exemplify the strategy of turn-taking. In my opinion they are rather cases of appropriate-and-extend but applied to the agents and not to the results of their work. For me, the turn-taking strategy refers to a close number of agents and it does not imply expansion but rather recursivity or iteration.

AGV I agree with the idea of recursivity (understood in a broad way) in this strategy, but I don't see why it should happen only in a closed group of agents, so I still think these are examples of turn-taking processes.

Some of the actions are carried out by individual agents, but most are undertaken by groups that remodel and rebuild the public space by cultivating together in turns, both sequentially in time and side-by-side in contiguous spaces, in a common act where each participant intervenes on a specific piece of the land. There are many instances of this kind of collaborative work, since the movement is very active in several countries. One of them is the building and establishing of the *Gandhi Garden* in Trenton, New Jersey, a public community garden developed by a group of local residents on the space of a former vacant lot.

In conclusion, all of these cases show that these three basic strategies for the advancement and coordination of improvised activity can help explain and give a more specific account of how an important number of actions in the built space function. They underscore that construction does not necessarily require a previous plan to be developed in a coordinated manner and to be both consistent with the expectations of the agents involved and coherent with the situation in which it takes place. Improvised action in building and the kind of agencies it involves are much more common in regular practices than has been acknowledged thus far. Therefore, they may have a much more consequential role in construction than the common focus on the single author notion of creativity suggests. All this can, on the one hand, help us revise our understanding of collaborative improvisation in built space and recognize and encourage structures and practices that facilitate those kinds of agencies. On the other hand, a more detailed study of improvisation in construction, a field whose fundamentally planned and controlled nature has been all too readily accepted and assumed, could significantly contribute to a more exact and developed understanding within action theory of the forms of unplanned activity.

LG You use the term improvisation in the theoretical framework of agency to explain how agency is constantly realized by agents. Space is performed and constituted by doing in this respect. Architectural works that also have a situated character are a kind of propulsion device made up of users who are both agents and makers. Improvisation is certainly a theoretical framework, but it is also an aesthetic category that comprises a very specific "class" of aesthetic and artistic practices. In this sense, we can also speak of an "aesthetics of improvisation." Does the relationship between agency and improvisation refer only to a particular class of artistic and architectural phenomena, or can we define it in terms of the conditions of the possibility of constituting aesthetic phenomena to develop a more general aesthetics that may not be art theory?

AGV I think some authors (among them, Bertinetto, for example) would argue that some kind of improvisation belongs to every form of aesthetic creativity, and in that respect, I believe certain elements of improvised action could be considered in terms of conditions of possibility of any aesthetic creation. But, at least in this context and for the purposes of this text, I am considering it as a particular kind of aesthetic, artistic and architectural practice.

ME The model of improvisation embeds creativity in the setting in a specific way. What kind of role would creativity play, if the model was taken from the context of political decision-making?

AGV I think that would depend very much on which kind of political decision-making we would take as a model: on the one hand, political decision-making can be completely planned in advance, structured hierarchically or respond to an individually-led and closed process, or, on the other hand, it can define a very collaborative context, opened at every stage of the process and where improvising and multiple inputs are welcomed. In that respect, as we know, sometimes political decision-making processes (often in activist environments) tend to share relevant traits with artistic and aesthetic practices. In any case, I think the relation of creativity, improvisation and political processes is a very interesting research space and I would like to explore it further, so thank you for the idea, Mika!

SH Ana's article is a profound account of three approaches to the discussion of agency in architectural design. Their discussion is introduced by the presentation of two extremely different and then rejected positions: of Tim Ingold's interpretation of medieval architectural design as a problem solving activity and Vasari's idea of design as a visual expression of an architect's or artist's ideas.

There are more promising ideas on designing, among them the ones presented by "The Agency," who proposed the idea of the architect as anti-hero and co-author, as sense-maker, mainly supporting three activities: "intervene," "sustain" and "mediate." A second interesting approach to agency is proposed through the Actor Network Theory. I agree with Ana's conclusion: this theory does not leave room for the intentions of people involved and thus eliminates critique and politicized practice.

Ana's preferred position is the third—improvisation, and the inspiration for this theory is jazz. This implies vision, inspiration, innovation, rules, and is radically temporal. It is best played in groups and open to collaboration, interaction and codetermination as Tim Ingold and Beth Preston stress ("sociogenerism"). Jazz also shows that improvisation demands quite a lot of resources: highly developed skills, a plan, a pre-existing structure and, as Preston argues, strategies.

Ana projects some of these strategies onto architecture: the "appropriate and extend strategy" (example: The Elemental Team/Aravena: *Quinta Monroy*); the "proliferate and select strategy" (difficult in architecture as not everything can be executed and then selected; example: the full scale models by URBED); and the "turn taking strategy" whose model is conversation (as in the *Public Loitering area* in Liverpool).

The paper is written in an excellent style, nearly twice as long as a common text and provides great insights into the process of designing and the role of agency in it. There are some questions though: the subject of the text as in most considerations of agency in architecture is the role of the architect. The question arises whether it is just "agency" you are debating—or is there a certain idea of (threatened) professionalism at work? In this respect I thought it is interesting to see that jazz musicians who are able to improvise freely are virtuosos on their instruments.

Second question: the fact that architects are not solitary geniuses but usually involved in many social, professional, institutional settings and networks is stressed by the Sheffield group working on agency—but one could argue that this was always known without being acknowledged. Why do we have to discuss it now?

My last questions are all on improvisation, as this happens to be the key concept of the paper: but who is the improviser in The Elemental Team's/Aravena's proposal for *Quinta Monroy*? Who is the improviser? What is the use of referring to strategies and possibilities of music or language when talking about architecture? What will be better done when architecture emerges in a process of improvisation?

AGV In response to the first question, on the role of the architect and agency in general in building, I agree of course that, as in jazz, virtuosos in architecture (and among them, architects) have more developed skills and can therefore improvise possibly in very rich ways. But here I am not so interested in "high performances," but in how it is possible that any "performance," any form of agency, that has not been fully planned beforehand, can actually take place, especially taking into account that it has to be developed in coordination or collaboration with other agents. And here, the architect's forms of agency are only one kind among many others.

To the second question: even if it was always known, it has not always been properly understood: To better understand—as these different theories of architectural agency try to—how these networks, institutional settings and most of all social contexts define both architectural practices and our ideas of building, as well as the roles of those involved in construction, is an important achievement not only from a theoretical point of view, but also offers an opportunity to improve practices and make them more collaborative, less hierarchical and more respectful and integrating of all the different forms of agency involved.

And about the last group of questions: the improvisers in The Elemental Team's *Quinta Monroy* are all the people that developed further in many different ways the basic structure proposed initially by the architects, the "unfinished and unprogrammed" space that demanded the active and unplanned forms of agency that shaped each dwelling.

Secondly, strategies of action recognized or well-known in music or language allow us to develop a deeper understanding of what is actually happening in other realms of action, such as building or architectural practices, by describing more accurately than the planning-instantiation model the interactions and collaborations that take place in at least some of those practices.

And finally, improvisational practices can, on the one hand, encourage and foster distributed forms of creativity in building—both socially distributed as well as temporally distributed—and, on the other hand and as mentioned before, they can also help facilitate and develop more collaborative and integrating processes in construction, where all forms of agency are recognized, accepted and given real spaces to thrive.

1   Tim Ingold, Making: Anthropology, Archaeology, Art and Architecture (London and New York: Routledge, 2013), 51.

2   Ibid., 55.

3   Ibid., 53. And here, as Shelby points out, templates or "molds," rather than drawings per se, would be the main means used by master masons to transmit architectural forms to other workmen: the master mason would draw designs onto planks that a carpenter would cut out and these would be used by the workmen for cutting the stone (See Lon R. Shelby, "Mediaeval Masons' Templates," The Journal of the Society of Architectural Historians 30, no. 2 (May 1971): 140–154). With this, the builders could face the important stereotomic challenges in fitting solids together to construct arches, vaults, etc. but their solutions did not come from exact pre-calculation and precision cutting, but from a "combination of rule of thumb and creative extemporization" that left room for individual differences and personal choices.

4   See John James, The Contractors of Chartres (Wyong, NSW: Mandorla Publications, 1979).

5   See David Turnbull, Masons, Tricksters, and Cartographers: Comparative Studies in the Sociology of Scientific and Indigenous Knowledge (New York: Taylor & Francis, 2000).

6   Ibid., 43. Turnbull connects his idea of "assemblage" (a term he borrows from the philosophy of Deleuze and Guattari) explicitly with "Foucault's epistemes, Kuhn's paradigms, Callon, Law and Latour's actor-networks, Hacking's self-vindicating constellations, (…) and Knorr-Cetina's reconfigurations" (p. 44), but finds that none of these are sufficiently encompassing for his goal.

7   See Jonathan Hale, "Ingold on Making – Agency and Animacy," bodyoftheory, https://bodyoftheory.com/2014/12/05/ingold-on-making-agency-and-animacy [accessed Dec 10, 2017].

8   In line, for example, with the ideas that Bruno Latour and Albena Yaneva propose in "Give me a Gun and I Will Make All Buildings Move" or Colin Lorne in "Spatial agency and practising architecture beyond buildings" (See Bruno Latour and Albena Yaneva, "Give me a Gun and I Will Make All Buildings Move: An ANT's View of Architecture," in Explorations in Architecture: Teaching, Design, Research, ed. Reto Geiser (Basel, Boston, Berlin: Birkhauser, 2009), 80–89; and Colin Lorne, "Spatial agency and practising architecture beyond buildings," Social and Cultural Geography 18, no. 2 (2017): 268–287).

9   See Beth Preston, A Philosophy of Material Culture (New York: Routledge, 2013).

10 See ibid., 15–43.

11 See Agency in Architecture, Footprint, no. 4 (Spring, 2009); Agency and the Praxis of Activism, Field Journal 3, no. 1 (December, 2009), www.field-journal.org; Architectural Research Quarterly 13, no. 2 (2009); and Perspecta: Agency 45 (2009).

12 Florian Kossak et al., eds., Agency: Working with Uncertain Architectures (London: Routledge, 2009).

13 Jeremy Till et al., Spatial Agency: Other Ways of Doing Architecture (London: Routledge, 2011).

14 See Jeremy Till and Tatjana Schneider, "Beyond Discourse: Notes on Spatial Agency," Agency in Architecture, Footprint, no. 4 (Spring, 2009): 97–111.

15 Ana Paula Baltazar and Silke Kapp, "Against determination, beyond mediation," in Agency: Working with Uncertain Architectures, ed. Florian Kossak et al. (London: Routledge, 2009), 131.

16 Jeremy Till and Tatjana Schneider, "Beyond Discourse: Notes on Spatial Agency," 97.

17 See Bruno Latour and Albena Yaneva, "Give me a Gun and I Will Make All Buildings Move," 81.

18 James R. Faulconbridge, "The regulation of design in global architecture firms: Embedding and emplacing buildings," Urban Studies 46 (2009): 2537–2554.

19 Rob Imrie and Emma Street, "Regulating design: The practices of architecture, governance and control," Urban Studies 46 (2009): 2507–2518.

20 Peter Kraftl, "Utopian promise or burdensome responsibility? A critical analysis of the UK government's building schools for the future policy," Antipode 44 (2012): 847–870.

21 See Coline Lorne, "Spatial agency and practicing architecture beyond buildings," Social and Cultural Geography 18, no. 2 (2017): 274.

22 Zygmunt Bauman, Wasted Lives (Cambridge: Polity Press, 2004), 31. Quoted in Jeremy Till, "Architecture and Contingency," Architecture & Indeterminacy, Field Journal 1, no. 1 (2008): 120–135.

23 Jeremy Till, "Architecture and Contingency," 120.

24 See Kim Trogal and Leo Care, "A quick conversation about the theory and practice of control, authorship and creativity in architecture," Architecture & Indeterminacy, Field Journal 1, no. 21 (2008): 136–145.

25 See Jeremy Till and Tatjana Schneider, "Beyond Discourse", 97.

26 See Jeremy Till, "Architecture and Contingency," 135.

27 Jeremy Till and Tatjana Schneider, "Beyond Discourse," 97.

28 Projects of this kind have of course existed in history in parallel to the canonical history of architecture. A good set of examples of this are the projects and groups from various contexts and times catalogued as cases of spatial agency in Jeremy Till et al., Spatial Agency.

29 See, for example, Kurt Evans et al., "Letter from the Editors," Perspecta: Agency 45 (2009): 3; and Colin Lorne, "Spatial agency," 276.

30 See Kossak et al., Agency, 1–18.

31 Ibid., 6.

32 Jeremy Till, Architecture Depends (Cambridge MA: MIT Press, 2009), 168.

33 Ibid.

34 Tomohiro Sugeta, "Agency: Enabling or Constrained? Thinking agency in architecture through the built works of Rem Koolhaas," in PG2014, School of Architecture and Built Environment at the University of Westminster (2014): 17.

35 Jeremy Till, Architecture Depends, 168.

36 Jeremy Till and Tatjana Schneider, "Beyond Discourse," 100.

37 On the other hand, and precisely in order to insist on reducing the architects' forms of control, in his book Architecture Depends Till presents the notion of "slack space," a space that is not overregulated and planned and where contingency may develop: it is "a space that is 'softer' than what it has replaced, insofar as it is not founded on the principles of abstraction, normalization, and order

that underpin hard space. It does not presume to control or divide in the same way that hard space does" (Jeremy Till, Architecture Depends, 133). He uses the concept of slackness outlined by William Connolly, who argues that any common ground should not be overdetermined by order and regulations, and consequently, this space of indeterminacy in building activity would favor both the empowerment of a diversity of agents and the development of their action in unplanned ways. However, once again, the focus of this approach is on the mechanisms used by architects to develop this idea in what he calls "Lo-Fi architecture": which kind of design supports it, instead of an analysis of which kind of actions or agencies are developed in this context. Despite this, the concept of slack space opens a new field of contingent activity and many of the projects reviewed from the perspective of this idea or from the notion of indeterminacy in Jeremy Till et al., Spatial Agency (both in their book and on the website) offer a good opportunity to study further those other forms of agency and their own strategies.

38 See, for example, Bruno Latour and Albena Yaneva, "Give me a Gun and I Will Make All Buildings Move".

39 See Albena Yaneva, The Making of a Building: A Pragmatist Approach to Architecture (Oxford, Berlin, New York: Peter Lang, 2009).

40 Thomas Gieryn, "What Buildings Do," Theory and Society 31, no. 1 (2002): 35–74.

41 See Bruno Latour, Reassembling the Social: An Introduction to Actor-Network Theory (Oxford: Oxford University Press, 2005), 46.

42 Kjetil Fallan, "Architecture in action: Traveling with actor-network theory in the land of architectural research," Architectural Theory Review 13, no. 1 (2008): 80–96, 90.

43 See Albena Yaneva, The Making of a Building.

44 Bruno Latour and Steve Woolgar, Laboratory Life: The Social Construction of Scientific Facts (London: Sage Publications, 1979).

45 Albena Yaneva, The Making of a Building, 197.

46 Ibid., 198.

47 See Colin Lorne, "Spatial agency," 271; See also Noel Castree, "False antitheses? Marxism, nature and actor-networks," Antipode 34 (2002): 111–146.

48 Lambros Malafouris, How Things Shape the Mind. A Theory of Material Engagement (Cambridge MA: MIT Press, 2014), 129.

49 Richard Rogers, "The Artist and the Scientist," in Bridging the Gap: Rethinking the Relationship of Architect and Engineer, the Proceedings of the Building Arts Forum (New York: Van Nostrand Reinhold, 1991), 146 (quoted in Jeremy Till, Architecture Depends, 99).

50 It is precisely for that reason that Tim Ingold and Elisabeth Hallam reject the characterization of creativity as innovation, since it only focuses on the results or the products of creativity and not on creativity itself, which they themselves describe as improvisation. See Elizabeth Hallam and Tim Ingold, eds., Creativity and Cultural Improvisation (Oxford, New York: Berg, 2007).

51 Alessandro Bertinetto, "Performing Imagination: The Aesthetics of Improvisation," Klesis – Revue philosophique, Imagination et performativité 28 (2013): 82.

52 Beth Preston, A Philosophy of Material Culture, 64.

53 See Alessandro Bertinetto, "Improvisation: Zwischen Experiment und Experimentalität?," in Proceedings of the VIII. Kongress der Deutschen Gesellschaft für Ästhetik, Experimentelle Ästhetik (2011), 1–12, 5.

54 Elizabeth Hallam and Tim Ingold, Creativity and Cultural Improvisation, 6.

55 Alessandro Bertinetto, "Improvisieren / Improvisation," in Künstlerische Forschung – Ein Handbuch, ed. Jens Badura et al. (Zurich: Diaphanes, 2015), 143–146, 145.

56 See Elisabeth Hallam and Tim Ingold, Creativity and Cultural Improvisation, 6–7.

57 For that reason, also for R. Keith Sawyer, who describes improvisation in connection with the works of Dewey and Collingwood, collaboration is a fundamental part of this process. R. Keith Sawyer, "Improvisation and the Creative Process: Dewey, Collingwood, and the Aesthetics of Spontaneity," The Journal of Aesthetics and Art Criticism 58 (Improvisation in the Arts), no. 2 (Spring, 2000): 149–161.

58 Elisabeth Hallam and Tim Ingold, Creativity and Cultural Improvisation, 7.

59 Ibid.

60 Beth Preston, A Philosophy of Material Culture, 7.

61 Alessandro Bertinetto, "Performing Imagination," 63. See also: Roland Borgards, "Improvisation, Verbot, Genie. Zur Improvisationsästhetik bei Sonnenfels, Goethe, Spalding, Moritz und Novalis," in Leib/Seele – Geist/Buchstabe. Dualismen in den Künsten um 1800 und 1900, ed. Markus Mauss and Ralph Haeckel (Würzburg: Königshausen & Neumann, 2009): 257–268.

62 See Charles Jencks and Nathan Silver, Adhocism: The Case for Improvisation (Cambridge MA: MIT Press, 2013), viii.

63 Ibid, 9.

64 George Herbert Mead, The Philosophy of the Present (Chicago: University of Chicago Press, 1932). Quoted in R. Keith Sawyer, "Improvisation and the Creative Process," 152.

65 R. Keith Sawyer, "Improvisation and the Creative Process," 152.

66 See Alessandro Bertinetto, "Improvisieren / Improvisation," 146.

67 Alessandro Bertinetto, "Philosophie und Improvisation," http://www.dienachtderphilosophie-berlin.de/_ressourcen/conferences/Alessandro-Bertinetto-Philosophie-und-Improvisation-nacht-der-philosophie.pdf, 3 [accessed Dec 10, 2017].

68 See Alessandro Bertinetto, "Improvisation: Zwischen Experiment und Experimentalität?," 3.

69 See Elisabeth Hallam and Tim Ingold, Creativity and Cultural Improvisation, 12.

70 David Sudnow, Ways of the Hand: The Organization of Improvised Conduct (Cambridge MA: MIT Press, 1978), 37.

71 Alessandro Bertinetto, "Performing Imagination: The Aesthetics of Improvisation," 82.

72 Ibid.

73 Ibid., 83.

74 See Georg Bertram, "Kreativität und Normativität," in Kreativität, ed. Günther Abel (Berlin: Universitätsverlag der TU Berlin), vol. 1, 273–283; Georg Bertram, "Improvisation und Normativität," in Im-provisieren – Paradoxien des Unvorhersehbaren. Kunst – Medien – Praxis, eds. Ursula Brandstätter et al. (Bielefeld: Transcript, 2010), 21–40; and Georg Bertram, Die Sprache und das Ganze. Entwurf einer antireduktionistischen Sprachphilosophie (Göttingen: Velbrück Wissenschaft, 2006).

75 Georg Bertram, "Improvisation und Normativität," 37.

76 See Alessandro Bertinetto, "Performing Imagination"; Alessandro Bertinetto, "Improvisation"; and Alessandro Bertinetto, "Jazz als Gelungene Performance. Ästhetische Normativität und Improvisation," Zeitschrift für Ästhetik und Allgemeine Kunstwissenschaft 59, no. 1 (2014): 105–140.

77 Ludwig Wittgenstein, Philosophical Investigations (Oxford: Basil Blackwell, 1953), § 83. Quoted in Georg Bertram, "Kreativität und Normativität." See also Alessandro Bertinetto, "Jazz als Gelungene Performance," 130.

78 See Alessandro Bertinetto, "Improvisation," 5.

79 Beth Preston, A Philosophy of Material Culture, 94–96.

80 Ibid., 95.

81 Ibid., 97.

82 See ibid., 96.

83 See ibid., 98–99.

84 See Gunter Lösel, Das Spiel mit dem Chaos: Zur Performativität des Improvisationstheaters (Bielefeld: Transcript Verlag, 2013), 107–108.

85 See ibid., 105. See also R. Keith Sawyer, Creating Conversations: Improvisation in Everyday Discourse (New Jersey: Hampton Press, 2001), 94.

86 "Connecting actions (Anschlussaktionen) in an improvisation can be understood as practices through which starting actions are recognized." Georg Bertram, "Improvisation und Normativität," 30.

87 Beth Preston, A Philosophy of Material Culture, 97.

88 Alejandro Aravena et al., "Quinta Monroy," ARQ, no. 57 (2004): 30–33.

89 Jeremy Till et al., Spatial Agency, 92.

90 Richard J. Williams, "Towards an Aesthetics of Poverty: Architecture and the Neo-Avant-Garde in 1960s Brazil," in Neo-Avant-Garde, ed. David Hopkins (Amsterdam: Rodopi, 2006), 211. Quoted in Jeremy Till et al., Spatial Agency, 44.

91 Sérgio Ferro, "Flavio arquiteto," in Arquitetura et Trabalho libre /Sergio Ferro, ed. Pedro Fiori Arantes (São Paulo: Cosac Naify, 2006), 100.

92 Pedro Fiori Arantes, Arquitetura nova: Sérgio Ferro, Flávio Império e Rodrigo Lefèvre, de Artigas aos mutirões (São Paulo: Editora 34, 2002), 83.

93 Camillo Boano and Francisco Vergara, "Half-happy architecture," Viceversa, no. 4 (2016): 58–81.

94 The idea is actually already present in Das Wachsende Haus organized by Martin Wagner and Hans Poelzig in 1932 in the context of the International Exhibition Sonne, Luft und Haus für Alle in Berlin. See Martin Wagner, Das wachsende Haus (Berlin: Spector Books, 2015).

95 Manuela Morales Delano, "Comunidad Andalucía. Ensayo Visual," Bifurcaciones. Revista de estudios culturales urbanos (2013). http://www.bifurcaciones.cl/2013/01/comunidad-andalucia/ [accessed Dec 7, 2017].

96 Peter Sulzer, "Notes on participation," in Architecture and Participation, ed. Peter Blundell-Jones et al. (London: Routledge, 2005), 154.

97 See Beth Preston, A Philosophy of Material Culture, 103–120.

98 Ibid., 119.

99 Jeremy Till et al., Spatial Agency, 132.

100 URBED: 2Up2Down. Progress Report (April 2012). http://urbed.coop/sites/default/files/2up2down%20Progress%20Report_April.pdf [accessed Dec 10, 2017].

101 Beth Preston, A Philosophy of Material Culture, 121.

102 See ibid., 122.

103 Jean-Francois Prost, Adaptive Actions. Space Residency Publications (2009), 10. http://aa.adaptiveactions.net/media/uploads/2012/05/1375/aactions-booklet15-web-lowres-02-pdf.pdf [accessed Dec 10, 2017].

104 Richard Reynolds, http://www.guerrillagardening.org/ggwar.html [accessed Dec 10, 2017].

Drawing on Language: "Aesthetic Research" as Experience and Expression

Jonathan Hale

Our actions and our given surroundings are the starting point of our self-knowledge, each of us being for himself a stranger to which things hold up a mirror. (Merleau-Ponty, Sense and Non-Sense, 73).

SEEING THROUGH PAINTING

Despite the common assumption (especially prevalent in architecture) that phenomenology is a fundamentally backward-looking philosophy (concerned with recovering lost meaning, lost unity, lost wholeness, and so on), I would like to suggest that the work of Maurice Merleau-Ponty (1908–61) in fact offers a radical alternative: a vision of phenomenology as a progressive and forward-looking method of discovery, and a way of understanding how embodied processes like drawing and painting naturally generate new forms and new meanings. [A] I believe this idea also helps to explain Merleau-Ponty's own interest in the process of making art, and why he uses it to illustrate his understanding of the peculiar nature of perception—and, more specifically, the intrinsic connection between experience and expression.

Merleau-Ponty sees the artist making paintings as a way of seeing the world, or experiencing the world in a particular way *through*

[A] ^{LG} I would argue that phenomenology, as a progressive and forward-looking method of discovery, concerns above all perception and how sensible patterns articulate perception. Drawing and painting are "aesthetic practices" or methods of discovery only on the assumption that discovery is always implied by perception.

the act of making paintings. Artistic images therefore are not seen as a "record" of experience, they are the artist's way of *having* that experience as such. [B] So, whether it is the artist making the work or the viewer who is looking at it, both are being invited to see the world in a new way. [C] Merleau-Ponty therefore suggests that rather than seeing the work as an object, and contemplating the meaning hidden behind it, we are instead being offered the chance to see according to it, and in some sense to re-live the artist's experience in our own bodily response to the image:

> Things have an internal equivalent in me; they arouse in me a carnal formula of their presence. Why shouldn't these [correspondences] in their turn give rise to some [external] visible shape in which anyone else would recognize those motifs which support his own inspection of the world? (Merleau-Ponty, The Primacy of Perception, 164).

This goes some way to explain what Merleau-Ponty means by the reversibility of experience and expression: in other words, if it is true that expressing the world in paintings [D] is actually an elaborate form of perception, then in fact all perception should be considered as at least a nascent form of expression. [E] [F] Perhaps a better demonstration of this idea in action comes with art forms that directly involve the moving body, such as in works of contemporary dance that are developed through the process of "contact improvisation." This involves one performer moving in response to the movements of another, although it is not always clear at any moment who is following who. In this situation, one performer's perception of the other is happening through the very act of performing, and therefore out of this perception they are, at the same time, both creating a visible form of expression. This also conforms to the more recent explanations offered by the neurobiologists Francisco Varela and Humberto Maturana who describe perception and communication as the "coordination of behavior"

[B] ᴸᴳ Phenomenology as a progressive method of discovery implies, further-more, a critique of aesthetic experience as a recording act, and, on the contrary, perception is the accentuation of the constitutive process.

[C] ᴬᴬ Taking Merleu-Ponty's *Cezanne's Doubt* as reference, I would tend to say that the idea is not so much to see or experience the world through painting but rather to understand through painting the phenomenologi-cal constitution of what appears. Consequently, a painting can be under-stood as a dispositive to access this understanding both in the process of painting and in the process of regarding the painting. However, there is a connection between both interpretations: to understand how the world comes to be phenomenally implies inevitably to see the world in another way.

[D] ᴬᴬ Following the line of thought expressed in my first comment, I would rather say that a painting is not so much "the expression of a world" (or "an expression of the world") but rather a perceptual dispositive that allows us to understand how the world (better, a world) comes to be in a phenome-nal dimension, i.e., how it expresses itself for us (the painter, the viewers).

[E] ᴬᴬ I think that, in spite of painting, perception can always be considered as a form of expression (as formulated in your quote of "Indirect Language and the Voice of Silence"): a particular form in which a thing expresses itself for and with the one to and with whom it appears.

[F] ᴸᴳ Or is it perception in its constitutive phenomenological meaning, as the condition of the possibility of expression, that is not like a recording act? As I mention above, perception seems to be the transcendental level of expression. We need a transcendental level to understand how the var-ious empirical meaning articulations have a sensible commonness that "emerges" in perception. Do you detect a relationship between expression and the "aesthetic conduct" that Alex Arteaga defines in his text?

ᴶᴴ Yes, although I think what makes the kind of aesthetic conduct that Alex discusses distinct from ordinary perception is the fact that it results in (or rather involves the production of) various more or less durable artifacts that are able to bear witness to the process.

between an organism and its environment (Maturana and Varela, The Tree of Knowledge, 195). In this case the two performers are, simultaneously, both organisms and environments. [G]

Merleau-Ponty's understanding of "motor cognition" also suggests that what we perceive in a given situation is determined by what we are able to respond to. In other words what "shows up" for us in an environment is only what we have the bodily-cognitive skills to enable us to deal with. So, our initial reaction to the affordances offered by a space is to invoke the bodily routines we will need to engage with them. [H] Therefore, if our possible actions are, in a sense, already prefigured in our perceptions, then we could even say that they *are* those very perceptions. [I] This conclusion also forms part of Merleau-Ponty's long-standing critique of the traditional Empiricist view of perception, in which the body is simply a receiving device passively bombarded with incoming stimulations. His alternative view involves a more proactive process where the body reaches out towards the world, moving in response to its solicitations and its own expectations. As the biologist Jacob von Uexküll famously suggested, this is why all organisms could be said to "specify" or construct the environment [J] *(umwelt)* in which they exist (Uexküll, A Foray into the Worlds of Animals and Humans). As the body is thereby already engaged in a particular form or "style" of movement and behavior, it is this behavioral aspect of the process of perceiving that Merleau-Ponty describes as our first act of expression. In other words—and whether we intend it or not—our behavior is also already a form of communication. [K] This is how he describes it in one of his key essays on art, *Indirect Language and the Voices of Silence* (1960):

> The movement of the artist tracing his arabesque in infinite matter amplifies, but also prolongs, the simple marvel of oriented locomotion or grasping movements. Already in its pointing gestures the body not only flows over into a world whose schema it bears in itself but possesses

[G] ᴬᴬ I totally agree. But this implies, in my opinion, that what results—the world or worlds emerging out of this "coordination of behaviors" is not the expression of one or the other performer but of the whole dynamic system they are part of.

ᴸᴳ How would you define the performativity of the environment?

ᴶᴴ I suppose the aim would be, as suggested by Alex's next comment, to preserve the simultaneity of the relationship—both organism and environment become mutually co-expressive during this process.

[H] ᴬᴬ Although I basically agree with the approach this formulation expresses—the approach precisely summarized in the former two sentences—I think that it is problematic to situate "affordances" before perception. On the contrary I would consider them to be a trait of the percept.

[I] ᴬᴬ I have again a problem with the chronological relationship you describe here and with the conclusion that follows. Addressing the first question, I would argue that the relationship between perception and action obeys a logic of simultaneity and mutual conditioning rather than a sequential one. Actually this relationship should be extended to the action of our sensory organs in the way Alva Noë formulated—especially in his paper with J. Kevin O'Regan on the sensorimotor approach. Accordingly, perceptions emerge out of the sensorimotor coordination, which in turn is conditioned by the emerging perceptions—I'm applying here the enactivist model of co-emergence. This model delivers an alternative to consider, as you do, an equation between actions and perceptions.

ᴶᴴ Yes, I agree, this was my aim, but it is sometimes too easy to slip back into conventional (and misleading) formulations! The principle of simultaneity is vital to preserve here.

[J] ᴸᴳ How can organisms construct their environments while interacting with them? Would you define the environment as a potential dimension of specification, or does the environment have its own performativity that is also part of the construction process?

ᴶᴴ I would see this as an emergent process, resulting from the organism's ongoing attempts to preserve its viablity, as Alex might say, in its given surroundings, and thereby it specifies (or perhaps "enacts" is better) its environment.

[K] ᴬᴬ Again in accordance with Maturana and Varela and in the original sense of communication: to make together.

this world at a distance rather than being possessed by it. … All perception, all action which presupposes it, and in short every human use of the body is already *primordial expression* (Merleau-Ponty, Signs, 67).

So, while the painting may appear to be the outcome of a process, in fact it is actually the beginning, [L] which is a consequence of the "paradoxical logic of expression" that the philosopher Donald Landes has recently described (Landes, Merleau-Ponty and the Paradoxes of Expression). [M] It also implies that becoming an artist involves behaving as an artist does, learning to perceive the world through the act of making art, rather than simply learning to make paintings. We might also usefully think of an architect as operating in a similar way, as someone who perceives the world through the process of drawing and design, a point I will return to towards the end of this chapter. Being an architect of course also involves adopting a certain "lifestyle" that includes a whole assemblage of special patterns of professional behavior, as sociologists like Pierre Bourdieu (Pierre Bourdieu, Distinction) have famously described. A key element of the *habitus* of any practicing architect is to experience the world by drawing it, and through the process of drawing—which the philosopher Andy Clark has recently called "scaffolded" thinking—to discover new ways of transforming it (Clark, Natural-Born Cyborgs, 11).

THE LANGUAGE OF EXPERIENCE

On this evidence, there is a reciprocal link between perception and action: a sense in which bodily movements could be said to generate perceptions, just as perceptions solicit further bodily movements. But Merleau-Ponty is also claiming a similar connection between experience and expression, suggesting that particular styles or habits of movement create particular forms of expression and they do this by eliciting responses from their perceivers according to the cultural memories embedded in those forms of behavior.

[L] | LG Is painting the beginning in the sense of being a generative practice?

JH Yes, I probably want to suggest this as a kind of beginning in the sense that might apply when an artist steps into the scene, like an actor appearing on a stage, and is therefore witnessed by the audience as inhabiting the space in the manner of an artist, i.e., beginning to produce a painting.

[M] | AA Again a chronological discrepancy: Could the painting be neither beginning nor end but a contingent agent throughout the process?

JH Yes, I agree. I think I use this terminology here more for rhetorical purposes!

The best way to explain this is through the example of language, which Merleau-Ponty himself returned to many times in his career. For him it served as a paradigm case for the influence of cultural forms and habits on our perceptions of the world, based on the idea that language is also, in essence, a form of expressive embodied behavior. If we recall the evolutionary argument that language most likely begins with unconscious bodily gestures, then this link between thinking and patterns of behavior becomes even more explicit (Corballis, From Hand to Mouth). The "cultural memory" embedded in linguistic forms can be understood in terms of what I would like to call a "deficit-and-surplus" [N] model of language, which also helps to illustrate the creative aspect of all forms of communication, including the process of drawing. The model suggests that when we attempt to communicate in language we end up saying both less and more than we intended, thereby generating both a deficit and a surplus in relation to the thought we were trying to express. The fleeting impression of a passing moment, or the "gut reactions" to unfolding experiences, can never be completely captured in the ready-made phrases that language offers up. But, the fact that we have to make do with this anonymous language created by others, is balanced by an unexpected benefit that arises precisely from this collective history. Rather than arriving fully formed, language emerges and mutates over time as a result of people using it, from previous attempts by others to capture thoughts as they continually bubble up and slip away. This means that it also carries more along with it than the present user can ever anticipate, suggesting ideas in the mind of the listener based on their own previous personal experiences. What is sometimes referred to as the "baggage" that preformed linguistic containers inevitably bring with them, suggests additional layers of meaning that go beyond the speaker's original intention. This results in a surplus of expression which benefits both the listener and the speaker, because as Merleau-Ponty pointed out: "my spoken words surprise me myself and teach me my thought" (Merleau-Ponty, Signs, 88).

[N]   ᴬᴬ It recalls the very fundamental phenomenological idea that we never see the whole thing but we perceive the whole thing-as-phenomenon, that is with a surplus of significance.

Merleau-Ponty is suggesting something here that goes against one of our common sense assumptions about language: the idea that thoughts exist fully formed in the mind prior to our attempts to communicate them. [O] He shows in fact that the use of language can itself bring thoughts into our minds. In other words that thought is *realized* through speaking, as opposed to being simply represented by it. Thinking in a sense therefore "reaches out" for language in order to know itself more precisely, as he suggests in this passage from his important later essay *On the Phenomenology of Language:*

> The significative intention gives itself a body and knows itself by looking for an equivalent in the system of available significations represented by the language I speak and the whole of the writings and culture I inherit. For that speechless want, the significative intention, it is a matter of realizing a certain arrangement of already signifying instruments or already speaking significations (morphological, syntactical, and lexical instruments, literary genres, … etc.) which arouses in the hearer the presentiment of a new and different signification, and which inversely (in the speaker or the writer) manages to anchor this original signification in the already available ones (Merleau-Ponty, Signs, 90).

So, while the richness of the world inevitably exceeds the ability of linguistic expression to capture it, language also serves as a set of tools by which worlds are continually [P] being created. Just as tools and buildings offer affordances for types of behavior, so language offers affordances for that peculiarly human behavior we call "rational thinking": [Q]

> Thus, by renouncing a part of his spontaneity, by engaging in the world through stable organs and pre-established circuits, man can acquire the mental and practical space that will free him, in principle, from his milieu and thereby

[O] LG This to my mind also means that language is a "medium" of constitution or, as Herder would say, a kind of morphogenetic process in which thought becomes sensibly articulated.

JH Yes, I think Merleau-Ponty would echo that. Sensibly articulated and thereby available to the speaker.

[P] LG If language is a performative medium, I would not speak of language as a "set of tools."

JH Perhaps not, again to avoid slipping back into an obstructive convention. Although, after technology theorists like McLuhan, I would tend to see less of a clear distinction between tool and medium, especially within the contemporary context.

[Q] AA These ideas on language could be as well formulated in terms of medium: language as a medium providing simultaneously enabling conditions and constraints for worlds to be constituted—through practices like different forms of writing and speaking actualizing the potentialities offered by the medium of language.

allow him to see it (Merleau-Ponty, Phenomenology of Perception, 89)

What Merleau-Ponty is also hinting at here is the important gap that remains between language and experience. The sociologist John O'Neill, who was one of Merleau-Ponty's early translators and commentators, suggests that this is also one of the problems inherent in both philosophical reflection and scientific analysis. Both involve a certain "liquidation" of the uniqueness of a particular moment in favor of its more generic but thereby also more communicable character (O'Neill, The Communicative Body, 90). In other words, we sacrifice a degree of fidelity to the distinctiveness of a personal experience in favor of labeling it with a readymade linguistic token which thereby renders it recognizable to others. This idea also echoes Merleau-Ponty's provocative claim that the museum "kills the vehemence of painting" (Merleau-Ponty, Signs, 63) by again subsuming an individual visual expression into the general canon of art historical movements. [R]

Alongside the apparent trade-off between these benefits and drawbacks of language, more important for Merleau-Ponty was to understand how language itself tries to overcome its own limits. He did this by making a distinction between what he called "speaking" and "spoken" speech, an idea first mentioned in *Phenomenology of Perception* but developed in detail in his later essays (Merleau-Ponty, Phenomenology of Perception, 202–203; Signs, 44–45). *Spoken speech* refers to the conventional language typically used in everyday conversation, including the kind of heavily codified functional terms that we use to communicate factual information. *Speaking speech* on the other hand involves the more obscure forms of literary language, the kind of poetic expressions that push at the boundaries of linguistic convention and test the limits of what can currently be said. It does this by creating a deliberate ambiguity in the relation between signifier and signified, as when poets use metaphor and allegory as techniques for opening up multiple possible layers of meaning. It can also happen through the

[R] | AA I basically agree with Merleau-Ponty, although a museum—or more specifically an exhibition, understood as apparatus or assemblage (see Mika's text)—can contribute to the opposite: to create and offer adequate conditions to unfold the expressive power of a painting.

JH Yes, I would certainly agree—and I think that this is just the kind of redefinition that many contemporary museums are attempting to achieve—promoting the museum as a site of creative production, rather than simple consumption.

way in which "spoken" speech is performed by the individual speaker, where a vocal emphasis or acoustic inflection might suggest a whole new layer of meaning:

> The spoken word (the one I utter or the one I hear) is pregnant with a meaning which can be read in the very texture of the linguistic gesture (to the point that a hesitation, an alteration of the voice, or the choice of a certain syntax suffices to modify it), and yet is never contained in that gesture, every expression always appearing to me as a trace … and every attempt to close our hand on the thought which dwells in the spoken word leaving only a bit of verbal material in our fingers (Merleau-Ponty, Signs, 89).

It could be argued that the ambiguity of "speaking speech" is also what allows language to gradually mutate and develop, as it provides a mechanism for the invention of new forms of expression and for the standard lexicon to evolve and expand. To explain this Merleau-Ponty borrowed a phrase from the historian André Malraux, claiming a positive and productive role for the kind of deviations from conventional usage often encountered in expressive language: [S] "It is just this process of 'coherent deformation' of available significations which arranges them in a new sense and takes not only the hearers *but the speaking subject as well* through a decisive *step*" (Merleau-Ponty, Signs, 91).

Hence one might describe what poetry tends to do with words as a "thickening of the surface" of language, in the sense that it often draws attention to its own materiality, [T] resisting any obvious semantic reference. By preventing the easy translation of signs into stereotypical meanings it tries to maintain the potential to invoke new meanings, while of course also risking being dismissed as meaningless:

> Because he returns to the source of silent and solitary experience on which culture and the exchange of ideas

[S] LG The problem seems to me to relate the productive role to conventional usages. This is also a crucial problem for performativity theories such as Austin's, which assume the performativity of linguistic acts as genuine creative agency but at the same time restrict the performativity to a narrow class of conventional phenomena. The challenge is to assume performativity without its conventional implications, and that seems to also be a strategy for defining phenomenology not as a genealogical discipline but as a theory of meaning constitution. For this, we need a transcendental level of analysis that explains how meaning depends on sensible cognition as production.

[T] AA And, I would like to add as an extension to the concept of "materiality," to its condition of medium.

have been built in order to know it, the artist launches his work just as a man once launched the first word, not knowing whether it will be anything more than a shout, whether it can detach itself from the flow of individual life in which it originates and give the independent existence of an identifiable *meaning* (Merleau-Ponty, Sense and Non-Sense, 19).

This suggests that successful communication involves both replication and reinvention, as we saw above when Merleau-Ponty claimed that even new expressions must be anchored in already available ones. This also seems to contradict slightly his attempted distinction between speaking and spoken speech, as it becomes impossible to draw a definitive boundary between them.

BETWEEN SPONTANEITY AND REPETITION

Another way of understanding this emergence of new forms in language is by looking again at behavioral practices like social conventions and habits. Like language they also have a vital double function, being both useful tools that enable us to operate successfully within a given environment, and at the same time forms of expression, whether we intend them to be or not. As with the limitations we have just described within preexisting patterns of speech, the bodily routines acquired from previous experiences are also never quite fully adequate to the unique demands of a new situation. But there are also two sides to this social equation: however closely we might try to conform to the behavioral norms of a given setting, our actual bodily performances inevitably fall short. In other words, even well-practiced habitual actions can never be perfectly reproduced due to the inherent inertia and unpredictability of our own physical embodiment. As suggested by Merleau-Ponty in his analysis of expressive speech, this "thickness," or ambiguity in the material embodiment of behavior is, again, what ensures that new forms will inevitably continue to be generated.

According to Gail Weiss's recent analysis of Merleau-Ponty's under-standing of habit: "even in the most sedimented patterns of conduct, ambiguity and indeterminacy are nonetheless present, guaranteeing that the repetition of old habits will never be a complete repetition of the same" (Weiss, Refiguring the Ordinary, 96). [U]

Merleau-Ponty's account of the acquisition and execution of behavioral routines therefore involves a somewhat counterintuitive conclusion: innovation is not only possible within these processes, it is, thanks to our own material embodiment, actually inevitable. This insight is vital to understanding the creativity and criticality inherent in all embodied activity—whether we are, like Merleau-Ponty, looking at art, literature, philosophy, or even architecture. [V] The key thing is that all these activities involve a certain level of creative randomness in the way that mistakes are inevitably generated even by genuine attempts at repetition. [W] These "copying errors" or mutations in the "DNA" of behavior will generate new possibilities for signification that can be re-tained if they turn out to be useful. In other words, a form of behavioral Darwinism seems to select and preserve beneficial mutations, just like in language when popular neologisms like "texting" and "trolling" are added to the official lexicon.

MATERIAL METHODS OF LOOKING

Merleau-Ponty also looked at painting to help him understand this process of emergence—a process he previously called the "springing forth of reason in a world that it did not create" (Merleau-Ponty, Phe-nomenology of Perception, 57). Towards the end of *Phenomenology of Perception* he introduced this connection of language and painting, highlighting the distinction between the two forms of speech that he developed in detail in his later essays:

> For the painter or the speaking subject, the painting and
> the speech are not the illustration of an already com-
> pleted thought, but rather the appropriation of this very

[U]   AA Another reason for the constant variation in the performance of embodied habits is their constant and inevitable coupling with the surroundings, in and with which they unfold, that is, their situatedness. A body never acts in a void and although it acts with the autonomy provided by its own form of organization—by its "operational closure" in Varela's terms—it is always in a dynamic and "structural coupling"—in Maturana's terms—with its environment, which is in a constant process of change.

[V]   AA Or, I would suggest to add, looking at each quotidian action.

[W]   LG Is repetition a representational practice?
        JH This is an interesting question, but I would probably answer it in reference to all kinds of practices, which—whether classed as, or aimed at repetition—are also inevitably representational—provided we operate with a relational definition of representation, i.e., by also considering who it might be representational for.

thought. This is why we have been led to distinguish between a secondary speech, which conveys an already acquired thought and an originary speech which first brings this thought into existence for us just as it does for others (Merleau-Ponty, Phenomenology of Perception, 409).

Writing is here, like painting, seen as a tool for capturing [X], something of the "sense" of a moment (Merleau-Ponty, Themes from the Lectures at the College de France, 13), rather like a fishing net dipped into the "stream of consciousness" to catch a fleeting thought before it slips away. Scholars of language evolution have likened this process to the growth of a mangrove forest within a tropical swamp, where the trees are able to create a relatively stable land mass by gradually trapping debris within their root systems (Clark, Natural-Born Cyborgs, 80–82). If words and phrases offer "islands of stability" on which more complex thought constructions can gradually be built, then this might also help to explain how the bodily practices of drawing and sketching can support the artist's thinking process.

One of Merleau-Ponty's examples comes from the work of Henri Matisse, based on a film of the artist in action which reveals the process of "thinking through drawing":

> A camera once recorded the work of Matisse in slow motion. The impression was prodigious … That same brush which, seen with the naked eye, leaped from one act to another, was seen to meditate in a solemn and expanding time … to try ten possible movements, dance in front of the canvas, brush it lightly several times, and crash down finally like a lightning stroke upon the one line necessary (Merleau-Ponty, Signs, 45).

Matisse's apparent hesitation in front of the drawing involved a choice of which line to commit to, which at the same time meant deciding which of the alternatives to reject. The fact that the lines remain visible in the final drawing allows both the artist and the eventual

[X] | AA I'm critical of the concepts of "appropriation" and "capturing" Merleau-Ponty and you use to describe the relationship between painting and language on the one hand and thinking, sense and the "stream of consciousness" on the other. These operations imply again a temporal difference: thinking or sense precede painting and speaking (or writing). I do not agree. I think, instead, that painting and speaking—as any other intentional act organized as a practice—perform thinking, that is, are enabling conditions for thinking or the emergence of sense (and meaning) to come about. A middle way—an integrative hypothesis—could be formulated as follows: painting and speaking are forms of intervention, of getting in touch and modifying the ongoing flow of emergence of sense. This alternative formulation recognizes the existence of a dynamic entity going on before painting and speaking are performed, but painting and speaking do not appropriate or capture this flow—this is an impossible operation: a flow cannot be appropriated or captured—but modulate it.

JH I would only add that I think what Merleau-Ponty is suggesting in this notion of thought as embodying itself in the material form of language is that it thereby becomes accessible to inspection (and reflection) in a way that it wouldn't be otherwise. But this is not meant to suggest that the thought exists already prior to its embodiment in language. I agree that thought must in fact be co-emergent with expression, but this process does also result in the emergence of more-or-less stable forms (whether words, phrases or paintings/sculptures, etc.) that do somehow mark a moment in time in their power to endure. But, as Merleau-Ponty also suggests, they thereby quickly expire and demand to be replaced by new expressions—to "extend the contract which has just expired," as he says in Signs, p. 95.

viewer to retrace the path of the process, again echoing the evolutionary mechanism that selects mutations that turn out to be beneficial. This is one reason why exhibitions of architects' sketchbooks can often be more compelling than the finished buildings themselves—seeing these various "roads not taken" can often give a better insight into the nature of the creative process. One benefit of the hand-drawn sketch over that of the hard-line CAD image is precisely this ability to retain the traces of previously abandoned lines. This allows the designer to spend time comparing alternatives while perhaps working on another area of the same drawing, literally providing a space to think "between the lines" before deciding which options to retain and develop further.

Another example of the productive possibilities of the kind of "constrained randomness" inherent in embodied behavior is described by the performance theorist Carrie Noland in her book *Agency and Embodiment.* In this text she makes direct reference to Merleau-Ponty's work on perception in her discussion of the multimedia artist Bill Viola, specifically his time-lapse video piece from 2000 entitled *The Quintet of the Astonished* (Noland, Agency and Embodiment, 66–72). In this work five actors are filmed performing a sequence of facial expressions, communicating the canonical emotional states of fear, anger, pain, sorrow and joy. By shooting the video at up to 384 frames per second instead of the typical 24, one minute of live action is extended to 16 minutes of viewing time. This allows previously unnoticeable facial movements to become visible in the finished work. Viola suggests that this blurs the normally obvious distinctions between one emotional expression and another, while opening up for the viewer's inspection the previously unseen transitions between them. In this way a whole set of ambiguous new expressions become available to be assigned to new meanings. The lesson to be taken from this, as with all the examples discussed, is that the embodied physicality of material processes is what puts them beyond our complete control, but by

the same token, ensures that previously unforeseen possibilities are inevitably and spontaneously produced. [Y]

This also highlights a characteristic moment of uncertainty in the early stages of the design process, where it is often difficult for the designer to know how or where to begin. Many architectural projects start with what can often seem like a mundane observational exercise, for example, simply making drawings of the existing conditions of a place without any preconceptions about what might eventually emerge. In the act of drawing the site quite roughly by hand—as opposed to simply photographing it in a precise or systematic way—a series of initial judgments can begin to be made about which features are worth retaining and which elements—for the time being at least—can be safely ignored. [Z] It is here where the productive gaps between image and reality can begin to create space for the designer's imagination to inhabit. [a] It could even be said that the action of simply drawing the world-as-it-is [b] seems to open it up for change, to "loosen the joints" of reality in order for things to be reconfigured. In other words—to use a familiar software analogy—the initial drawing of the existing conditions allows the world to be "unlocked for editing."

CONCLUSION

Merleau-Ponty's description of language as an embodied, material, phenomenon suggests that all material practices entail an element of creativity and criticality in their use, hence my initial claim at the beginning of this chapter that phenomenological analysis should be seen as a *prospective,* rather than a *retrospective* activity. According to Merleau-Ponty's account, it is in the very act of using language that we discover what it is that we wanted to say. [c] In other words, as a vague or half-formed feeling becomes a linguistically mediated thought, we discover something important about what it was that we were trying to express. We discover something about its similarity to what we—and others—have said before, and how it draws from the collective pool

[Y]   AA According to this conclusion, with which I agree, the "islands of stability" are simultaneously (new) "swamps of instability."

[Z]   AA I think that in the process of drawing you describe, some other intentional acts precede the "initial judgments." I think that this process of drawing—of getting in touch with the emerging environment by drawing, or simply of thinking through drawing—modulates the constitutive power of perception and consequently the phenomenon or network of phenomena that will come to be the object of judgments.

[a]   LG It is important to protect design as a process of openness and media constitution that goes beyond images. The gap between image and reality needs to be explored, referring to the aesthetic possibilities of architecture as means of constituting space.

   JH I agree, there is also the interesting gap between the designer's intention regarding how a space might be occupied by the ideal user and how it is actually occupied once the building is finished and handed over.

[b]   AA From a phenomenological point of view, "drawing the world-as-it-is" can only be accepted as a game, as an "as if"—drawing the world as if it would be like it appears. This process of drawing—and I'm coming back here to my first comment relating to my interpretation of *Cezanne's Doubt*—can be understood as a kind of implicit "aesthetic epoché": suspending the validity of the world by facing the world in order to investigate its constitution. Of course the motivation of the drawing architect is different from the phenomenologist's, but the commonality I see is their interest—mostly implicit in the first case and always explicit in the second—of addressing the emergent world, the world-to-be by facing the world-as-it-appears.

   JH Yes, I should at least have said "attempting to draw the world as it is …," or as it appears to be.

[c]   AA Or better: what can be said, not only by us and beyond our very personal will of saying (it).

of shared meanings that has been steadily growing since the dawn of human communication.

Through the act of expression, therefore, a new dimension of experience becomes possible. Another aspect of the world becomes available to us in linguistic form, and therefore—at least to some extent—both repeatable and communicable. At the same time, both its form and meaning remain inevitably mutable, as each time an expression is re-used, it is altered—however minutely—by both the context and the manner of its performance. Each new iteration again throws into question the connection between the form of the signifier and the content of the signified—a mechanism of renewal and reinvention that allows the language to mutate and evolve: what Merleau-Ponty described as a process of "coherent deformation."

Acts and arts of physical making should therefore never be seen as trivial, mechanical processes of unthinking or "blind" repetition. This is something that often happens when distinctions are made between "untutored" vernacular crafts and so called high or "academic" art; between folk and classical music or between everyday building and "capital A" architecture. A common theme in this debate is the privileging of high-altitude conceptual analysis as the sole means of critical reflection. I would like to propose instead a form of "embodied critique" that is intrinsic to material practices [d]—natural engines of innovation that are constantly and inevitably generating new forms, which should also be seen as constituting an implicit critique of all previously generated solutions. Even the process of selecting which of these new alternatives might be worthy of retention and further development should be seen as a variant of the kind of "environmental selection" seen in natural evolution. To do this we would need to include in our definition of environment the full material context of the work, in other words, the full range of social, cultural, conceptual and technical conditions.

[d] [LG] Is not this "intrinsic level" the transcendental one I mentioned before?

ME It would be interesting to read a couple of lines more about "innovation" in this context. How does innovation relate to invention? Esa Kirkkopelto has written some valuable passages about innovation, invention and institution in relation to artistic research. His text might be a productive point of reference here: Esa Kirkkopelto, "Artistic Research as Institutional Practice," in Artistic Research Yearbook 2015 – From Arts College to University, ed. Torbjörn Lind (Stockholm: Swedish Research Council, 2015), 49–53. https://old-publikationer.vr.se/en/product/arsbok-kfou-2015-fran-konstnarlig-hogskola-till-universitet/ [accessed Dec 17, 2017].

JH Thank you, yes, this would be an interesting theme to develop further. A straightforward, pragmatic, response would be that I tend to use the term "innovation" more often, referring to an incremental step beyond what has been done previously, and "invention" when referring to something more radical, perhaps a move that breaks an existing paradigm, something less commonly achieved in architecture! I hadn't previously considered these two terms in relation to your third one, "institution," but I think Merleau-Ponty would be sympathetic to that idea.

References:

Bourdieu, Pierre. Distinction: A Social Critique of the Judgement of Taste. London: Routledge, 2010.

Clark, Andy. Natural-Born Cyborgs: Minds, Technologies, and the Future of Human Intelligence. New York: Oxford University Press, 2003.

Corballis, Michael C. From Hand to Mouth: The Origins of Language. Princeton NJ: Princeton University Press, 2002.

Landes, Donald A. Merleau-Ponty and the Paradoxes of Expression. London: Bloomsbury, 2013.

Maturana, Humberto R., and Francisco J. Varela. The Tree of Knowledge: The Biological Roots of Human Understanding. Boston, London: Shambhala, 1992.

Merleau-Ponty, Maurice. The Primacy of Perception, and Other Essays on Phenomenological Psychology, the Philosophy of Art, History, and Politics. Evanston IL: Northwestern University Press, 1964.

Merleau-Ponty, Maurice. Sense and Non-Sense. Evanston IL: Northwestern University Press, 1964.

Merleau-Ponty, Maurice. Signs. Evanston IL: Northwestern University Press, 1964.

Merleau-Ponty, Maurice. Phenomenology of Perception. Abingdon, New York: Routledge, 2012.

Merleau-Ponty, Maurice. Themes from the Lectures at the College de France 1952–1960. Evanston IL: Northwestern University Press, 1970.

Noland, Carrie. Agency and Embodiment: Performing Gestures/Producing Culture. Cambridge MA: Harvard University Press, 2009.

O'Neill, John. The Communicative Body: Studies in Communicative Philosophy, Politics, and Sociology. Evanston IL: Northwestern University Press, 1989.

Uexküll, Jakob von. A Foray into the Worlds of Animals and Humans: With a Theory of Meaning. Minneapolis: University of Minnesota Press, 2010.

Weiss, Gail. Refiguring the Ordinary. Bloomington IN: Indiana University Press, 2008.

Exploring Edges and Taking Place: Reflections on Environment and Architecture

Lidia Gasperoni

The notion of environment, which today is mainly connected to theories of ecology and the idea of sustainability in architecture, belongs intrinsically to the framework of philosophy of perception and cultural studies. It concerns the reflection on the attitudes we assume when we perceive our surroundings. This attitude deals thematically, first, with the relationship between us and the perceived surroundings (also called nature); second, with the media that allow the representation of the environment; and third, with the correlation between architecture and landscape in constituting the environmental field.

The aim of my paper is to regard *perceived surroundings not as a field of appropriation and representation but rather as the environment in which we are immersed and that emerges in the act of perceiving it.* This is a paradigm shift—which I will define by means of the concept of *"Umwelt"*—in terms of how the three topics ("perception," "media," and "landscape") are approached. First, the relationship between mankind

and nature is understood as a fusion between the two rather than two separate spheres of experiencing reality. Second, representation deals with a process of resonance between subjective perception and objective reality that is in fact a process of constitution and the emergence of reality itself within perception. Shaping representations, media are therefore not instrumental but performative practices [A] by virtue of the fact that representations are sensible matters. Third, architecture is not an isolated constitution of the environment—architecture is not merely built environment. On the contrary, it has a share in the emerging environment. And landscape is not a complementary part of architecture; rather, it is its regulative dimension, performing the site and the edges of perceiving architecture as built structures.

In this paper, I will first investigate the notion of environment and its philosophical framework. I will then specify the threefold paradigm shift introduced above, showing how perception, practices and landscape are mutually related dimensions of environmental constitution. Delving deeper into this paradigm shift, I will consider three aesthetic practices related to each of them. The aim of this paper is to stress the theoretical relevance of philosophical theories for contemporary efforts to design the environment. Philosophy is, in my view, a process-related form of thought that aims to retain and improve new design practices and to be a generative reflection on aesthetics.

THINKING OF THE ENVIRONMENT AS *UMWELT*

Before I delve deeper into the threefold paradigm shift concerning the way we understand perception, practices, and landscape, I want to specify the common theoretical framework that is based on the notion of environment—along with the notion of *Umwelt,* which Jakob Johann von Uexküll refers to and distinguishes from "surroundings" *(Umgebung). Umwelt* is not simply a notion that stands for the environment but rather a way of conceiving the environment: *Umwelt* is a specific view of the environment which, according to Uexküll, implies a critique

[A] AGV As it happens again below, I think the text would benefit from a more specific clarification of the idea of media.

LG The medium is the condition of possibility of a practice. Practices and media are correlated, but they are not synonyms. The practice is the medium in use, and it represents the empirical and concrete realization of a medium. The medium is in this regard not a specific technical device but a sensible organization of meaning: for instance, the image in its abstract meaning is a medium, a space of possibilities realized by practices in the act of painting, drawing, taking photos, and so on. Media are performative because they mark and articulate borders that are conditions of possibility of the sensible configuration of meaning, so that we can realize certain things with the medium "image" and other things with "spoken language" or "haptic gestures." In this regard, media are intrinsically "performative" because they mark boundaries. This limitation does not imply a static semantics or the predetermination of our access to meaning; rather, it deals with philosophical exploration of the sensible articulation of meaning without being a merely physiological investigation or a new form of embodiment theory, instead being their transcendental foundation and extension. Media need to be performed if their limits and sensory boundaries are to be revealed, however. And practices are the empirical exploration of media because they stress and tend to the borders of sensible articulations, revealing the constraints on their possibilities and developing their own semantics.

of a positivist conception of science, re-establishing the role of the subject who perceives, interprets, and constitutes objects—including so-called scientific objects:

> All reality is subjective appearance. This must consti-
> tute the great, fundamental admission even of biology. It
> is utterly vain to go seeking trough the world for causes
> that are independent of the subject; we always come up
> against objects, which owe their construction to the sub-
> ject (Uexküll, Theoretical Biology, XV).

Referring to Immanuel Kant, but at the same time extending his vision of sensibility, Uexküll stresses the function of sense qualities and the different types of organization sense data achieve through knowledge. As Giorgio Agamben, relating to Uexküll's theory, points out: "Every environment is a closed unity in itself, which results from the selective sampling of a series of elements or 'marks' in the surrounding *(Umgebung),* which, in turn, is nothing other than man's environment" (Agamben, The Open, 41).

Umwelt is therefore dependent on human perception, which builds its edges, marking the surroundings. Perception is thus not the result of the relation between two different relata but the synthetic process itself, which makes experience possible through marking and organizing sensible variations. *Umwelt,* as organization and constitution, allows the subject to perceive both its separation from the object and the constitutive role *taking place* within its surroundings. This kind of hiatus between *Umwelt* and surroundings is the particular form of human positionality. [B]

Uexküll distinguishes the world of animals from the world of human beings, referring to the grade of perception of one's own environment within one's surroundings: while other living beings perceive their surroundings as their own environment, human beings further distinguish their own environment from other surroundings that, for other living beings, are merely their own specific environments. Helmuth

[B] ᴬᴬ Would you be open, as the enactivists are, to accepting that this is not only a peculiarity of humans but, basically, that is, accepting differentiations like the ones you make in the following paragraphs, of all kinds of living beings?

    ᴸᴳ I am open to accepting that this differentiation belongs to all kinds of living beings, but only if this assumption is not an ontological one. The distinction between *Umwelt* and surroundings is not a given border that marks the difference between human and non-human beings but rather a space of sensible articulation modulated by practices that realize our environment. The main problem in this regard has an aesthetic origin, and it emerges in the perception of practices by articulating this space of difference. The challenge is to find a methodological assumption in order to make visible this space of difference concerning the practices of other living beings as well, without reducing their richness to humanistic purposes or assuming that agency also presupposes intentionality. If this assumption is not ontological but phenomenological, the question is how we can relate this space of differentiations to other living beings in order to reflect on the constituted nature of the *Umwelt,* which is not a neutral surrounding but is rather constituted by perception.

Plessner develops a similar distinction, defining human positionality as *eccentric* (Plessner, Die Stufen des Organischen und der Mensch, 364). The animal condition stands for a constantly ongoing process of perception: living beings occupy a centric position and lose themselves in the here and now; they live in the center but not as the center. By reflecting on the perceived and distancing themselves from the immediate body, human beings experience and become aware of their centric condition as, at the same time, a frontal position with regards to the outer world. Human beings therefore live in awareness of their centric position in an eccentric relation to the surrounding field. In this condition, they acquire a new level of liveliness, experiencing the edges or boundaries of their center, thereby overcoming perception tied to the here and now and exploring the richness of their bodily perception *(Körper)* beyond the immediate condition of the living body *(Leib).*

Eccentric positionality is an experience of both acquisition and deprivation. On the one hand, becoming aware of one's own center is a moment of openness to the animate world; on the other, it represents the moment of losing immediate perception (within the here and now) and the beginning of awareness of the difference between subject and object. [C] As Plessner points out, in the eccentric position there is no longer a surrounding field, and that field becomes the outer world. In this conflation between surroundings and outer world, the former loses its environmental character, and the outer world is experienced from the perspective of the inner world (Plessner, Die Stufen des Organischen und der Mensch, 367). At this moment, the hiatus between subject and object risks being read as an ontological difference that marks the history of dualism in philosophy and defines perception as a space of appropriation. On the contrary, stressing the environmental character of perception can lead to a new form of monism as mediation and metamorphosis of reality that depends on the activity of the subject, who is an aesthetic maker and agent of the environment. In this sense the difference between subject and object is a heuristic

[C] | AA Do you mean that our "eccentric" position excludes for us categorically the possibility of immediacy? An argument to answer this question with "no" could be found in the fact, if I understood you right, that our eccentricity does not substitute our "centricity" but extends it.

> LG If the eccentric position is meant as a dualistic space, then if there were no exploration of the hiatus that accompanies it the immediacy would be excluded; phenomenological practices of immediacy would be neglected and would not be implemented. The eccentricity extends and embeds the centricity. But the centricity does not directly mean immediacy, which is in this regard possible not as an ontological condition but as a phenomenological exploration of our perception modulated by practices.

one: it is a space of possibility, in which the subject discovers the presence of the object in its difference. For this kind of monism we need a more radical accentuation of the generative value of perception and practices.

Thus the specification of the environment as *Umwelt* and the eccentric positionality of human perception have relevant implications for the conception of both perceptive qualities and the function of medial practices in spatial constitution. If there is a hiatus between subject and object in the eccentric position of human perception, then the problem is to understand how perception in this hiatus has a constitutive function. In the inner world, there is a manifold scale of states of perception, which are the constitutional parts of the hiatus in the sense of openness to the animate world; hiatus therefore means, even in its etymology, a movement of distance through an opening gesture in the shared world.

Also for Uexküll and Plesser, this hiatus is a *space of thresholds within a place of distance and openness,* exploring different intensities of perceptive qualities—Uexküll refers to a threshold as "the just perceptible difference between two intensities of a quality" (Uexküll, Theoretical Biology, 63). I will explain this aspect in the next section according to Kant's definition of quality and Gilles Deleuze's interpretation of Kant. This exploration of thresholds on the part of perception depends on practices. Life realizes itself only in active execution, as Plessner says (Plessner, Die Stufen des Organischen und der Mensch, 384). The constitutive function of practices will be considered in the second section.

THE THREEFOLD PARADIGM SHIFT: PERCEPTION, PRACTICES AND LANDSCAPE

With this conception of the environment as *Umwelt* in hand, I shall now consider the threefold paradigm shift introduced above. The notion of *Umwelt* provides a helpful focus in uncovering, first, the generative value of perception within the surrounding field; second, the

performative value of practices; and third, the constitutive role of land-scape. With each paradigm shift I shall introduce an aesthetic practice of emerging environment. Not only is this threefold paradigm shift a theoretical framework, but it also grounds the practical unfolding of *Umwelt* through aesthetic practices.

1. PERCEIVING THE GENERATIVE VALUE OF POSITIONAL EDGES AND THE MINIMUM OF ARCHITECTURE

Reflecting on the constitutive meaning of perception is crucial to un-derstanding the relationship between human beings and the surround-ing field as a *displacement of perspective.* Although Kant is known as the philosopher who defined the transcendental laws to which nature must submit in order to become an object of knowledge, he confers an essential role upon perception as a moment of constitution—a role that was radicalized by Johann Gottfried Herder in his revision of the schematism theory (Gasperoni, Versinnlichung). Thus, sensibility plays a constitutive role in cognition. Senses also stand for qualities and anthropological values: they are not just transmitters but, accord-ing to a broad reading of Kantian schematism, sensible media that organize perceived thresholds into sensible forms—with and without conceptual content. Sensibility is closely connected to formation and organization. This is why Deleuze refers to Kant's notion of intensive magnitude in his book *Francis Bacon: The Logic of Sensation,* which is a critical reflection on the epistemic and aesthetic value of perception and its configuration beyond the realm of a dualistic approach.

Deleuze points out how, in the chapter in the *Critique of Pure Reason* on the anticipations of perception, Kant introduces the notion of a grade as the infinite approximation in perception to the zero level of stimuli. Kant calls this kind of grade an intensive magnitude, and thus it is intended not only as a quantitative diminution or graduation but rather as a space of perceptive intensity between real perception and its absence or negation. In this in-between, there is, as Kant ex-plains, "a continuous nexus of many possible intermediate sensations,

whose difference from one another is always smaller than the difference between the given one and zero, or complete negation" (Kant, Critique of Pure Reason, A 168, B 210). This is a kind of approximation that for Salomon Maimon will assume an ontological meaning, and for Deleuze an aesthetic meaning. It is interesting to note that Kant uses poetic, expressive language to describe this intensive kind of magnitude, which "can also be called flowing, since the synthesis (of the productive imagination) in their generation is a progress in time, the continuity of which is customarily designated by the expression 'flowing' ('elapsing')" (Kant, Critique of Pure Reason, A 170, B 211 f.).

The revaluation of the quality of perception involves rediscovering the function of the senses—viewing them not as physiological sensors but rather as modalities of articulating perception in virtue of grades and thresholds. In perception, sensorial shifts and modulations become more important than the functional structures of the senses. Space and time are not perceived as discrete entities but are rather approached originally as diffuse qualities.

In the "Anticipations" chapter, Kant comes closer to the problem of the intensive magnitude of perception, which is "always merely empirical and cannot be represented a priori at all (e.g. colors, taste, etc.)" (Kant, Critique of Pure Reason, A 175, B 217). Intensive magnitude is a condition of possibility of perception whose matter (which is called "sensation") cannot be anticipated at all. The materiality of sensation is an unknown inflow that is perceivable only through sensible organization. In any case, Kant seems to confer a systematic role to materiality, which also plays a crucial role in the later-described "schematism without concepts" (Kant, Critique of Judgment, B 145 f., A 143 f.). This is a sensible organization with a direct reference to material perception without dissolving itself into raw materials. This art work is a material whole that has compositional [D] but not conceptual value. It is a work that is itself present as a new object without conceptual content; it is a form of genesis par excellence that does not correspond to the

[D] AA It would be useful to elaborate more specifically on the relation between the compositional articulating aspects of perception and the compositional value of aesthetic objects, since it is presented as one of the key elements of your approach.

> LG The notion of composition is a key element of my theory of *Versinnlichung,* intended as a theory both of art and of sensibility. The sensible articulation of meaning is not just a sensible expression that can be various and multiform at the empirical level. This expression is not only the material that is transformed within perception and works of art but a matter of organization, of *Gestaltung* and composition—as Deleuze, reflecting on Kant's aesthetics, and both Dieter Mersch and Gerard Vilar suggest. The composition is the perceptive space of stressing the boundaries of media through aesthetic practices.

naked material but rather implies the practice of reflecting the form of the object. [E] As Deleuze notes:

> By form, here, we must not understand the form of intuition (sensibility). For the forms of intuition are still related to existing objects, which constitute sensible matter within them; and they make themselves part of the knowledge of these objects. Aesthetic form, on the contrary, is merged with the reflection of the object in the imagination… Only design counts, only composition counts (Deleuze, The Idea of Genesis in Kant's Aesthetics, 61).

The compositional value of sensible cognition by perceiving one's surroundings does not only concern aesthetic reflection [F] on works of art. On the contrary, asserting the constructed character of science, according to Uexküll, involves revealing the richness of the impressions, both of the subject and of the object, that are created by virtue of perception and organization. At the same time, senses mark the flowing boundaries between human beings and the environment. Precisely because the human being is a "border crosser" between the inner and the outer world, [G] his perception of the environment is a form of dwelling that is both a perspective and a constitution. *Senses are thus modalities of environmental configuration, and* Umwelt *an epistemic term for perception and its organization.* Focusing on the quality of perception as exploring space also means approaching the sensible realm beyond semantic efforts to define objects with a precise label. This space has poetic contours, and this definition has both a concrete and an epistemological framework.

Voiding functions and opening space is the main aesthetic practice represented by James Turrell's work at the Mendota Hotel—that is the *first aesthetic practice* I relate to perception. Georges Didi-Huberman describes this work as follows: "Thus, space emptied itself out in order to become a site of withdrawal and imminence concerning the gaze itself: *a looking into,* as Turrell calls it, counter to any gaze

[E] AGV I understand you mean "reflecting on the form of the object"; is that correct?

LG I mean "reflecting the form of the object" as a kind of mirroring of the object into the imagination as the generation of an object, based on composition. Deleuze uses the term "form" in the sense of "aesthetic form," which is both the reflection and the creation of an object that is not part of the "given" knowledge of objects and that liberates it in the imagination as a new form of composition.

[F] AA Until this point I could read "reflection" as "mirroring" but here I'm not sure that this is what you mean. In which sense are you using "reflection" here?

LG In this sense, I use reflection as "reflecting on something," as investigating, but also in the sense of reflection a posteriori on works of art without perceiving them as devices of composition and transformation.

[G] AA Is it possible in such a "worldly" approach to make a distinction between "inner" and "outer" world?

LG Maybe not. But I wanted to indicate the philosophical debate in which we are engaged when we try to overcome this dualism, describing human positionality as "border crossing" and perception as a dwelling, as disappearing contours of space.

searching for an object *(a looking at)*" (Didi-Huberman, The Man Who Walked in Color, 42). Disclosing the openness of space beyond the functional place involves exploring edges and thresholds, remaining at the boundaries of that place, and realizing practices of entering into perception and its diffuse senses. Turrell in this way explores grades of intensity and mutation with regards to perception. At the same time, he uses photography as an aesthetic practice in order to explore the constitution of a new place in the empty space, which is a paradox. As Didi-Huberman points out:

> [T]he deserted place is not a simple place where there would be nothing at all. In order to provide visual evidence of absence, there must be the minimum of a symbolic alliance or its fiction (which, in one sense, is the same thing). In order to present the unlimited, there must be a minimum of architecture, that is to say, an art of breaks, partitions, and edges (Didi-Huberman, The Man Who Walked in Color, 52).

Thus, the limit of experience depends on the minimum of architectural constitution as the perception of an environment exploring edges. Perception—as in Kant's definition and Deleuze's interpretation—has an intensive dimension that must be a magnitude in order to be experienced. Turrell makes this magnitude real, exploring the edges between its absence and emergence. This is not only an aesthetic or perceptual experience, but is rather a genuine architectural act of constitution which is "local and not transportable" (Evans, Translations from Drawing to Building, 159). As Didi-Huberman notes, Turrell's chambers are "architectures where the operation of edges—extraordinarily subtle and complex articulations of elements, volumetric and chromatic planes—*constitutes the site itself where seeing takes place*" (Didi-Huberman, The Man Who Walked in Color, 54). Turrell's work at the Mendota Hotel reveals the constitutional value of perception through the modification of the conditions that make place

perceptible. The constituted space is not an illusion but rather a new realm of *virtuality* (Schürmann, Erscheinen und Wahrnehmen, 80). At the same time, this work is the effort of aesthetic practices which realize the presence of multiple perceptions and the destabilization of functions. The next section develops a more fine-grained account of the generative value of aesthetic practices.

2. THE PRIMACY OF PRACTICES AND THE FUNCTION OF DESTABILIZATION

Far from reducing surroundings to atmospheric representations, the problem is to explain how space is perceived as being constituted for a subject within his or her specific environment—which is different in perception and representation. It is perhaps startling that Uexküll's book ends with a chapter on the observer, who relates himself or herself to the environment with his or her own specific depth. In order to explain the different intensities of perception, Uexküll refers to the paintings of Holbein, which are characterized by a specific richness that gives an elevated realness to the object (Uexküll, Umwelt und Innenwelt der Tiere, 252). *How we perform reality* [H] *also constitutes the richness of the environment as* Umwelt, *and this process depends essentially on practices.*

A performative account of media involves evaluating the function of constitution practices, against the constituted products. Coming back to minor practices is, for instance, the main aspect of Michel de Certeau's reflection and implies, among other things, a new revelation of walking and traveling as practices of space constitution. Referring to the city, de Certeau describes it as an "operative concept" that is not abstract but rather based on urban practices. To analyze space, he suggests focusing on "microbe-like practices" that, according to Michel Foucault's analysis of the structures of power, "draw their efficacy from a relationship between procedures and the space that they redistribute in order to make an 'operator' out of it" (de Certeau, The Practice of Everyday Life, 96).

[H] AGV What does "perform reality" mean?

LG To perform reality is, phenomenologically, to transform and constitute perception via practices.

The operations of walking belong to such microbe-like practices, which are often forgotten and devoured by the map-marking of the city. In truth, the transcription of paths and trajectories both fixes and destroys the operative and performative power of walking, which is a doing:

> These fixations constitute procedures for forgetting. The trace left behind is substituted for the practice. It exhibits the (voracious) property that the geographical system has of being able to transform action into legibility, but in doing so it causes a way of being in the world to be forgotten (de Certeau, The Practice of Everyday Life, 97).

> On the contrary, walking is a "space of enunciation" which is a present, discrete, and phatic articulation of constituting space. The walker actualizes certain possibilities of space constitution, and "he makes them exist as well as emerge" (de Certeau, The Practice of Everyday Life, 98). His movement is an errant one that establishes a new rhetoric of space—which de Certeau refers to as the idea of "residing rhetoric" (de Certeau, The Practice of Everyday Life, 100). This is at the same time a new style and use of space that tries to reactivate the fullness of spatial perception, rediscovering the childhood experience of space. Space is read in this sense beyond the geometrization of architects, who measure space and bring it within a disciplined dimension. Space is not linear anymore; it is a discrete unity, and its narration becomes a performative practice of its becoming. The performative character of practices turns them into media, agents. [1] Jane Rendell notes how de Certeau focuses much more on the space as a dynamic dimension rather than place, which risks becoming lost and static. On the contrary, Rendell argues that "in 'practising' specific places certain artworks produce critical spaces." The place is thus the "single articulation of the spatial and site as a performed place" (Rendell, Art and Architecture, 19 f.). Rendell relates to walking as a practice of discovering spaces:

[I] | AGV Which idea of agency are you proposing here? In this formulation, it appears to be equivalent to that of medium, but I guess this is not your intention. I think it would be useful to characterize how you understand agency more closely and elucidate in particular its relation to media. Also, are practices agents? I would think that in the example above the people walking are the agents in question; if you mean practices become agents by constituting space, it would also be clarifying to specify it. And if that were so, would that then be the case for any kind of practices?

LG I relate the notion of agency to media. There is an essential connection between performativity and agency. The latter concerns neither primary human intentionality nor the inner dynamics of the creative process. In my answer to the first comment, I explained why media are both performed and performative. This distinction also implies two different kinds of agency: when media are performed, the agents perform practices in the sense that they execute practices and adopt the phenomenological attitude of the constitution of the environment; when media are performative, they are agents at a transcendental level of definition of the conditions of possibility of environment constitution and experience. This latter kind of performativity is related to media as conditions of possibility, to practices as aesthetic constitution, and to us as developers of practices and thinkers of their constitution and semantic enrichment.

Through the act of walking new connections are made and remade, physically and conceptually, over time and through space. Public concerns and private fantasies, past events and future imaginings, are brought into the here and now, into a relationship that is both sequential and simultaneous. Walking is a way of at once discovering and transforming the city; it is an activity that takes place through the heart and mind as much as through the feet (Rendell, Art and Architecture, 190).

Travel is also a practice of inventing space: "Travel (like walking) is a substitute for the legends that used to open up space to something different" (de Certeau, The Practice of Everyday Life, 107). Travel is the concrete experience John Dewey refers to in order to explain what a medium is. As he explains in *Art as Experience,* "not all means are media" (Dewey, Art as Experience, 205). Defining the concept of media, Dewey distinguishes between external and intrinsic operations. This distinction concerns all the affairs of life, of which traveling is a concrete case:

> Sometimes we journey to get somewhere else because we have business at the latter point and would gladly, were it possible, cut out the traveling. At other times we journey for the delight of moving about and seeing what we see. Means and end coalesce. If we run over in mind a number of such cases we quickly see that all the cases in which means and ends are external to one another are non-esthetic. This externality may even be regarded as a definition of the non-esthetic [J] (Dewey, Art as Experience, 205).

Dewey defines this internal, immanent perspective as an aesthetic one: from an instrumental point of view, you can travel or study only in order to attain goals, or you can experience, from a performative, internal point of view, [K] each step of a journey or process of

[J] | AA Do you think that it would be possible to establish a relationship of equivalence between Dewey's concept of externality and Danto's one (see Gerard's text)?

> LG I think that it is possible to relate Dewey's concept of externality and Danto's concept only if the externality is meant as something that is merely instrumental from an aesthetic point of view, attached and not essential to the work of art. With respect to the function of the text when it comes to explaining works of art, it is crucial to understand whether this discursive dimension is a compositional practice or merely an external description that remains instrumental with respect to the work and covers the lack of composition of the work. Reactualizing the concept of composition as the notion of an internal aesthetics that defines a new autonomy of the aesthetic experience may also, in its constitutive multimediality, benefit from Dewey's reflections on media.

[K] | AGV It would be important to clarify which idea of performativity is being used in the text, since it is one of the key concepts in your approach: here it seems to be just equivalent to "internal point of view" (and below this appears several times again). For some definitions of performativity, though, this could be problematic.

> LG Performativity can be described as an internal point in the sense of the immanent transformative potential that media and practices have, for instance. Media as mere tools are not performative but rather instrumental and external to the process they support and in some cases make possible. Performativity also deals in this sense with the consciousness and attitudes we have when dealing with media and practices.

learning as an essential rich part of the full path. This last perspective reinforces the function of each aesthetic practice in learning. Education in this sense should be a performative act, the formation of a new perception in order to enrich the perception we have of ourselves, community and life. This is why Dewey was an inspirational figure for the experimental approach to education adopted at Black Mountain College.

The question of an immanent and intrinsic approach to phenomena is deeply connected with the question of imitation in art. There is a first meaning of imitation as a kind of external reproduction which uses media and tools as external instruments. But there is also a second meaning of imitation, which is a *going into,* an active going into phenomena in order to capture and transform their essence. An intrinsic approach to meaning constitution does not necessarily imply a critique of imitation in its totality; rather, it implies the defense of a performative view of imitation counter to an illustrative description of media in perceiving.

Coming back to practices points out the expressive and sensible performing of meaningfulness by virtue of media that are in this sense conditions of possibility of aesthetic practices. As Dewey notes: "There are then common properties of the matter of arts because there are general conditions without which an experience is not possible … [T]he basic condition is felt relationship between doing and undergoing as the organism and environment interact" (Dewey, Art as Experience, 221). An aesthetic practice is in this sense not restricted to the production of artifacts but is rather a specific distribution of the sensible, which for Jacques Rancière has a political implication with respect to representation. Aesthetic practices are "'ways of doing and making' that intervene in the general distribution of ways of doing and making as well as in the relationships they maintain to modes of being and forms of visibility" (Rancière, The Politics of Aesthetics, 13).

Aesthetic practices cannot be abstracted from the attitude they stand for. Space constitution thus occurs in the distribution and transformation of a basic level of perception: *a political environmental acting.* In *A Thousand Plateaus,* Gilles Deleuze and Félix Guattari describe the tension and mutual relation between the smooth space and the striated one. These are two conceptual extremes that Deleuze and Guattari explain with reference to the sea and how we experience it. While the striated space is a metrical and organized matter, the smooth space is an intensive dimension, in which the line is a vector. The latter is "a space constructed by local operations involving changes in direction" (Deleuze and Guattari, A Thousand Plateaus, 478). The smooth space is not a space without signs or traces but rather a space that stands for an attitude of experiencing space beyond its representational control—and it can be compared to de Certeau's analysis of pedestrian paths as an attitude of improvising routes which are not traceable without forgetting their intensive knowledge. Deleuze and Guattari's smooth space

> is filled by events or haecceities, far more than by formed and perceived things. It is a space of affects, more than one of properties. It is haptic rather than optical perception. Whereas in the striated forms organize a matter, in the smooth materials signal forces and serve as symptoms for them. It is an intensive rather than extensive space, one of distances, not of measures and properties (Deleuze and Guattari, A Thousand Plateaus, 478).

The sea is the archetype for the smooth space, and 1440 stands for the historical moment of its striation, mapping and translating the originally experienced path into reproducible traces. These spaces are a "mode of spatialization, the manner of being in space, of being for space" (Deleuze and Guattari, A Thousand Plateaus, 482); they are modes of voyage, which for Deleuze is deeply bound to the notion of intensity introduced above, according to Kant's anticipations. *The*

concept of a medium thus stands for a performative approach to prac-
tices, [L] against a mechanical or instrumental approach to the tools that
constitute sensible representations.

In the aesthetic research work of Alex Arteaga, practices are processes of making possible and opening new modes of perception, dealing with the dwelling aspect of grasping meaning by perception. That is *the second aesthetic practice* I consider. Destabilizing meaning is one practice of releasing meaning from conventional constraints, as the work *transient senses* shows. Practices of discrepancy overcome the distinction between truth and illusion. The expression "optical illusion" is paradigmatic of the dualism, but it makes no sense in destabilized perception, which explores edges as practices of openness and not of intentional constraint. As Arteaga states:

> "Inside" and "outside" are fully constituted and stable intentional objects. They are phenomena with clear meaning. However, when these meanings are destabilized—in this case through the intervention of a particular construction—they make evident their phenomenal status. They show that they are constituted, that is, that they are the emerging result of certain kinds of interactions (Arteaga, Architecture of Embodiment, 2).

This destabilization has a cognitive function of extending perceptive meaning. [M] Exploring the constitution of phenomena depends radically on practices such as walking, recording, editing and installing, which configure the variety of perception in a perceptive modulation—which Arteaga calls "aesthetic conduct" (Arteaga, Embodied and Situated Aesthetics, 24). The practice is in this way also a form of behavior and participation of the subject, whose attention opens up to passivity. Passivity—as Arteaga notes—is not understood "as a lack of activity but rather as a specific kind of activity. Passivity denotes here a way of actively being-in-the-world, a variety of action receptive to other actions, focused—in an unfocussed way—on

[L] | ^{AGV} I think it would be illuminating to explain concretely this concept of medium and especially to elaborate further on the relation between media and performativity.

    ^{LG} See my reply to the first comment.

[M] | ^{AA} What do you mean with "perceptive meaning"?

    ^{LG} "Perceptive meaning" is the meaning that is constituted, articulated, and modulated in perception.

its adaptation to those actions that touch the passively acting body" (Arteaga, Architecture of Embodiment, 6). In this sense, *media* [N] *have the function of revealing new possibilities of experiencing phenomena as environmental practices.*

3. RELEASING LANDSCAPE

Related to the environment, spatial re-presentation becomes the *pre-sentation* of a new outcome that constitutes manifold interrelations between object and subject. Taking place as a practice of being aware of the act of constitution that is perception does not involve the onto-logical fusion or conflation of subject and object. On the contrary, this awareness motivates the subject to grasp the constitutive value of me-dia as practices of performing reality—also at the level of the percep-tion of everyday objects or states. In this sense, media are conditions of possibility of the relation between subject and object, and this relation has the transcendental value of performing reality. The distinction be-tween subject and object is thus the difference of a displacement of perspective, articulated and shared in aesthetic practices as practices of experience in the realm of perception within the environment. [O]

Perception is not about an experience of the surface of phe-nomena that emerges as fixed semantic schemes and conventional functions. On the contrary, phenomena are looked for, explored and constituted in their immanence. Immanence is the mediated essence of phenomena as aesthetic practices. Edges are the magnitude of the intensity of our perception of phenomena from an eccentric position-ality, from which we do not surround but are rather *in* the environment. Coming back to practices, therefore, implies a new view of the rela-tionship between object and subject that implies at once a new con-ception *taking place* at the boundaries between architecture and land-scape, territory and earth. As Deleuze and Guattari point out:

Subject and object give a poor approximation of thought.
Thinking is neither a line drawn between subject and

[N] | AGV Again, which are the media you are referring to in this case?
LG Media are the conditions of possibility of practices; they are both performative and performed. See my reply to the first comment.

[O] | AA This passage reinforces my doubts on the distinction you make between "media" and "practices." On the one hand you used these two concepts as synonyms—"media as practices"—but on the other hand it would be possible to understand, as I do, that practices actualize the potentialities—the conditions of possibility—offered by media.
LG Media and practices are correlated, but they are not synonyms. See my reply to the first comment.

object nor a revolving of one around the other. Rather, thinking takes place in the relationship of territory and the earth (Deleuze and Guattari, What is Philosophy?, 85).

Architecture is a performative act of composition that marks the territory and articulates its movement. Architecture as intervention is thus the perception of landscape. Sensations are organized by architectural interventions in a kind of schematism that can have a specific function or can be the composition of a new function. Architecture, like other forms of art, shows that art depends on composition—as I noted above according to Deleuze—which is a specific transition from the material into the composed sensation, also called by Deleuze a "block of sensations" (Deleuze and Guattari, What is Philosophy?, 164).

In particular, architecture composes precisely at the level of animal activity a territory in which pure sensory qualities emerge "not only in the treatment of external materials but in the body's postures and colors, in the songs and cries that mark out the territory. It is an outpouring of features, colors, and sounds that are inseparable insofar as they become expressive" (Deleuze and Guattari, What is Philosophy?, 184). This philosophical concept of territory aims to show its compositional character as a whole of sensations rather than a generic notion of territory as an ensemble of immediate synesthesia. The territory is qualitatively porous; it is a *habitat* that brings different qualities of perceptions and spaces together. As Deleuze and Guattari write, referring precisely to Uexküll:

> Every territory, every habitat, joins up not only its spatiotemporal but its qualitative planes or sections: a posture and a song for example, a song and a color, percepts and affects. And every territory encompasses or cuts across the territories of other species, or intercepts the trajectories of animals without territories, forming interspecies junction points. It is in this sense that, to start with, Uexküll develops a melodic, polyphonic, and contrapuntal

conception of Nature (Deleuze and Guattari, What is Philosophy?, 185).

This notion of territory implies a new consideration of the relations and internal tensions between architecture and landscape, which are all too often distinguished from each other on the basis of practical functions. The mutual correlation between landscape and architecture requires truly a new consideration of border areas and dismissed places—which Rendell relates to the concept of *expanded field* referring to the spatial practices of Stalker—Laboratory for Urban Interventions (Rendell, Art and Architecture, 188). The borderlines between architecture and landscape have the double function of demarcation and the prioritization of architecture, against the non-built environment. The borders become places to be, beyond the drawing of a semantic frontier between the built environment and disused land. Architecture is considered in ways that go beyond its practical function and is at a fundamental level an intervention into space, and thus the constitution of a structural principle by orienting our habitat (Awan, Schneider, and Till, Other Ways of Doing Architecture).

The notion of *Umwelt* also marks a paradigm shift for architecture that is sometimes the antithesis of this approach. As Ian Simmons observes, "architecture after the industrial revolution, however, positively celebrates its release from the forces of nature… In other words, the construction made by architecture, both physical and symbolic, is that of the high-energy industrial world, which is the outcome of centuries of adherence to the idea that nature had to be overcome" (Simmons, Interpreting Nature, 115).

Gilles Clément emphatically maintains that the relationship between human beings and nature is that of fusion, and he suggests the idea of "symbiotic humanity" (Clément, The Emergent Alternative, 276). Nature is therefore interesting not only for scientists but, as Clément notes, referring to the work of Roberto Burle Marx, for artists too (Clément, The Planetary Garden, 25). Both experiment with nature in

creative ways, which does not mean that they create nature but rather that they show, experimenting with practices and methods, how nature is also a product of creation. A new perspective on the relationship between nature and human beings entails, on the one hand, a new kind of openness to practices and to practicing knowledge; on the other hand, it entails granting a new status to the landscape, going beyond fixed classifications—and Clément shows how the principle of a *garden in motion* arises from the explosion of the garden as an expression of ordinate thought (Clément, Le jardin en mouvement). This is *the third aesthetic practice* I relate to the mutual relation between landscape and architecture. New ways and practices of exploring the landscape are part of an "emergent alternative" in defining the environment, as Clément explains:

> The word "environment", used to describe the world around us, implies that humans do not belong to this *mis-en-scéne,* that the human is situated behind, above, or elsewhere, but not within the environment. Ministries of the environment—ministries of the surroundings—see the creature and its landscape as a complex ensemble to be analyzed in order to quantify it, not as a living space in which humanity, to the same degree as all the other living entities, find itself *immersed* (Clément, The Emergent Alternative, 268).

> As he writes further, "[o]ne needs to *immerse* oneself, to accept oneself as an entity within nature, to revise one's position in the universe, no longer above or in the center, but rather *within* and *with*" (Clément, The Emergent Alternative, 269). This method of resistance marks the very shifting interest in perception and its edges described above—perception and edges which emerge from the encounter with different environments and which are ways of experimenting with the impreciseness and depth of representation (Clément, Manifeste du Tiers paysage).

The transformation of our approach to environment, along with the redesigning of the material environment, does not involve interpreting the objects of representation in an immediate way. There can be no approach to materiality without *critically* viewing objects as hybrid constructs that are materialized by virtue of practices and media that are the conditions of possibility of the design environment. As Uexküll notes, in an observation which marks a suitable conclusion to my reflections on the concept of *Umwelt* and its implications: "Peasants and gardeners … are not students of Nature, unless they happen to have acquired the art of interrogation" (Uexküll, Theoretical Biology, X). *There is in conclusion no environment without the exploration of its emergence.* [P]

[P] AA This conclusion seems to me to be problematic. The exploration of the (emergence of the) environment seems to be a condition of possibility of its own emergence but, how can the exploration precede the emergence of the object of exploration? According to the enactivist approach, the environment emerges spontaneously out of the coupling between autonomous and heteronomous units and its exploration—an intentional reflection—can only take place after the environment is sufficiently constituted— or to be precise, while the environment is in its process of constitution but enough constituted in order to be "object" of inquiry.

LG The environment as *Umwelt* stands for a philosophical approach that deals with the constitution of the environment and moves us to explore its emergence. This is not an onto-genetic level of analysis that aims to explain the emergence as a starting point of the environment but rather a phenomenological approach that tries to deal with the emergence not as immediacy but rather as the experimental exploration of the emergence, which implies—as Kant also observes—an infinite grade of perception.

[FULL TEXT]

ME How to perceive practices? Or, the other way around: how to practice perception? In Finnish language there is no evident equivalent to the word "practice." If the perception of practices is mediated through language, then we need to make linguistic distinctions in order to get access to the richness of practices. In Finnish we need to think of the richness of practices with the help of the following distinctions: "exercise," "rehearsal," "training," "convention" and "hobby," which makes the questions related to "practice" rather complex.

LG "To perceive practice" is a practice, and it requires a multitude of practices. There is no passive perception of practices to capture their sensible meaning. On the contrary, we are dealing with a particular kind of asymmetry that plays a crucial role, for instance, in design practices. Practicing perception is the key relationship between observing, learning and developing practice because for that we need "practical" knowledge in which these levels are interrelated. The perception of practices is mediated not only through language but through embodied practices.

SH Lidia's text is very dense. It refers to many ideas on perception, on practices, on aesthetic conduct and on the role of architecture in landscapes. As its basic intention I understand the introduction of philosophical positions into the discussion of environments, here identified with Jakob von Uexküll's concept of the *"Umwelt."* Lidia is mainly interested in Uexküll's understanding of the ability of humans to understand themselves as the center of their environment. For my comment I choose two subjects among the interesting issues alluded to in the paper. First I want to mention the productive idea of linking the notion of perception to practices: The discussion of Michel de Certeau's walking or traveling practices is indeed a major example for aesthetic approaches to the perception of environments and for their ability of constituting space. With Dewey Lidia argues for the educational role of these practices supporting a felt relationship between organism and environment in their interaction, a key notion of the text I assume. A second remark concerns the notion of landscape: In this text landscape seems to be identified with territory, with region, with environment and even with "nature." Possibly this is motivated through the reference to Gilles Clément who expresses his strong intention to defend nature's beauty and resources and who also refers to Uexküll's concept of *"Umwelt."* But still I would defend that it makes sense to understand landscape as a special term related to the, interestingly not exclusively European, tradition of a basically aesthetic approach to vast territories. This also implies that architecture can be read and built as a structure within landscapes—even if one may debate whether today's architecture already respects the manifold ways of perceiving, the huge wealth of possible aesthetic practices and the richness of environments to a satisfying degree.

> LG The reference to landscape and landscape architecture aims to show that, starting from the environment as *umwelt,* as constituted nature within perception, how we grasp the relationship between architecture and the "unbuilt" surroundings changes. Gilles Clément tries to overcome this boundary by revealing the value of boundaries as environmental explorations. The boundary becomes a space of constitution, and architecture can be read, of course, as a structure within a landscape, as a process of performing the space of perception that depends on aesthetic practices.

References:

Agamben, Giorgio. The Open: Man and Animal. Palo Alto CA:
    Stanford University Press, 2004.

Arteaga, Alex. "Architecture of Embodiment." Lecture given at
    the School of Architecture of the Royal Academy of Fine
    Arts in the framework of the International Lecture Series.
    Copenhagen, March 17th 2016.

Arteaga, Alex. "Embodied and Situated Aesthetics: An enactive
    approach to a cognitive notion of aesthetics." Artnodes
    20 (2017): 20–27. https://artnodes.uoc.edu/articles/ab-
    stract/10.7238/a.v0i20.3155/ [accessed Jan 10, 2018].

Awan, Nishat, Tatjana Schneider and Jeremy Till. Spatial Agency:
    Other Ways of Doing Architecture. London: Routledge, 2011.

Clément, Gilles. Le jardin en mouvement. De la vallée au champ
    via le parc André-Citroën et le jardin planetaire. Paris: Sens
    & Tonka, 1991, 258–277.

Clément, Gilles. Manifeste du Tiers paysage. Paris: Éditions Su-
    jet/Object, 2004.

Clément, Gilles. "The Emergent Alternative," in Architectural The-
    ories of the Environment, ed. Ariane Lourie Harrison. New
    York: Taylor & Francis, 2013, 258–277.

Clément, Gilles. The Planetary Garden and Other Writings. Phila-
    delphia: University of Pennsylvania Press, 2015.

De Certeau, Michel. The Practice of Everyday Life. Berkeley CA:
    University of California Press, 1984.

Deleuze, Gilles. "The Idea of Genesis in Kant's Aesthetics, "Ange-
    laki. Journal of the Theoretical Humanities 5, no. 3, (2000):
    57–70.

Deleuze, Gilles and Félix Guattari. What is Philosophy? New York:
    Columbia University Press, 1994.

Deleuze, Gilles and Félix Guattari. A Thousand Plateaus. Minne-
    apolis: University of Minnesota Press, 2005.

Dewey, John. Art as Experience. London: Penguin, 2005.

Didi-Huberman, Georges. The Man Who Walked in Color (Minne-
    apolis: Univocal Publishing, 2017).

Evans, Robin. Translations from Drawing to Building and Other
    Essays. London: Architectural Association, 1997.

Gasperoni, Lidia. Versinnlichung. Kants transzendentaler Sche-
    matismus und seine Revision in der Nachfolge. Berlin: De
    Gruyter, 2016.

Kant, Immanuel. Critique of Pure Reason. Translated by Paul
    Guyer and Allen W. Wood. Cambridge: Cambridge Univer-
    sity Press, 1998.

Kant, Immanuel. Critique of the Power of Judgment. Translated
    by Paul Guyer and Eric Matthews. Cambridge: Cambridge
    University Press, 2000.

Plessner, Helmuth. Die Stufen des Organischen und der Mensch.
    Gesammelte Schriften, IV. Berlin: Suhrkamp, 1981.

Rancière, Jacques. The Politics of Aesthetics: The Distribution of
    the Sensible. New York: Continuum, 2011.

Rendell, Jane. Art and Architecture. A Place Between. London:
    I.B. Tauris, 2006.

Schürmann, Eva. Erscheinen und Wahrnehmen: eine verglei-
    chende Studie zur Kunst von James Turrell und der Philos-
    ophie Merleau-Pontys. Munich: Fink, 2000.

Simmons, Ian. Interpreting Nature: Cultural Constructions of the
    Environment. London: Routledge, 1993.

Uexküll, Jakob von. Theoretical Biology. Boston MA: Harcourt,
    1926.

Uexküll, Jakob von. Umwelt und Innenwelt der Tiere. London: For-
    gotten Books, 2015.

Aesthetic Research.
An Exploratory Essay [A]

Alex Arteaga

1.

We search. Constantly.

We are incessantly modulating the course of our actions. First of all, to make them possible, to continue making them possible. To continue making possible to adequately insert our actions-to-be into the flow of a dense fabric of action configured with other actions, which are conditioned—sometimes enabled—by our actions and which constrain—sometimes enable—our actions.

We search, constantly, uninterruptedly, in order to continue acting—to continue inter-acting. To continue realizing our ability to act—to inter-act. [B]

[A] JH I enjoy this text in many ways, but especially as piece of poetic writing. It seems to exemplify an idea of life as continuous flow that is developed later within this text and others in the book. This idea suggests that if (a) life is interrupted it might not always be able to resume—if dormant for too long it might lose its viability. I therefore find it a little challenging to intervene in a useful way during the body of the text, without feeling like I am interrupting a vital process and threatening its viability!

[B] DM To start with search in order to understand research means starting with its genuine etymological root. Research stems from search; however research obviously addresses a specific kind of search. So starting with search requires a thorough observation of the shift from one to the other. But search does not only mean to inter-act with the world. Instead I would like to claim that, in the first place, searching and desiring are co-relative. Searching in this view is a part of our longing, our striving for something. Both are mutually related to each other, and both point at a fundamental human practice, not necessarily a goal-oriented action, but a vague and indeterminate longing, a desire, as it were, for nothing specific, however a desire that sometimes is rewarded with some contingent findings. Searching, therefore, is more important than discovering, more important also than success and fulfillment. There is search because there is alterity, not in terms of capturing it, incorporating or absorbing it, but there is something other that attracts or affects us, touches us, speaks to us, provokes us.

> AA I basically agree with your comment Dieter but I would like to make some remarks. First, I agree that search does not mean to interact. I didn't mean it in my text. My point was that action—and therefore, necessarily, interaction—is the condition of possibility for any search. We come to search because we interact: we act with others. Accordingly, I agree with the first aspect of your last point—"there is search because there is alterity"—and I would add that this alterity is not distant: we are in touch with it, we interact with it. Second, I tend to interpret the kind of longing, striving or desire for something vague, for a non-specific object as expressions of the motivation of maintaining or maybe in this case rather extending or intensifying the viability of our actions, the fluidity of our existence, of our interactions. The fulfillment of the kind of desire you succinctly describe expresses itself as an experience of expansion, in my view, of possibilities of action. Therefore, I agree that search, understood in this way, is not object-oriented and consequently, cannot be about "capturing" or any similar operation.

We search in order to continue being able to adequately braid our actions with other actions which are operatively present—before they, perhaps, appear perceptually, before they, if this comes to be the case, are perceptually constituted as "other actions," as "the actions of others," as a not-me-in-action. An "other"—or "others"—which, through its intimate relation to my-self, through the radical intimacy of the mutual touch, operates as the necessary counterpart, as a dynamic whole "out there"—as the-other-of-my-self, the otherness of my selfness.

A diverse other, acquiring its singularity as the otherness of my singular self. A multiple other, a myriad of acting others, subsumed in this singular other—the environment, my environment, my world, the world, a world-for-me.

A singular other thus mirroring my singularity, the singularity of this plural, diverse self I call my-self from no other spot than this self recognizing itself through its participation in the dense meshwork of its world.

A worldly "selfless self."[1] A self emerging as a "project of the world." A world only possible as and through the realization of this self-recognizing-self while and because it cognizes its world.[2]

A world—<u>my world, the world of this my-self [c]</u>—also as a place of and for a myriad of acting others. Others interacting with one another, I guess, but certainly interacting with me, noticing immediately and in an unmediated way the constant alterations of my embodied self, of this self that notices also immediately and in an unmediated way—first operatively, as an alteration of the dynamics that connect one another—that they/it notice(s).

A radically active, plural otherness only possible as such—as other, as this other, my other, the other of my-self—by virtue of its dynamic coupling with a self—an active, plural self—which acts by virtue of its selfness—the embodiment of its own organization—enabled by the dynamic coupling with its otherness.

[C] | DM Here I would prefer to avoid any implicit egological perspective. Ex-
pressions such as "my world" or "my-self" prerequisite an already constituted me, a self as being already given or formed and contoured—by
what? The self is not primordial, but secondary in relation to the other.
The outcome of this is that search mainly is a function of the riddle and
strangeness of the world. Therefore I can only find and, literally, de-fine
myself through appearance and reception beyond intentionality. Hence,
intentionality first and foremost comes into place by secondary reflection
and repetition. Both produce a certain awareness, a refinement of search,
turning it into re-search.

AA I basically agree with your comment. I think neither that the self
precedes the world nor that the world precedes the self. I think, according to the enactive approach, that self and world co-emerge:
they arise simultaneously in a continuous process of mutual conditioning. It is on the basis of this strong interdependence between self
and world—of this "structural coupling" in terms of Maturana—that I
talk about "the world of a self" the same way I could invert the terms
and talk about "the self of a world." I also agree with your second
point: the world becomes strange to (its) self and this is the origin of
search. This is coherent with the idea of the co-emergence of self
and world: there is a disturbance in the process of co-emergence
and this manifests for the self as estrangement. And I also agree
with your comment on intentionality if we understand this term here
as the will-based performance of certain intentions generated, as
you wrote, through reflection. This refers, as you remarked, to research. Nevertheless, if we understand the word intentionality phenomenologically as the unavoidable aboutness of the self's actions,
intentionality is constitutive for the self's realization—and the arising
of its world.

And vice versa.

And so on.

We search, constantly, in order to maintain this "so on."
      To maintain the continuity, the fluid consistency of the realization of our acts in touch with other acts—without interruption, without break-in-between, neither between them nor between them and the acts of others.
      An extremely dense and complex succession of actions—we would say, if we would reflect on this continuum, if we would come back again and again to it (if we would re-flect) and singularize sections of this unceasing flow as distinct actions, if we would construct, better, re-construct, continuity as a chain of singularities: an artifact created by certain forms of reflection.

We search continuously, with the same continuity of the actions which are, at the same time, the object, the goal—if we are not able to conceive and accept the existence of goalless actions, of a radical absence of teleology—the medium and the realization of the search.

Our acts, thus, as search.
      A search without distance—between the search and its object, between the search and the searcher, between the search and its field, between its ostensible parts or moments.

A radically continuous, immanent search.

An invisible search. Invisible because we see, perhaps, our actions and, probably, their consequences—objectified, apparently, outside of the realm of action.

A search hidden under two layers of visibility linked to one another by direct causality: what we do and what follows.

We search, constantly, without being aware of the search because we are constantly finding without being aware of our findings: ways of continuing to act, of continuing to inter-act, of navigating our world without noticing, most of the time, any friction.

We search through our acts—due to our acts, because we act, by acting, as action—for "something in them": an aspect, a constitutive trait of the actions, a capacity embedded and realized in and through the actions themselves.

We search for the activation, for the maintenance, for the operative realization of a twofold ability to adapt: to our actions—to their uninterrupted flow, their smooth succession without a gap—and to their counterpart—the actions of our environment, the perturbations of the surroundings touching our acting body, constantly, uninterruptedly.

We search, incessantly, in action, through the very same actions we are realizing and in which we are searching for ways to sustain their realization by sustaining its adaptation to its own flow and, simultaneously, to the flow of the other actions with which our actions develop their course.

We search, by acting—in/through our actions—for ways of enabling to keep the touch touching, [D] to keep the dynamic contact between the acting body and its active surroundings, to maintain the possibility of inter-acting. Not of re-acting but instead of radically, constitutively, immanently acting-with. Of in-corporating: of maintaining through action the stream of embodiment, the incessant realization of structurally connected bodies in action—the touching actions of the body's surroundings, the body's not-itself but with-and-for-it-self—while and through acting.

We search, immanently, for ways to continue participating in the dynamic system that our actions contribute to enable, that enables the realization of our actions and that constrains—constantly, continuously, along and throughout their course—their realization.

We search by acting—implicitly, through and in each single action—for adequate forms of participation in this complex dynamic system in, through and by virtue of which every single action becomes possible and comes to be.

We search for ways to maintain the viability of our actions.

We search for the maintenance of the viability of our actions, contributing in doing so to maintaining the viability of the whole system.

We support, through the subtle, persistent maintenance of our adaptability, the dynamic system which supports the maintenance of our adaptability.

A closed, multilayered, self-supporting meshwork of mutually adapting, reciprocally supporting actions.

A medium—our actions—in a medium—the whole system.

[D] DM I fully agree with the interrelation between action and touching. Western metaphysics has always privileged the eye or the optical system and underestimated the tactile system. The visionary system always already presupposes distance and, hence, abstraction, while the tactile is comprised of the immediate dialectics of touching and being touched and is therefore related to the experience of existence. Before there is something—as a finding—there is something unknown, unassigned and even unsettled that has already touched us and gives rise to a "being-there," a "thatness" or just an irritation that my perceptual senses cannot ignore. Therefore search is primarily related to "being in contact with," whatever the "with" means. Before there is something as something, there is something as "touch," as a "given existence" which I also would like to call a "gift." Thus, if we search constantly, by acting (and also by responding), we, at the same time, receive gifts we never wished for. Findings, in the first place, are gifts or donations given by no-one.

Two interlaced, mutually conditioning media enabling through their interlacement their possible continuity—and, as a constitutive aspect of it, the viability of our actions through and with it.

We search—constantly, implicitly, silently, humbly, operatively, below the line of the perceivable but in constant touch with it—acting—by and through each single action—to make the next, not yet existent action possible—the next, not yet given moment come to be.

I'm not writing about anything special, anything extraordinary. I am trying to look into the inner structure of the quotidian—into its inner infrastructure—into the operative virtuosity of every single small action we perform everyday, every moment, since we open our eyes and find, or better, lay down our path through the day. [E]

I am writing about the way our feet adapt to the ever-changing floor allowing the rest of our organism to make a new step, about the way our hands adopt precise shapes changing constantly, fluidly, to allow the realization of each interaction—opening a door, shaking another hand, using a utensil adequately, caressing another body, configuring the gestures that allow the communication, the collective micro-realization of the fundamental common: the intimate touch that joins, mostly in an implicit way, our body to other bodies.

I am writing about, or better, I am trying to get in touch through organizing words, through pressing keys on my laptop and seeing how signs appear on its screen, through the way we are constantly articulating words—with one another and with the realization of the agency of each object, of each picture, of each material, of each other speaking voice that our speaking voice meets in the course of its own articulated production.

[E] | JH I think this is an important aspect of the enactive view of perception (as put forward by Alva Noë et al.), but also has an interesting link with the idea of the mind as a "prediction machine" suggested by Andy Clark and others exploring so called "predictive processing" within the brain. If we are constantly searching, in the sense described here, it is perhaps also because we are constantly projecting forward our perceptual (motor cognitive, in Merleau-Ponty's terms) anticipations of what we are about to experience, (based on our sense of what kind of situation it is that currently confronts us) and with this comes the need to find out if those predictions are correct, or, perhaps more precisely, to attempt to correct them, in order that they conform to what we have apparently just experienced, and to prepare us better for the next time we experience it.

    AA Without negating our ability to anticipate, I feel a certain resistance to admitting prediction as the basic operation of our conduct. Writing this text I have been rather envisioning a situation of "radical present": acting while neither knowing what is the next step nor the ground on which it will be made.

I'm writing about, or better with, the intimate howness of each silent touch, of each quotidian, irrelevant, banal—we would, unfairly, say—contact, with the viability of our acts emerging out of each minimal encounter, of each realization of the plasticity of our constant realization as bodies among bodies, of our ability of finding, or better of co-generating ways to realize this ability and, simultaneously, its conditions of possibility.

I am writing about, with and as a realization of the very quotidian search for ways to act—to inter-act—to do—and sometimes to make—to continue doing, to continue being active in, with and through the world—the world that supports our actions and is co-constituted by them.

I am writing about and in touch with something invisible, unnoticed, non-objectified, ungraspable, simply because it is continuously performed, because it is inseparable from everything we do, from everything that happens—underlaying it, supporting it, being what makes it possible "from within" (within the systems of relationships) and therefore occluded by everything we do and everything that happens.

I am writing about and with(in) the constitutive search of the quotidian, of every gesture, of every single act—even those which will never come to be but were possible and even would have been possible.

I am observing, looking at and for—going about, around, wandering—the searching nature of (our) nature.

And there, in the silent, meaningless but senseful quotidian life, we do not stop.

We act. We search—implicitly, intimately, continuously, by acting, through action—for the next possible action, for the next adaptive turn

of the course of our actions, for our viability through the subtle network of possible actions we share with our environment before they, some of them, are actualized, realized.

We search through action for the following possible-because-adequate move.

But sometimes the smooth concatenation of actions breaks down and our actions appear [F]—they appear right in this moment, they break then the silence of their operativity and appear. The medium—actions as medium of their own course—collapses and disrupts its necessary invisibility, the implicitness that confers to our actions their medial power.

Our minimal, quotidian, apparently insignificant actions appear right then when their viability is interrupted. They appear—as non-viable.

They appear because of their sudden lack of viability. They appear as absence—the absence of their actualization—as the impossibility of coming to be, as the impossibility of being realized, as the interruption of the fluid transition between potentiality and actualization, between possible because potentially adequate and actual because success-fully adapted.

Our actions appear then as their current impossibility, as a momen-tary loss of smoothness in the contact, as the temporary suspension of fluidity in the silent, intimate, operative dialog with other actions. [G]

Blockage. Maybe simply disruption. [H]

[F] DM The fascinating approach of the text is its very meticulous reconstruction of the turning-point between acting as searching and its moment of rupture and conversion into the reflective mode of re-research and re-cognition with certain emphasis on the "re"—the attempt to understand thoroughly the progress from doing to thinking. Arteaga's way of argumentation reveals itself as strongly anti-reductive.

[G] JH There is also here a suggestion of the idea that perceptual events might be better understood not as isolated percepts but as momentary fluctuations (or perturbations) in an otherwise continuous flow of perceptual activity. In this case life itself (organic/metabolic processes) could be thought of as fundamentally rhythmical in character, and therefore that the things that stand out, or show up, for us as objects, things or events, are actually rhythmic modulations in a constant flow or interchange of energies and information between the organism and its environment. For me, as an architect, this idea echoes Gottfried Semper's claim regarding the primacy of rhythm in the emergence of art as a practice of ordering (or organizing) of things in the world. For Semper the knot was seen as a kind of *Ur-form* of human making, the primary artistic unit out of which all other forms of making might have emerged. The knot in a piece of string could be seen as a modulation of flows, whether acting as a mnemonic device, or as a technique for measuring the speed of boats.

[H] DM This I consider as the most important part of the argumentation: starting with a phenomenology of search as incessant action, a striving for understanding and discovery as the very nature of our being-in-the-world, which often remains latent, unconscious and almost automatic and ending with cognition and knowledge. In the first place therefore acting seems to be a constant flight, a getaway, a permanent restless doing; and then, all of a sudden, a startle, a perturbation, a disruption happens which interrupts our continuation. Arteaga calls it a temporal nano-existential impossibility. It forces us to turn our head, to look twice and to start with reflection, in one word: to turn search into re-search. The main idea here is, that this which makes us think, derives from negativity. However there is still a certain indeterminacy: the undecidable decision between a rupture or impediment as cut, as distinction, as difference that makes differences, and just as a meaningless break or interruption that blocks our ability to understand. Maybe this undecidability remains contingent.

AA I basically agree with this comment. Nevertheless I would like to introduce a difference that for me makes a big difference. For me thinking begins with the first, minimal action. According to the enactive approach—and furthermore with the ideas formulated in the framework of the theory of autopoiesis—cognition is not the performance of "higher skills" but rather every contribution to the incessant process of sense-making, that is, of co-emergence of selves and worlds as significant entities. Consequently, there is no difference between acting and thinking—furthermore, there is no difference between organic activity and thinking. There are, undoubtedly, different varieties of thinking as different forms of action. Thinking, therefore, does not begin, but I certainly agree, that there is a form of thinking that has a "negative" origin: it does not work and we have to find a new way to make it function. Following this line of thought, I would reformulate the distinction described at the end of the comment: there are "meaningless breaks or interruption" but they all are senseful.

Temporary, maybe, minimal paralysis: cut apart, standing beside—out of play, momentarily excluded from the dynamic meshwork of interactions, of mutually supporting actions.

Out of the world. Only for an instant, maybe. Maybe nearly unnoticed and forgotten away with.

Unexpectedly, we do not know how to proceed. We did not know before, but we did not need to know. We were acting—simply acting.

We were navigating, smoothly, the emergence of sense that our interactions enabled and that supported the realization of our actions—without noticing it, without needing to notice it. Without knowing—being knowledge an artifact articulating a satisfactory description and/or explanation of the phenomenon to which the one who knows refers.

We did not know. We did not need to know. We were simultaneously co-constituting and performing [1]—that is, performing in both meanings of this term—the viability of our actions in, through and with the shared field of action that enables and constrains this viability.

But now the continuity is perturbed, the fluent adaptive performance and the unfolding of its performativity collapse.

And suddenly, unexpectedly, we do not know—perhaps we even say it, we speak it out. We do not know what's next—what is going to be, what could be the next move, the next gesture, the next displacement, the next turn, the next sound, the next word.

"It does not make sense"—we would say, perhaps—"it does not make sense anymore."

Nothing dramatic, but existential—nano-existential, we could say: the affirmation of a temporary impossibility.

Nothing special. Again, nothing extraordinary.

[I] | DM The idea here is obviously the duplicity between constitution and per-
formance. Often in philosophy both are separated: as long as we perform
our action, there is no need for reflection; and as soon we reflect, we are
unable to act. To take this incompatibility between practice and theory for
granted is here very rightly thrown into question. And the cautious steps
forward of the text, its slow moves and its hesitation is necessary to identify the subtle oscillation between both and the turning-point where things
suddenly become different.

> AA As I argued in my answer to your last comment, I definitely try to
> integrate constitution and performance: each act is potentially an
> act of phenomenal co-constitution.

The temporary lack of sense—the break down of the emergence of sense—and the impossibility of simply continuing to act appear simultaneously, as two sides of the same phenomenon. Or better, addressing it from another perspective, with another conceptual strategy: the impossibility of acting, the interruption of the adaptation, of the flow of actualization of our agency, expresses a gap of sense, the discontinuity of its dynamic and relational constitution.

The impossibility of acting—of simply making the next step, of simply saying another word—objectifies, in the moment of its disruption, the immanent operativity of sense. It brings to light, it makes explicit the implicitness of a so far constantly successful search, of the searching component of action that is collapsing now, that requires a modification in its performance in order to once again accomplish its performative function.

And then we stop. We have to stop.

We cannot do anything but stopping because we don't know how to proceed now (and now we need to know because of the implicitness of the emergence of sense, the unspoken, the "unsayable"[3] viability of our actions has lost, temporarily, its silent voice).

We stop because we don't know and need, ineluctably, to know—or at least to sense—how it goes further, how we can successfully couple again, how we can restore the fluency in the realization of the coupling with our environment.

We stop and consider.

We wonder—probably in an unspoken way, implicitly, rather touching, tentatively, around, sounding our closest domains, our habitualized spheres of action—what's next, how to do what we want or maybe

need to do, what can be the next gesture, the next move, the next sound, maybe an articulated one, the next word. We speculate about—we look and we look for—how can it—the realization of the connective dynamics between my-self and my-world—go on.

We stop and revise, revisit, reconsider. We look and explore again and again—the circumstances, what has happened, how everything in a surrounding time and space appears—in a fuzzy way, sounding, slightly touching with our fingertips, the possible, the plausible, the feasible.

But also, if necessary, if it still doesn't work, analyzing, grasping, dissecting, manipulating.

We look for right choices—we have to choose, now, explicitly, we have to decide, now, in a strong maybe even literal meaning of the word, we have to cut off a caesura, to bring dislocated parts together. We consider and, if necessary, we judge possible actions as adequate ones and discard, explicitly, others instead of simply, implicitly, adequately performing our actions.

We estimate, compare—iteratively, again and again.

We do not move forward—not yet. We keep on standing, still blocked, and see—what appears out of our iterative considerations. Repeatedly, over and over, again and again.

We no longer search-in-action. We are not simply doing, performing our actions, finding, without noticing—that we search, that we find—through each action the next action to follow.

We begin, thus, incipiently, to re-search. [J]

We step out of the unnoticed fluidity of our unnoticed search-in-action and situate ourselves spontaneously—maybe, at least at the beginning, in the moment we stop—in the position of the observer.

We observe the phenomena that we constitute and throw them in front of ourselves—our provisorily non-viable self, the domain of this temporary impossibility, the environment that appears now as incoherent, as non-transitable. [K]

We ob-bjectify now operative presences that have been dodging explicitness in order to maintain their fluidity.

We take distance—we could say, repeating an uncritically accepted formulation—without breaking the connections. We generate a space—without abandoning the field, without fully retreating—in which we can provisorily inhabit the non-viable.

We camp. We create a provisory shelter, a protected base out of the flow that flows now without us—or better, without our contribution—but always stay in touch with it.

A place—an incipient observatory, a germinal lab, an inceptive studio—in and from which to observe, to con-sider—to watch the moving stars, to see with the stars and get oriented again, to watch the stars with the stars and let con-stellations (patterns, forms) arise: new, explicit forms of guidance.

An alternative performative framework. An extra-ordinary sphere born out of both the impossibility of simply continuing to act and the imperious necessity of restoring the lost viability.

A new way of organizing action through which we expect to find out new possibilities to act—to inter-act—again.

[J] | DM Here we arrive, after a long journey over more than half of the text at the very aim of the exercise: gradually shifting perspective from searching as a fundamental human practice to the empire of (scientific or artistic) re-search. And still at this point the difference between art and science remains unsettled. Thus at this point we have to say that the difference between both is not general because both are originated in the same source: a split or rift, as fissure or caesura in everyday life experience.

AA I completely agree!

[K] | DM It seems to be a tiny crack that chances everything: a small cut, a hardly noticeable transition, a displaced syncope, an inconspicuous detail that makes the world incoherent and forces us to reinterpret our understandings. However this is exactly what I mean by the moment of alterity: the incomprehensible or mysteriousness. Here we have to say that it happens, without knowing why, because the longer we look at things (or at our neighbor) the stranger it or he or she seems. There is always something uncanny in the world, but the most uncanny thing is the social other, the other human being.

AA Yes, I agree situating alterity in this moment. It is the most radical alterity, the most primitive, original not-knowing: the provisory lack of sense—way beyond a temporary absence of meaning.

An enabling field for a second-order acting: looking—reiteratively, even systematically, methodically—for the adequate, for the convinient action—the action coming-with, moving-with, enabling, again, common actions.

There, in our observatory, we look for a solution, rather for a dis-solution—of the blockage, of the knot that tieds our activity, that keeps ourselves out of play, that hinders the dynamic touch, the connection, the fluid realization of the structural coupling that maintains the possibility of our selfness through the viability of the common. [L]

Research, thus, firstly, incipiently, minimally defined, as an alteration of our constant, unnoticed, operative search for the maintenance of the viability of our actions, of our dynamic being-with-the-world.

A necessary, unavoidable alteration of the constant, continuous search in order to achieve the same goal—now made explicit, now objectified—with different means.

A new field of practices that allows us to actualize, in a different way, the constraints of the same medium: action.

Research thus, primarily, as a temporal alteration of the quotidian search. As an intensification first and foremost through repetition, through iteration, through visiting the incipient gap again and again, through revisiting the problematic spot in front of which we stopped, we had to stop, in order to see—to see it differently, to allow it to take a new form, the one that provided conditions of possibility for us to find out, again, how to restore the viability of our conduct.

[L] JH This also reminds me of the work of Arakawa and Gins, and their poetic writing on the idea of a kind of immortality that might result from this kind of interdependence or merging of a stimulating environment and a stimulated body. In other words, how a productive interchange between living and non-living might begin to erase the typical distinction between these two realms.

> AA Following this thought, the categorical distinction between autopoietic (living) and heteropoietic (non-living) units—one basic idea on the enactive approach—could be diffuse to a certain extent. My way to contribute to blur the boundary is to consider the attribution of agency to heteropoietic entities.

If "the formal organizational properties distinctive of mind are an enriched version of those fundamental to life or more precisely, the self-organizing features of mind are an enriched version of the self-organized features of life,"[4] the organizational properties distinctive of research are an enriched version of those fundamental to the quotidian, unnoticed search implicit in each action. [M]

2.

The search—the continuously flowing, implicit seeking for immediate viability of each unnoticed act, of each act to be—and its iterative, repetitive, explicit, even systematized, methodologically organized variant [N]—the re-search—both are interventions in a twofold articulation: in the articulation of our own acts—the organization of inflections in the continuous actualization of our own agency—and, simultaneously, in the articulation of our actions with the flow of other actualized agencies with which our actions are in constant, mutually constitutive touch. Search and research, thus, as an intervention in the conjunction of two articulations—the articulation of a dynamic ownness with the dynamics of an otherness.

But we can try now to come closer. We can pursue another strategy in order to overcome the apparently conspicuous differentiation between ownness and otherness, between the spot from which we observe and an outside subsuming the rest—the not-me, the not-self, the vastness of the other, of all others.

[M] ᴶᴴ Yes, I agree, and I have tried to make a similar point in relation to Dieter Mersch's paper.

[N] ᴰᴹ If we look at the dialectics of search and research from this angle—as suggested—research is not necessarily linked to certain procedures and methods. Method—Greek met'hodos—originally means to follow a pathway. The pathway is already preordained. I have to follow the lines, on the beaten tracks, with no real alternative, otherwise I risk going astray. Research, without method, means to work heuristically, intuitively, like a wanderer who has no clear goals or draws circles. Research, although organized, therefore does not necessarily need to be disciplined. However for scientific work some minimal criteria are essential, which does not hold for artistic research. Also science adheres to instruments, to documentation and archives which make its results readable, while art is confronting us with the non-understandable. However we should not claim distinctions between both too early, for what is true for creativity and intuition or inspiration in art is often also true in science. Both seem to have more in common than we normally admit. And here again, it seems to be prudent to argue step by step in order to make our distinctions rigorous (and here, I think, we have to keep in mind, that art and philosophy share more things in common than art and sciences. Arteaga's phenomenological approach, his way of thinking—as an artist and as a philosopher, implicitly indicates this).

ᴬᴬ I basically agree with this comment. I would like to point out that I consider the method—the pathway—originally to emerge from the research and not to precede it. Like in the poem of Antonio Machado, often quoted by Francisco Varela, "there is no path, we lay down a path by walking." It is the repetition that constitutes the act of walking, which enables the configuration of methods. And once re-cognized—by walking, by re-searching—they can be described, taken out of the flow of the search and considered as reference, without any prescriptive or deterministic function, for future research processes. I am claiming here a circular continuity between re-search and method.

We can take a perspective now that allows us to overcome the seemingly natural, the ostensibly given differentiation between my actions and other actions. A perspective that allows us as well to overcome the concept of interaction—a first attempt to transcend, to go beyond, or, more precisely, to climb across the ownness of what we tend to call our actions, without negating the difference, their demarcations, their limits but establishing, additionally, a mutual causality or, at least, a reciprocal conditioning between mine and other actions.

We can try now to address the situation of immanently, intimately, radically shared agencies, of constitutively intertwined actions, by activating the etymological configuration of an alternative term: conduct—to lead with.

A term that allows us to resituate, to intensify the function of the commonness that informs each singular action: the commonness underlying, enabling and constraining each action. The commonness being the most fundamental source of agency—of agencies, without the necessity of further specifying—and not the result of a subsequent, supplementary confluence. The commonness which allows every single action to develop in the very way it does, which modulates its course, which enables and constrains its realization.

A commonness—I would say in a first move, just to compensate established positions but not yet fully expressing mine—that does not follow individuality: it is not an addition, a supplement, a con-sequence, a result of an addition qualified by the use of prefixes like "multi," "inter" or "trans," but its most fundamental condition of possibility. [0]

Or better—to try to come even closer to the specificity of the relationship between this kind of commonness and the singularity of each action, to try to avoid a reductionist description establishing a unidirectional causality, formulating now, specifically, my approach—a

[O] | LG Would you agree with the definition of this commonness as a transcendental level of agency? It seems that the way in which you differentiate individuality and commonness precisely addresses the difference between the empirical and the transcendental level. The first deals with the contingent constitution of our activity, to which agency belongs, while the second concerns a condition of possibility of agency and is independent of the individual acts of constitution.

> AA I am trying to blur the categorical differentiation between individuality and commonness and to situate the common as a necessary condition for possible individualizations. And I guess I agree with your comment situating my approach close to a transcendental perspective related to the contingent—and consequently common—constitution of agencies.

commonness that enables each single action while, simultaneously, the realization of each single action constrains the common: a relation of mutual conditioning possible to be described as a system of co-emergence—the co-emergence of the singular and the common.

A relationship between the singular and the common, determined by the simultaneity of their mutuality: the singular and the common developing at the same time, reciprocally conditioning one another in the most intimate manner—without being able to trace a clear delimitation between both spheres (unless we take the distance that analysis requires and produces, unless we step out of the experience that presents action operatively, in its course, from its "inside": not the inside of one actor, not the inside of the own, but the inside of the whole dynamic meshwork, the inside of the common action). Or better: the common inside of action, the inside of the radically shared agency—a radicality that blurs the boundaries of the own and of the single without excluding the identification of different nodes of agency: different ex-pressions of the common, different ways of inhabiting the common, of actualizing it, of in-forming it.

Search, thus, and re-search as well, as the immanent drive of each action to ensure the possibility of the common action, the common of all possible actions—the withness of the lead, the viability of the share ductus, of the path laid down, inevitably, together—of each action as con-duct.

Search and research participating in the immanence of an immanence: the immanence of action in the immanence of the common—and the other way around.

Search and research as two ways to realize a constitutive trait of each conduct: the attempt to enable its viability by enabling the common—by looking for ways of maintaining the possibility of the immanent, constitutive coupling, or better, trying again to overcome the duality of ownness and otherness: the further viability of the implicit, aprioristic interlacement of a myriad of selfless micro-dynamics, the inherent coalescence of a tide meshwork of vibrant particles, the most fundamental commonness of their possible common ductus.

3.

Departing, thus, from the common, taking the common as a base or better—trying to overcome another duality, the one formulated as a constructive metaphor in terms of base and superstructure, a duality expressing on the one hand an irreversible sequence and on the other hand a unidirectional dependence—departing from the co-emergence, the simultaneous and mutually conditioning constitution of the common and the singular. Departing therefore from the impossibility of a pure singularity—and consequently, from the impossibility of an absolute commonality—we can take now, again, the perspective of a single unit—let's say one of us—the perspective provided by the experience of its participation in the field of shared agency in which it unfolds its own one.

We take now a first-person-perspective—pluralized in order to allow, in a fictional way, to perform the writing/reading as a shared process—and we focus on one specific conduct, on one variety of

engagement in the common in which it participates. A variety of conduct I term aesthetic conduct.

We establish contact with a new entity. We begin now to be in touch with it.

And, let's say, we stop there: we maintain the touch, we indwell the contact, we inhabit the possibilities enabled by the performance of our sensorimotor skills—by the fundamental, relational and dynamic unit of motors and sensors that enables the primary constitution of phenomena, that allows us to perceive, and, before that, to realize operatively the presence of a presence-to-possibly-be, to notice it without inscribing it, to sense it, to incorporate it in the process of emergence of sense we are participating in.

We relate to this new alteration of the otherness. We operate with this new presence in the domain of potentialities that we begin to share and shape basically by actualizing our sensorimotor skills: the connective and connecting patterns developed throughout a long process of embodiment.

We are and remain, literally, in touch, in a sensing/moving contact enabled and constrained primarily—I would tend to say "exclusively" to make my point clearer—by the spontaneous realization of our sensorimotor logic: the field of possibilities enabled and constrained by the habitualized link, the embodied connection—the interdependence implemented as and through organic matter, as and through flesh—between sensors and motors.

Our active relationship—the articulation of our conducts, the dynamic actualization of our agencies—results now, primarily, out of this spontaneity: out of the uninhibited, uncontrolled actualization of the closeness of the systemic network that allows our movement to unfold, to realize its direction and velocity by virtue of the activity of our own sensors, which in turn develop their activity—the transduction of environmental perturbations, the basic communication, the first doing-together—by virtue of the conditions provided by our movement.

Conducting ourselves aesthetically means, therefore, firstly, to allow the spontaneous unfolding of our sensorimotor skills to lead our common course.

Moving, now, according to the work of our sensors, and sensing through moving—being led by the mutuality of sensors and motors for the contingent constitution of our selves and our world—we have to recognize the agency of another skill at work, situated as well in the join of sensing and moving.

We have to recognize that we "are moved" as well—and, perhaps, that we "are sensed" as well.

The use of the passive form, [P] the grammatical introduction of passivity in order to address, now, emotionality as another inalienable driving force in this variety of conduct I call aesthetic, intensifies the problematization of the ownness-otherness issue and at the same time the definition and demarcation of the first term of this pair: Would I say that it is me who acts, when the driving force is the spontaneous enfolding of the sensorimotor patterns? (I know—being knowing the "possession" of a descriptive and/or explicatory artifact—that they are "my" patterns—that they "belong" to "my" body, that they, better,

[P] | ^{DM} Looking at different methodological approaches—goal-orientation, repeatability, generalization, and exoterian (open to public) verifications— seem to me one criterion to distinguish between artistic and scientific research, because in art there is no clear target, often artistic work insists on its irrepeatability, its non-generalizable singularity and its subjective idiosyncrasy. Looking at different understandings of the role of identity, consistency, and logic in science on the one hand and contradictions in art on the other, also seems to be essential. However, with respect to perception and the senses, one of the main differences between both is the difference between active and passive. The text here is hinting at this. But starting with search as activity seems to miss the trait of art from its beginning, because aesthetics genuinely is based in a primordial passivity, for perception firstly is reception. Everything here depends on the under-standing of search—as an active exercise or, as it is meant by Arteaga right from the beginning, as an inter-action or inter-relation that starts from otherness, responding to its attraction, its attack or urgency. Here, I think, we arrived at the most important point of the consideration, worth a second thought. Scientific work, with the help of technology, is intervening into the world and therefore violating it in order to reveal its inner truth, while art is touching it by being touched by it, being moved by it, leaving it as it is, just challenging its inner contradictions in order to show its com-plexity, its non-reductive riddles, its incomprehensibility. The first (science) sticks to certainty and therefore to the visible, the audible in one word: that what can be identified; instead art sticks to the tactile, the uncertain, the singular and unspecific. Therefore art is "intensifying doubts," making our experience of the real more unstable, more abyssal. The radicalness of art results from this.

> ^{AA} I agree with this comment. There is only one, classic problem: the term "passivity." The way you characterize art (research) at the end of your comment presents art as a form of activities different from the ones performed in the realm of science. Both are fields of action. Perception, and reception, are as well forms of action. If, I'm implicitly positing in this text, there is no no-action, what we tend to qualify as "passive" can only be understood as a variety of action. I see the fundamental differences between "passivity" and "activity" in the role of will and the level of distribution of agencies. I refer to passivity as a form of action which is not will-based and consequently does not pursue the achievment of a goal, and allows other agencies to become more relevant in the interaction. To ex-press these or related ideas we tend to associate touch—a goalless, sounding touch—with passivity, although we can "touch" and "be touched" also by the agency of images and of vibrant bodies if we look and listen "passively."

constitute "my" bodily "mine-ness"—but: would I still recognize this conduct as "mine," as the conduct of "my"-self? Would I recognize my-self when other skills of mine—will and target-oriented acting—retreat (they have to retreat!) in order to allow my sensorimotor self to act spontaneously? Is this will-less, this dis-oriented, aim-less, goal-less self—furthermore: is it a self?—still my-self?).

And moreover, further intensifying the doubt: How should I interpret the "e" (this shortened "ex") that qualifies motion in this concept: emotionality? How should I connote this presumable exteriority? As I did before, saying that "I am moved," locating implicitly the motoric source of an emotional experience somewhere "out there" while affirming the interiority, the ownness of sensorimotor action?

Only an exhaustive and comparative phenomenology of emotionality and the sensorimotor self could help here. But incipiently, as a trial—as an essay—I would tend now to accept, speculatively, that both, senso-motoric and emotionality, express the realization of "our" skills—skills situated right there, in the boundary, between our skin, its sensors, our muscles and what might touch our skin—may be this is the primary place of aesthetics ...

Despite the attribution of my actions' source to one or the other side of my skin, emotionality brings about another quality of action: a direct, immediate and unmediated action mobilizing the whole organism—the organism as a whole, as an organized whole—in, maybe, the most intimate touch, the most touching touch, the most intensive touch with the new perturbation of its environment.

A holistic alteration of the embodied organism, changing at once—immediately and in an unmediated way—its disposition toward its otherness and, maybe, as well toward itself varying its disposition toward the whole system self-world: coloring it, modifying, exhaustively, its

tonality, its overall and most basic texture. Modifying, thus, fundamentally, radically although temporarily, the primary framework of action. Generating—or probably better, manifesting—a fundamental contingent layer—a layer between potentiality and actualization, between the structure of our agency and its realization: a medium, I would tend now to say, acknowledging its character of basic all-over setting of conditions of possibility for the realization of our conduct.

The actualization, the spontaneous—again, meaning not constrained by any functionality, by any instrumentality triggered by the performance of our will and our ability to set a goal, to "devaluate the present by projecting on a future, on a not here and now"[5]—unfolding of our emotional skills, our capacity of fundamentally, extensively, implicitly, potentially connote—not as an addition to a denotation, but as its condition of possibility, as marking together the field in which singularities will be marked, will be signified—the environment in its process of becoming environment: the process in and through which our surroundings—the necessary accomplice of our emotional action, of our emotion as action—turn to acquire a significance, turn to be an environment-for-us.

Aesthetic conduct: a form of participation in the common enabled and constrained fundamentally by the spontaneous, unpremeditated and thus radically present unfolding of the logic of the sensorimotor and the emotional.

A radical form of touch: of being, intensively, exhaustively, intimately, silently, attentively in touch.

An implicit but radical attentiveness—a basic awareness of the innermost touch of touch—through which the commonness of the common acquires an undeniable experiential expression.

A variety of conduct that allows the intensification—through the neutralization of our capacities of control in favor of the realization of our most basic forms of vulnerability: the constitutive fragility of the sentient organic matter—of the receptiveness to other agencies without strengthening their otherness but rather the commonness, the contingent character of the shared agencies.

Aesthetic conduct, therefore, as primarily and the most radical form of participation—of realization of the common.

4.

We search. Constantly.

We search for maintaining, maybe increasing, the viability of our conduct by dynamically modifying the disposing of the skills that structure our agency—our capacity for transformative action.

We connect, distribute, activate, repress, limit the actualization of our skills—in different degrees, on different levels, with different timings—configuring variable and complex networks: the infrastructures of multiple varieties of conduct, of different ways of participation in the common.

We search, also, aesthetically. [Q]
        We search letting our sensorimotor and emotional skills—our most basic connective skills (perhaps disregarding even more basic

[Q] | DM Here it becomes clear, that aesthetic search, and hence aesthetic research, signifies only one mode of the most general search-practices that characterize our being-in-the-world. However, it seems necessary to me to distinguish between aesthetic and artistic search and also aesthetic and artistic research. Aesthetic search is more general, while artistic search and research seem to be more specified; the first includes all investigation based in what Gilles Deleuze called "percepts," while the latter addresses a peculiar way of thinking, that forces open normative limitations, not as an end in itself, but as a way of reflecting them and demonstrating their inner illegitimacy. Therefore the constant emphasis of the concussion, the break and disrupture of order, a plea for more noise, more nothingness than sound being. So just pointing at aesthetics, at least in my view, wouldn't be enough to found art and in art the way of artistic re-search.

AA This is an important issue, thematized extensively in Gerard's text. An exhaustive comment on that will exceed the limits of a comment. So just to sketch the guidelines of my approach: first, yes, I think it is important to note the difference between the aesthetic and the artistic; second, I consider art to have undeniably aesthetic roots, that is, I think that for a practice to be considered artistic, it has to be rooted in a form of being-in-the-world I term aesthetic conduct; and third, I don't think that all aesthetic practices are artistic because not all fit in with the normativity that the (social) art (system) has been consolidating throughout its history—yes, I think too that art breaks normative limitations but it does it in the frame of its own normativity.

ones that enable metabolization, like breathing, eating, drinking or excreting)—lead the search.

"Letting them lead": releasing the control of another skill—will—and, probably before that, of another one—rather a close network of abilities: to identify, select and fix targets.

Letting our conduct not be driven by the determination and achievement of goals.

Breaking temporarily with another variety of action, with a different disposition of our organic activities centered in an incisive, projecting, narrowing, engraving, manipulating participation in our world: an instrumental use of our body, a functional conduct demanding our body to work, to accomplish certain functions determined by a body, the very same body, that does not present itself to itself as a body but as a superior, disembodied entity that governs, subdues, controls "its" body, the body that "belongs" to it, that serves it.

Breaking temporarily with an ostensible disembodied self that organizes itself—its undeniable bodily self, it-self, inevitably, as body (not the body that "belongs" to this emergent sense of self but that enables its emergence without appearing as such).

Breaking with the instrumental organization of our skills by a functional self, an organization that simultaneously enables the functional self to emerge and to maintain itself—a self that subdues its body, that makes out of "body" "its body," in order to subdue its environment.

An egocentric self that reduces body and environment to means and stages for its own accomplishment.

Aesthetic conduct—aesthetic participation, aesthetic being-active-with-the-world—thus, as one possible alternative to functional conduct.

A non-tensed, non-controlled conduct. A provisional suspension of a variety of engagement imposed by a single component of the whole system—the target-oriented will of a single unit—blocking the spontaneous formation of intentionality—the vector linking the unit to its surroundings, orienting their coupling. Blocking the tendencies emerging out of a non-hierarchical unfolding of our most fundamental connective skills—out of the communication, the intimate dialog of the common.

A temporary interruption of cont-rol: of rolling-against—against everything that resists, that opposes itself to the realization of the goal previously fixed by a singularity. Against the radical common: the common emerging out of itself, out of the spontaneous communication between its parts.

We search aesthetically, letting the adaptive actions—the actions-to-be, the possible actions because possibly viable—be informed by multiple agencies in touch: by converging contingent agencies.

We search for the viability of our conduct by disposing the skills that configure it in a way that allows for the emergence of the viable out of the fluid communication in a field of shared agencies.

We search reinforcing, extending, radicalizing the we, the common, letting it happen by intensifying the porosity of the touch—letting the viable arise out of the spontaneous performance of the viable.

But maybe, from time to time, it does not work. It simply does not work, and we have to stop and modify the search, make it explicit—explicitly organized, systematic, even methodic. We have to re-search.

Without ceasing to realize our agency in an intimate network of agencies, without renouncing to the lead of our coordinated sensors and motors, of our ability to be moved as a whole by and to the outside—to be e-motionally moved—we begin then to develop another form of awareness of it—of the way we are acting, of our aesthetic participation in the common.

We can realize—in a tight combination of both meanings of the word: understanding by doing, or even tighter, understanding as doing—the specific actions we unfold by acting aesthetically—again without imposing, without overwriting what is happening, but simply realizing it, noticing it, following it.

We can, thus, begin to turn our actions into practices—our aesthetic conduct into a network of aesthetic practices—and consequently our aesthetic search into aesthetic research.

We are, then, inevitably, inhabiting a thin space: a line, a boundary, a limit. The boundary that simultaneously separates and joins the spontaneity with which we move-by-being-moved and a certain degree of control, a minimal, iterative resistance to simply allowing everything to happen but without hindering that everything can happen: a minimal, subordinated reactivation of our will in order to come back again and again to what is happening—in order to reflect.

       In order to organize—minimally—the spontaneous unfolding of our most basic organization.

In order to practice instead of simply acting—without blocking the simplicity of our aesthetic conduct.

We are inhabiting then, unavoidably, the boundary in which the realization of a purposiveness—our fundamental and ineluctable intentionality: the constitutive aboutness that links us with the not-us—without purpose—without adding, without imposing any other intentions—is possible.

We research aesthetically: we let the connective dynamics of this field of shared agencies in which we are acting now unfold spontaneously in order to enable new possibilities of action, of viable action, to emerge and simultaneously to notice—and, perhaps, to notate—the forms the paths take: in order to allow unforeseen trajectories of sense in new, emerging fields of intelligibility to be disclosed.

We research aesthetically in order to (yes, there is an intentionality in this form of conduct, in this form of research, but it is operating in the background, it is, let's say, suspended, abandoned, ignored, as a way to let the non-intentionality or better, again, the spontaneity of our fundamental, unavoidable intentionality to unfold) realize forms of viability that we—now in a narrow meaning of the plural—cannot conceive by ourselves, cannot pro-duce—cannot lead to our outside—cannot make, cannot de-sign—cannot mark out of the flux, in which they appear and in which they should find an articulation.

We research aesthetically to mobilize the inherent cognitive power of the common to find ways through the common to understand it. [R]

[R] DM … but also, in part, to escape from it, to find new and yet unknown ways of co-existence, of cooperation, of communication and thus, the social.

AA … which are new ways of understanding these concepts (and new ways of understanding, that is, of constitution of co-existence, cooperation, communication and the social).

ME "We […] And so on." This highly selective quote highlights the gesture of exploration conducted throughout this text. Its textual habitus builds on a series of more or less recognizable philosophemes that privilege continuity and contact instead of gaps, adaptability and flow instead of blockages. In a word, its key gesture is "con-." With this gesture the text delimits its scope and unfolds its exploration within the horizon of what might be called the "paradigm of construction." It clearly does not engage with all those matters that we find in the basket labeled "the sublime." The specific form of research envisioned in the text—"aesthetic research"—departs from the "common," "establishes contact" with new entities and finds its "most radical form of participation," that is, "realization of the common," in "aesthetic conduct." In my view, this implies that the search described, or more exactly, notated in this text tracks down "the aesthetic" in terms that avoid questions of desire, paradoxes and the pathic fracture lines of experience. I am not sure whether "coherence" has its roots in hairesis or not, but the compelling co-herence of Alex's text, lives off the basic choice of privileging the "con-." As a consequence, my comment might appear as heretic, as a choice to depart from the common otherwise, diabolically, questioning the value of consensus. Another variety of aesthetic search?

AA My intention is not to privilege the con- over what you nicely termed "the pathic lines of experience." I'm trying to escape the duality of con- / dis- by developing an inclusive approach able to articulatedly encompass both tendencies on two bases: first the fact that, whatever happens, life—as a process of sense-making—goes on and second that this is unavoidably a common endeavor—a constant and plural process. Adaptability, as the performance of plasticity, is one of the main skills not to avoid or exclude "gaps," blockages," "desires" or "paradoxes" but rather to recognize and legitimate their function in the process or better networks of processes of sense-making. And examining the aesthetic way of participating in these processes, I would only accept the term "constructive" in its etymological interpretation: to structure with—to assemble or arrange together. I'm not interested in a concept of coherence based on any form of heresy but on the unavoidable necessity of, in all possible forms including all variants of separation understood as a structural element, "sticking together"—of maintaining structural coupling, to put it in Maturana's terms. Following this line of thought, it is, somehow, always about allowing the emergence of common senses—consensus. Aesthetic conduct and, beyond, aesthetic research can contribute to that in a very specific and powerful way.

1 See Francisco J. Varela, "Organism: a Meshwork of Selfless Selves," in Organism and the Origins of Self, ed. Al-
   fred I. Tauber (Dordrecht: Kluwer, 1991), 79−107.
2 Paraphrasing Maurice Merleau-Ponty in: Maurice Merleau-Ponty, Phenomenology of Perception (London:
   Routledge, 1962).
3 See Dieter Mersch, Epistemologies of Aesthetics (Zurich:
   Diaphanes, 2015).
4 See Evan Thompson, Mind in Life: Biology, Phenomenology and the Science of Mind (Cambridge MA: Harvard
   University Press, 2007).
5 Paraphrasing Pep Quetglas in Pep Quetglas, "Cometa de
   seda en ráfagas de viento," in Arquitectura de la Indeter-
   minación, Yago Conde (Barcelona: Actar, 2000), 16−21.

Artistic Composition as Research

Dieter Mersch

1.

The meaning of the term *artistic research* (or "research in the arts") is in no way clear, nor is it clear if the concept is really productive in any way, and this despite the fact that it has been the object of a dedicated discourse for over a decade now. A survey of the diverse, multifaceted uses of the term might help us better understand the scope and relevance of the debate. The term is currently used in at least six different senses: (i) [A] *First,* it is used to denote a specific form of contemporary artistic production that is distinguished from other historical forms. This usage demands that one follow tradition and distinguish art on the one hand from a wholly different artistic practice of "research" on the other. In a sense, this use of the term describes a certain discipline, one genre among others, or a certain artistic style. A defining characteristic of this mode of artistic research is the use of scientific—and primarily natural scientific—methods, as well as methods

[A] | AA I would call this mode of artistic research "appropriative" ("appropriation" is a term you use in relation to Lucier's use of Dewan's discoveries): it is based on the adoption of practices, methods and materials of natural and social sciences by the arts. Could this variety of artistic research also include the appropriation of concepts developed and used in the humanities and research results of the sciences? And what about goals: does this type of artistic research share goals of the research in these other fields?

> DM I fully agree with the terms "appropriation" or "appropriative artistic research"—indeed this way of research is very pragmatic, capturing methods or results from other sciences, using or misusing them as material for artistic reflection. I also would like to call it a "weak" form of artistic research. Here is not only relevant the collaboration between art and natural science as it often seems to be; there are also a lot of projects that use ethnographic methods or historical "recherché" and source-interpretation. All kinds of sciences, be it economics, natural sciences, social sciences or the humanities are included. But in my view the goals between artistic and scientific research are different. Often art is challenging scientific results, teasing out their very limitations or looking from the side, revealing the unseen or disregarded. However we also have to admit that in "appropriative" or "applied artistic research" there is a lot of trivial and tautological work that does not provide any new insights on scientific methods or results.

borrowed from anthropology and the social sciences. These methods are adapted and transformed for artistic purposes. [B] Either they have a secondary, supporting status in the artistic process, or they help bring new phenomena to bear, as when a material is produced that is subjected to special artistic treatment or when findings are produced that remain singular and have no relation to scientific propositions. (ii) *Second,* artistic research is concerned with the professionalization and valorization of the arts in their relation to the sciences, which have highly developed institutional structures and their own forms of qualification and specialization. Accordingly, this use of "artistic research" signifies the attempt to make the arts academic, in particular in the wake of the so-called "third cycle," which has the aim of allowing art schools to award doctoral degrees in the arts. Whatever avenue this venture might take, the win would be that art schools could recruit professionals from their own ranks rather than having to rely on the universities. [C] But, of course, whether or not this would really be a win is contested. (iii) [D] *Third,* it is no matter of coincidence that the debate over artistic research took off as part of the discourse on "postmodern" art. This is why some see artistic research, or research *in, through,* and *with* art, as not simply being one genre of art among others, but rather as *the* adequate articulation of artistic practice in the postmodern era. This type of artistic practice is no longer aimed at composing a work, but rather at remaining provisional and tentative, which is often accomplished by using collective or participatory methods to perform the artistic process as a search or exploration, thus crossing out the principle of authorship. In short, for this mode of artistic practice, the journey is the destination. It adheres to a processual logic without advance knowledge of what will be gained or whether there will be a conclusive result at all. (iv) [E] A *fourth* aspect of artistic research that might be listed here—even though it has now taken on a life of its own— is the critique of institutions associated with it. Our era is dominated by the sciences, and in particular the technological sciences, which

[B] AA Does this mean "to make art"? If this would be the case, I would not consider this case a variant of artistic research but simply as a case of artistic appropriation.

DM Here I would like to say that it depends on the character of the work. Sometimes there is only a duplication of scientific work, sometimes artistic research, in using or distorting scientific methods, that opens up new trajectories of research and insights. So generally speaking, we have to have a thorough look at it in order to decide whether it is simply an application or appropriation or a true artistic reflection.

[C] AA This "win" occludes, in my opinion, several losses: first the implicit acceptance that art does not belong originally to academia and therefore that academia is reduced to scholarly work; second, the acceptance that, in order to enter academia, art has to adapt to already established modes of work (in this case, modes of research) that define academia—an academia that, again, excludes art originally. Even accepting the original exclusion of art from academia, it would be more enriching—for both art and academia—to approach their approximation as a process of interchange and mutual transformation: both—academia too—should be open to being modified—in its case, to be extended, critically radicalized—as a result of this encounter.

[D] AA My problem with this type of artistic research relates, again, to the question of whether this is simply a mode of making art or performing research. Of course, by making this distinction I depart from the idea that not every form of artistic practice is research—although it can contribute to knowledge, understanding or have a positive epistemic effect or, simply, as you write later, an "epistemic dimension."

[E] AA I would tend to consider this fourth mode not so much as a specific variety of artistic research but rather a constitutive aspect of all kinds of artistic research, although considering this kind of activity not necessarily as a "critique of sciences" but rather as an alternative, and consequently as a critique, to the monopoly of science on research.

have claimed the concept of research for themselves, monopolized research funding, and in doing so have not only sought to grant themselves a privileged form of legitimacy, but also a privileged status more generally. Given this situation, some working in the arts have sought to establish an alternative conception of research that rejects the norms of the hegemonic notion of what research is in order to make clear that natural scientists are not the sole proprietors of research activity and that artists, too, engage in it. In this usage, artistic research is at once a critique of science. Still, it raises the question as to what the defining features of such "research in art" are. (v) [F] Related to the fourth usage, the *fifth* involves the general notion of a democratization of research or of research for "everyone." It runs against both the institutionalized, exclusive form of research reserved for elite scientists and, more broadly, the conventional concept of research as such. The point here is no longer a search for alternative forms of knowledge, whether it be *aesthetic* knowledge in contrast to scientific knowledge or something else, but rather a search for alternatives to the established modes of research as such. It takes part in today's seemingly all-pervasive *critique* of the established or the establishment and thus engages in a critique of the sciences' claims to power. In this usage, artistic research is a utopian project, a declaration of war in the name of which something new and different is supposed to take place, something that although implied by the concept of "research" has not yet been revealed, a *metabasis eis allo genos* or shifting of the terrain. What this something might be, however, remains open. (vi) Finally, the *sixth* use of the concept represents the position that research in the arts is nothing new, but rather that art has always engaged in a certain practice of research. The position states that art and research are not opposites, but rather that artistic research simply reveals what artistic activity—that is, forming and composing—does anyway. Art has been ascribed an epistemic dimension and been coupled with a claim to knowledge and truth in different ways since the arts gained their autonomy, from Leonardo

[F] | AA It would be easy to integrate the modes three, four and five as a new, historically based, and normatively defined art type. Nevertheless, my question remains: what makes this type of art a form of research?

DM Research is not a clearly defined notion. As you put it in your own article: research is primarily a kind of search, that is constantly redefined by recursion and recurrence. Especially the fifth version cannot be clearly separated from activism. So the notion of research is only used pertaining to an extension of the normativity of scientific research as it was institutionalized during the nineteenth century. Hence research here includes a critique of academic institutions which, as it is said, install a social hierarchy that artistic research tries to deconstruct. Critique—that is the general paradox of it—participates in the criticized and therefore cannot offer a positive vision. However, in general, the six variations only serve as clarifications, how the notion of research is used in the entire debate.

and the art of the Baroque to the discovery of aesthetics by Alexander Baumgarten and G.W.F. Hegel. The sixth usage of "artistic research" states that today's hot topic simply addresses something that *genuinely* belongs to the arts *in their very origins.*[1]

2.

My concern here is not to judge the value of these various uses of the concept, nor is it to take a position in the debate. Rather, it is simply to map out the various points of tension and the issues involved. This, however, quickly leads one to the observation that the most vaguely used, least well-defined concept in the whole debate is that of "research" itself. What is "research"? The concept's lack of clarity is nothing surprising given the fact that it is not limited to a single sphere of activity and that its very essence resists subordinating it to a set of norms. In the end, "research" signifies an ensemble of different activities that cannot be reduced to one single form of praxis. The meaning of "artistic" research and, more specifically, "research *in, with* and *through* the arts"—the prepositions here signify directions, approaches that the arts themselves take in this process of research— might be shot through with ambiguity. But it should not be forgotten that there is no *one single* form of scientific research and that the entire history of Western philosophy as metaphysics has dedicated itself to the problem of how to provide an adequate foundation for scientific thinking, how to legitimize it *as* science and how to define the criteria for what constitutes scientific "research," that is, it has dedicated itself to the problem of determining what principles science must adhere to and safeguarding it from illegitimate use. Similarly, it should not be forgotten that the sciences themselves, above all in the nineteenth century, have differentiated themselves according to their objects and methods and have undertaken their own critiques of knowledge and method in order to protect themselves as individual sciences from abuse. But the field of research is so expansive and vast that any

attempt at an exhaustive survey would be futile. The following is thus limited to a few points that might be seen as holding considerable significance for the debate on "artistic research." First, almost all scientific disciplines—from the natural sciences to the social sciences to the humanities—agree that, at least since the early modern period, "science" has long been inextricably bound up with an *exoteric* ethos. This means that the sciences are "public affairs" that have to be accessible to public debate and thus to public judgment and critique. Moreover, an irreducible feature of the economy of the sciences is the development of concepts and theories that are, for their part, associated with particular methods. In the end, it is pretty much redundant to say that the most minimal form of scientific statement consists in the construction of "knowledge," which is to say in the formulation of reasoned or reasonable judgments articulated in the form of a proposition, which has the formal structure of "A *is* B," expressing "something as something else." [G] Every scientific claim adheres to a certain logic; only the methods, the "how" of the procedure, and the way in which it is articulated and mediated provide material for debate. In general, these ways are, at least according to classic theories of science, divided up into three types: deduction, induction, and abduction. The latter denotes the practice of formulating hypotheses, which is always done with a good bit of intuition and inexplicable inventiveness that have strong overlaps with artistic process and creativity. This is just one example of the commonalities between art and science that subvert the traditional strict division between the two. Both clearly require a creative sensibility, a similar form of passion, and a similar dedication to precision, all of which creates a web of tangential points that makes their borders flow into one another like a *Möbius strip.* What's more, in the 1950s C.P. Snow spoke of "two cultures" in the sciences, pointing out the discrepancies and lack of mutual understanding between the natural sciences, whose practitioners often lack any kind of aesthetic or literary education, and the humanities, which seem to be capitulating

[G] AA This restrictive definition of "knowledge" can be a very useful basis in order to assert that artistic research does not necessarily produce knowledge. This assertion can be founded on the widely accepted hypothesis that artistic research does not necessarily develop in the medium of language and consequently cannot produce such a "proposition."

DM I fully agree, however the goal of the article is finally to show, that knowledge in itself is unstable and that we have to divide positive knowledge as it is produced by—in specific—natural or empirical science, and critical or reflective knowledge. The peculiarity of the latter we find in philosophy. Philosophy reflects upon its own conditions; and in my view also art is referring to the very conditions of art as music—understood as art—is reflecting music in its musical compositions. In other words: I vote for a very strong picture of art.

in the face of the former's rise and sometimes even proudly trumpet their ignorance of mathematics. The differences between their respective conceptions of "research" correspondingly reveal a radical split: while the natural sciences work with empirical and—particularly in the case of physical cosmology—speculative methods with the aim of discovering laws, the humanities are interpretive and their research inductive, because its only material are sources and texts that are always open to multiple readings. These strict divisions are outdated and must be filled out by the social sciences and anthropology, which are distinct in the fact that they seek to observe something of which they themselves are a part. [H] The division of the faculties thus has to be reconsidered. But beyond all that, the progress of technology has confronted the world of science with a sort of third power, namely the culture of the so-called "technosciences," which exist in the medium of experimentation and whose criteria of truth is the realization of the experiment itself. In short, for technoscience, research consists in the construction of models, and their validity is tested on the basis of whether they function and can be applied in the real world.

Thus, over the course of centuries, the sciences have created institutions, rules, and norms that circumscribe the limits of research as a scientifically recognized, collectively accepted practice. This seems not to be true for the arts, however, as they adhere to different criteria: their methods are often singular and not part of a canon, accessibility to public debate is not paramount, and neither is fulfilling the rules of verifiability and reproducibility. [1] Clearly, when we speak of research in the context of art—research *with, in,* and *through* art—we are talking about *something different* than research in science, even though this does not mean that the two have nothing in common.

3.

Descriptions of the idiosyncrasy—or perhaps obstinacy—of artistic research have often drawn on Hans-Jörg Rheinberger's concept of

[H] AA Accepting, as I do, that the act of observing—or even before that of simply "getting in touch"—makes the observer, inevitably, participate in the object of observation, this assertion, proper to the social sciences and anthropology, is valid for every form of research.

[I] AA Is the problem here to "adhere to different criteria" or rather to have a different goal at least on an explicit level? The concept of research as means to produce or achieve knowledge has been, as you describe, at the center of the scientific system since a solid, coherent and widely accepted definition of this term would provide solidity and coherence to the whole system. But this has not been the case in the arts. "Research," until the emergence of the term "artistic research," has not been seen as central, relevant or even of existential relevance for the art system. Artists have not invested any energy to define this term as constitutive for their collective.

DM The idea is (i) firstly to say that we can extend the notion of research to all arts and also over time. For instance: Baroque mannerism as research through a multi-layered reflection on images as mirror or in meta-pictures; serialism in musical composition as research on combining the four basic elements that structure music; classical ballet as research on overcoming gravitation, performances as research in the delimitation of human body and human relationships and so on. (ii) Secondly, research in the arts is not bound to the experiment or laboratory but to the studio and hence, at least in fine arts, similar to the alchemist's kitchen. In terms of this, artist's research also dealt with color as painterly matter, its effects, but also with form and construction and so on. (iii) Thirdly, looking from this angle, artistic research turns out to be completely different from scientific research, even from research in the humanities, because there are only singular practices rather than methods. This also means that in my view every single artwork on its own is already a kind of erratic research practice, so that art always starts anew rather than sticking to already established and widely accepted solid practices. Therefore the goal of my considerations is to emphasize the differences between research in the arts and research in sciences instead of underlining their similarities. And this is a difference in action, in institutional self-understanding, in criteria as well as in aims, tradition, archive and reason. Also: scientific research is very much based in the ideal of repetition, while artistic research is singular and individual and, thus, a practice that cannot be retrieved.

"experimental systems" and Bruno Latour's actor-network theory. Both approaches have their origins in the study of the history of science and science and technology studies, which over the past fifty years have shaken to the core long-unquestioned views of science held by philosophers and theorists of science. Rheinberger's primary concern was to analyze the role played in the experimental practices of the natural sciences by technical instruments and media, happenstance and intuition, non-scientific ideas like symmetry, and concepts borrowed from other discourses. He called these supposedly external factors "inscriptions." Bruno Latour coined the term "actor-network": to be read as one word, actor-networks consist of semiotic systems of signs that play a constitutive role in the construction of theories and their public representation. For Latour, the mode of production is decisive. He sought to show that scientific findings rely on a series of often discontinuous transformations, such as that from a living being into a biological sample, a sample into a microscopic element, the element into an image, and the image into a piece of evidence that can be presented to the (scientific) public. For their part, each step is itself a series of multiple discontinuous moments. Science and the process of scientific research do not form a seamless line of transparently logical stages. Rather, they are speckled with all kinds of opacity, and the way scientists bridge these opaque moments by using metaphors has more affinity with the artistic process than many of them might like to admit; on the other hand, sometimes scientists are so enthusiastic about this aspect of their work that it seems as if they might be happy to call themselves artists.

Thus, both Rheinberger and Latour sought to radically question the supposedly obvious differences between art and science. In doing so, they not only forged a new understanding of science, but also a *new understanding of art*. After all, if scientific research has affinities with the arts, then the inverse that the arts have affinities with the sciences must also be true, so that it seems justified to look for

similarities and overlaps in their methods and practices and, in the end, to call at least some aspects of both "research." Thus, it should come as no surprise that this vocabulary is in particular used to describe forms of art that work with methods that approximate those of the natural sciences. Some examples include the use of certain biochemical and genetic processes like in the so-called "bio-art" of artists like Eduardo Kac, the use of certain mathematical or stochastic processes to create sound, like in the works of Iannis Xenakis and Robert Ashley, or the exploration of sound waves, amplification, and recording techniques in so-called "sonic art" and computer music or in the algorithmic compositions of artists like David Cope and his program *EMI*. [J] These artistic forms are made possible by complex experimental arrangements that make it easy to view them through the perspective of Rheinberger's concept of "epistemic things" or Latour's theory of semiotic transformations. However, just as important is the fact that they rely on the application of technological tools and instruments to such an extent as to blur the line with the natural sciences and their dependence on technology. This brings us to the broad field of "sound studies," which would be inconceivable without methods and technology borrowed from the natural sciences. At the same time, many have asked whether the field of sound studies constitutes anything more than a presentation of interesting effects or experimentally produced technological artefacts, as it has a tendency to foreground the possibilities opened up by technology rather than grapple with fundamental questions of aesthetics.

4.

The difficulties of forging a hybrid of art *with* natural science and technology can be explored using a well-known example that not only makes clear the pitfalls and dangers of such a practice of composition, but also its potential—namely, Alvin Lucier's 1965 piece *Music for Solo Performer.* The piece draws on Edmond Dewan's experiments on the

[J] | AA These are, as you write, varieties of artistic practices or procedures but: are they forms of research? I feel a recurrent irritation throughout the text which is caused by a problem in the syllogism underpinning implicitly some basic argumentations: if scientists research and artists work similarly to scientists, it follows that artists research. I don't think that this is necessarily true. The conclusion can as well be, simply, that artists make art in a similar way to how scientists do research. To appropriate one aspect of a system—in this case practices or methods—does not mean necessarily the adoption of other components of the system—for example goals—and even less of the whole system.

DM This passage argues with certain clichés in the debate on artistic research: that indeed artistic research is similar to scientific research, that there are at least some intersections in practice and understanding. Often this is stated with reference to Latour or Rheinberger. I refuse this. The argument is to start with the opposite point in order to show that art differs completely from what we mean by scientific practices. Look at sonic art or David Cope's algorithmic compositions which use mathematical methods in order to produce music, but I would even call that music (maybe musaque). Here the artistic approach is nothing but a maidservant for science. This is not to say that any adoption of scientific method leads into rubbish—but here, I think, we have to have a closer look at that which really happens in an artistic piece. Therefore (see below), I try to look closely at Alvin Lucier as an example who seems to use brain-wave methods from physics and turns them into acoustic phenomena, but what he is doing with it jumps out of the array and provides us with new insights about art and the artist themselves rather than about brain activities.

physics of brain waves, which he sought to measure with instruments specially designed for the purpose. The basic idea of the piece was to make audible the alpha waves streaming through the human brain, which have to be filtered out from the scramble of a number of other frequencies.[2] Because their frequencies move somewhere between eight and fourteen hertz—that is, outside the range of human hearing—and the waves are very weak, they have to be amplified to be heard at all; additionally, the amplification also has to make them louder than the background noises and the sounds of the measurement instruments themselves. This requires a whole arsenal of machines: EEG, electrodes, transformers, amplifiers, speakers, etc. All of these things were part of the apparatus used in experiments on the physics of the nerve system, which physicist Edmond Dewan was researching in the 1950s and 1960s.[3] Dewan was interested in uncovering the physical foundations of consciousness. He explicitly dismissed philosophical theories of consciousness, which remained stuck in the old Cartesian body-mind dualism. Dewan, in contrast, wanted to prove that body and mind were one by bringing brain waves under conscious control using methods influenced by Norbert Wiener's theory of cybernetics. But what distinguishes alpha waves from other brain waves is the fact that they only start flowing when the brain is in a state of rest, a state in which it is in a sense not doing anything but is also not in a state of sleep. The extremely low frequency of alpha waves makes them paradoxical: when a subject is focused on something and their eyes are open, the brain's electrical activity is higher than when their eyes are closed and their body motionless in a state of meditation. Alpha waves are produced by the harmony of inner peace—they stop the instant the subject opens their eyes. [K]

So much for the physical facts. Dewan's discoveries were met with astonishment and it was not long before they were being used by the military and air force; but otherwise, they did not attract much interest outside the world of medicine, munitions, and neurology. Lucier

[K] | JH Could this also be related to the way in which hallucinations are gen-
erated in conditions of sensory deprivation? As if the body is somehow
hungry for stimulation, and in fear of stasis (fear of death) and therefore
produces its own stimulation as a way of arousing activity, resisting entropy and staving off death.

DM I have to admit that I don't know. It looks similar to sensory
deprivation, but whether it is the same effect seems to me questionable. Clearly there is that hunger for stimulation, but maybe the
alphawaves are an effect of concentration rather than resistance
to death.

came up with the idea of using Dewan's methods for composing music, transforming the latter's scientific inquiry into an aesthetic experiment. Lucier's goal was not simply to exhibit the particular quality of the sound of alpha waves. The radicality of Lucier's piece lies in how he appropriated Dewan's experiments on the materiality of consciousness by making audible the classical oppositions that for centuries dominated aesthetics as a theory of art, namely, the oppositions between concept and work, the idea and its realization, compositional intention and performative result. The common view of artistic production sees its beginnings in some kind of idea that is then translated into the form of a composition; it is an intuition that is stamped onto the material, thus making the idea perceptible. Lucier sought to deconstruct this naïve belief by modifying Dewan's method into an artistic experiment that pulled the rug from beneath classic oppositions like mind and material. In doing so, he revealed something wholly new. [L]
The piece was premiered with John Cage in 1965. In the performance, Lucier sits in a chair; attached to his head are electrodes connected to speakers in such a way that their vibrations stimulate percussion instruments, which begin to make noises as if they were being played by a ghost. In other words, pure thoughts, or, more precisely, Lucier's mental state of not thinking were, in a highly indirect fashion, transformed into a concert. The actual sounds that were created could not entirely be controlled: they depended on the strength of the waves transmitted, which for its part was dependent on how relaxed the performer was. The point was thus not the sounds themselves, which were more or less contingent. The "wit of the experiment" was expressed in the relation between control and the loss thereof, which was born out of the mind-bending fact that alpha waves only show themselves in the moment of sheer *inactivity*. [M] Thus, the more the performer sinks into a state of contemplation, the more they "just sit there" in an entirely "unproductive" state, the more music is produced. The artist does nothing—music just *happens*. [N] Thus, it happens when

[L] AA The opposite interpretation is possible as well: this piece shows with absolute clarity how an idea—the use of alpha waves to make music—is realized. In my opinion, if we interpret Lucier's motivation to make this piece in the appropriation of Dewan's discoveries in order to make music, there is, at least on the level of Lucier's motivation, nothing new. (This is pure speculation. I believe that Lucier did not create this piece "as a demonstration of a physical fact" as he wrote in his other piece *I am sitting in a room*).

   DM My argument is that Lucier's art-piece belongs to an avant-garde approach (which in my view is pure research in and through arts; even more: we have to reinterpret avant-garde in terms of artistic research). This means that he does not simply use the alpha waves to make music—this would be a typical sonic art simplification—but he uses them against the grain, so to speak anamorphoticly and thus ironically, in order to reveal an artistic statement on the artist's production of ideas. So not the sounds and thus the results are interesting but the arrangement, the concept.

[M] LG The performing act as a kind of inactivity, not as a controlled action that makes something happen, is a kind of concrete realization and development. But is it possible to define another kind of "methodological performativity" as the process of "aesthetic preparation and disposition"? I would explain this kind of performativity as both "theoretical" and "practical" experimentation within the media and circumstances that enable production and implement the intensity of performativity—also by inactivity.

   DM Clearly there is practical experimentation needed to realize the piece, and Lucier himself described his failure at the beginning because nothing happened (he wanted too much, so no alpha waves emerged—unless he gave up and stopped desiring!).

[N] AA In my opinion, this is the radical novelty of this piece and its fundamental contribution to the field of music and to the concept of music: a radical break between activity—and particularly virtuosity—and the production of art. Here music emerges and the composer creates the enabling conditions for this to happen.

   JH As suggested above, could this also be related to the point I raised in my own paper regarding the designer's dilemma at the beginning of a project—faced with a blank sheet of paper and no idea of where/how to begin designing. By not trying to come up with new ideas, but simply by repeating (i.e., drawing) what already exists, new possibilities inevitably begin to emerge … ?

   DM I don't think that the piece is about emergence, but, as you suggest, through emergence something happens that shifts the entire established dispositive and, hence, our understanding of music and musical production as such. Therefore, by the way, John Cage was so interested in this piece (he helped Lucier to realize it on stage), because the whole piece works as a vexation: there are some sounds but the sounds hint at a background, the conditions of their production, some ghostly magic which resembles a hollow form …

nothing is happening. As Lucier wrote in his *Reflections:* "The harder you try, the less likely you are to succeed; so the task [is] performing by not intending to …"[4]

5.

In short, the example demonstrates that art does not conduct some kind of idiosyncratic research by means of a different scientific method, but neither does it follow the path of scientific research. [O] First and foremost, art *makes claims about art itself.* Thus, the object of the discourse of artistic research is art's research into itself. [P] Art's "auto-research" encompasses an exploration of art's media of production and the circumstances under which it is produced; it entails an exploration of the praxis of art itself, its aesthetics and aesthetic categories; and it entails an exploration of the distinction between art and non-art and how this limit might be transgressed, a transgression that always implies displacing the limit and making something new out of it. Our inquiry into the relationship between the concept of "research" and the arts and the particular usages of the concept of "artistic research" seems to demand that we focus less on the explicit act of "doing research" and more on those places where the "foundation" of research *reveals itself*—after all, research is primarily a form of searching and thinking. In other words, we should not ask "what is research," but rather "what is thinking," or, more precisely: What are the specific features of aesthetic or artistic thinking? [Q] Or, to put it in yet a different way: rather than engaging with the problem of artistic research or research in, with, and through the arts, we might be better off inquiring into the relation between aesthetics and knowledge, [R] a classic question that has been around since aesthetics was established as an independent branch of philosophy. Posed by Baumgarten in his foundational work on aesthetics, it has been formulated anew again and again by Hegel, Martin Heidegger and Theodor W. Adorno, especially as regards the relation between art and truth. But philosophers have

[O] ᴬᴬ This affirmation presumes that Lucier's piece is or can be considered to be research which I do not necessarily agree with.

[P] ᴬᴬ There are two problematic aspects in these sentences. The first and minor one refers to the terms "claims" and "discourse." I don't think that art makes necessarily any claims or produces any discourse. Lucier's work is a good example of that. The second problematic aspect is that the primary and ineluctable object of artistic research is art itself. I agree that, on the one hand, research on production means and circumstances, as you write in the following paragraphs, is needed to make art as it is also the case for all human activities: we need to know how to make what we want to make. On the other hand, I agree that since the all-over medium of art is exposition (Michael Schwab)—or simply, to show (Dieter Mersch)—art shows itself by showing whatever art shows. But this is not enough to consider art as its own object of research. Art showing itself in showing art can be considered as an unavoidable side effect.

> ᴰᴹ I agree with respect to claims and discourse in art; clearly art does not claim or make statements—art shows. However the notion of discourse or of claim is, so to speak, nothing but a phrase, a façon de parler. A better word might be: recognition, or insight which is meant. Pertaining to the other point I disagree. But I think the reason for the disagreement or rather antagonism is that I would like to put forward a rather strong notion of artistic research which is linked to reflectivity. Therefore I still stick to knowledge—knowledge in terms of reflexive knowledge or recognition, therefore I compare artistic research with research in philosophy (which also sticks to reflectivity), and therefore I distinguish very strongly between research through singular artistic productions and scientific research as method-led enterprise.

[Q] ᴬᴬ I agree on that: the question is "what is aesthetic and/or artistic thinking"? But I disagree that this question is a different one than this other one: what is doing artistic research? My reason is simple: aesthetic and/or artistic thinking is thinking by/through doing (aesthetic and/or artistic research).

[R] ᴬᴬ I totally agree. But, according to the concept of "knowledge" you presented in section 2, I think that the counterpart of "aesthetics" here should be another concept—a wider concept, not reduced to "reasoned or reasonable judgments articulated in the form of a proposition." A possible alternative—the one I would opt for—is "cognition." Another one could be simply, again, "thinking."

generally posed the question in a way that obscures the specificity of aesthetic thinking by forcing it into the straitjacket of philosophical thinking and its language, thus subordinating it to the hegemony of philosophical discourse. [S] The price to be paid for this, of course, is that philosophy always implements an implicit hierarchy that begins with the indeterminacy of the image at the bottom, moves on to the abstract, structural nature of music at the next level, and places the linguistic arts and poetry at the top of the tower, above which, as Hegel put it, "[t]hought and reflection have spread their wings."[5] Aesthetics has always produced such hierarchies. Indeed, it itself has been the victim of such hierarchization, which is why it generally plays second chair in the concert of philosophical disciplines, a devaluation that continues today. It is clear that whatever answer to the question comes out of this traditional framework, it is going to be unsatisfactory. [T]

So how to take a different approach? If one flips through the catalog of concepts that the philosophical tradition has drawn upon in its thoughts on art, it becomes clear that language and the proposition always receive privileged treatment, that primacy is placed on concepts and categories, judgments and propositions. This even holds for Immanuel Kant, who at least viewed aesthetics—as intuition—and logic as equals mediated by the "schematism," which does the real imaginative labor. Again and again, philosophy has attributed aesthetics and the arts with a mysterious power that does more to obfuscate their specific mode of thinking rather than clarify it. In opposition to this, and in contrast to discursive propositions or judgments or the copula as the foundation of every proposition, we should speak of the "singular logic of the aesthetic," its "uniqueness," which engages in its own "autonomous" mode of producing knowledge. [U] In doing so, we are led to the conclusion that aesthetics constitutes its own form of thinking that is distinct from both scientific and philosophical thought and that works with different media and techniques than the "proposition," predication, and the "something as something" relation. The

[S] AA And, I would like to add, subordinating or at least exclusively treating this issue in the medium of philosophy—language—and with its specific set of practices—writing.

[T] JH As I mentioned also in relation to Ana Garcia's paper, Terry Eagleton outlines this tension in a useful way in his book *The Ideology of the Aesthetic.* He emphasises the idea of "embodied knowledge" and the skills of aesthetic judgement for which rules cannot be written down and learnt: these skills, like craft processes, must be gradually developed in the "workshop of long experience," as Heidegger would say.

[U] AA Taking again the concept of knowledge you formulated in section 2: is it adequate—and even possible—to talk about aesthetic knowledge production?

DM It depends on what we understand by knowledge. Section 2 took knowledge in its traditional philosophical understanding—and the strategy of the essay is to take this understanding in order to deconstruct it through art and transform its meaning.

constitutive, decisive elements of aesthetic thinking are, on the one hand, *composition as its principle of work,* and on the other, *perception as its medium.* [V] The aesthetic is rooted in *aisthesis.* This might sound like a tautology, but the point is that the arts (and above all music and the "visual arts"), *whatever* they do and *however* they do it, they do it in the medium of perception. When they speak, show, or judge, they always "argue" in the mode of "percepts" (Deleuze) or perceptions, and in such a way that they "put them together" in the sense of a "com-positio." Composition [W] is a joining or "joint," a *"Fuge"* (for its part a key concept of Heidegger's late philosophy). It denotes less a musical fugue—a polyphonic form of composition using counterpoint and repetition—and more a joining of heterogeneous elements that allows them to retain their heterogeneity, such as in artistic montage or in the collages of various materials made by Dadaist and Surrealist artists. Decisive is the fact that the heart of this *synthesis* is not the copula "is" or "to be," which are the A and O of predication and which forge an ontological relation or describe something *as something,* thus defining it in the world of symbols. Rather, the synthesis of the joint uses the "and" of joining. It is a *conjunction* that does not use an "as" and thus does not produce signification or meaning in the strict sense, but rather associations. [X] Conjunction and disjunction belong together in the artistic process of joining. More precisely, their principle is not that of identity, symbolism, or meaning, but rather that of *difference,* fracture or *diremption,* concepts that underscore the non-unified and fragmentary. Joints are both spatial and temporal. Just as collages—and above all those of Dadaism—made explicit the points of separation and pasting and thus the violence and heterogeneity of the collage, so too does musical composition revolve around connections and continuations, which in truth constitute shifts and transitions that make the disparity and discontinuity of the parts manifest. The same can be said of the layers, palimpsests, and concealments of Art Informel, which seeks to foreground the non-unitary, irreconcilable, disjointed dimension of its

[V] AA I think that to define—at least in a narrower sense—perception as medium, is problematic: would it be still possible to consider "video" or "sound," just to mention two examples, also as media? Would it not be better to conceive of perception instead as a form of action?

DM But are there sounds or videos without perception? Both are perception-media (*Wahrnehmungsmedien*—in difference to computational media, etc.). Maybe this is a matter of language: and I am often struggling with wordings between English and German.

[W] LG It is interesting to note how the notion of composition arises in Deleuze, considering the genetic value of Kant's schematism and in particular of his "schematism without concept." This form of schematism is a composition that generates new sense and is in this way an extension or radicalization of the schematism which—as you write—"does the real imaginative labor." The composition in this sense is the constitution of sensation, not as a first operation of combination but rather as a genetic production that emerges from the work—as you say later, as a "surplus."

DM Right.

[X] AA I consider it problematic to define the type of "copula" constitutive for artistic composition in terms of linguistic units. If art is not prelinguistic but, as you wrote in your book *Epistemologies of Aesthetics,* "unsayable," should the specific variety of artistic copula rather not be defined in the medium of language?

DM Right! I completely agree. I should have added this to the article: since we are sticking to linguistic discourse and talk about art in propositions we always already start with the wrong medium. So every notion we offer in order to describe art and artistic practices serves only as metaphor (or hints at something which remains unsayable).

materials. A partiture, a series of happenstance events, a sonic cluster-ing: all are "com-positionalities," a word in which the key is the hyphen, which is to say, the split that does not close but rather remains open, resisting, despite the tendency to close, all conclusions.

In analyzing artistic production, Adorno spoke both of "con-figuration" and "constellation," using both more or less as synonyms. Against the common understanding of the word, the prefix "con" in "constellation" should be read less as a "with" or "together" and more as a "fraying." The figurations inscribed into the "fray" are characterized by an indeterminacy or openness, just as the literal meaning of con-stellation denotes a collection of *stellae*—stars—that can be combined and configured in various ways, because the figuration is not inherent in them, but is rather imposed upon them. Adorno also said that music "resembles a language," but not one that "is" language, but rather one that confuses anyone who takes it literally, precisely because musical compositions cannot be subordinated to judgment and definitions. As Adorno stated in his studies on Beethoven and in his *Aesthetic Theory,* the language that music resembles remains "judgment-less synthesis." One might add that in art, this synthesis constantly engages in de-syn-thesis, evoking a *diabolon* in the *symbolon.*

6.

One final, yet decisive point should be added. After all, a montage is not just some empty combination of random stuff. It's not enough to just throw something at the wall. Sure, every configuration of things, sounds, colors or other percepts has some sort of aesthetic dimen-sion. This is true even of trash. But the "artistic" in artistic production, that which makes a "composition" into an artistic event goes beyond mere combination: it evokes a *surplus.* I use the term "surplus" not to denote something determinate that could be pointed at, but rather the specific "more" that goes further than the assembly of individual ele-ments, that which makes *this* assembly into an "interesting object," into

a composition that "makes us think." The sum is more than its parts, but the essential, "out-standing" moment depends on the kind of sum, the particular modality of artistic exertion and "work on perception" [Y] that distinguishes this perceptible object from others. This is why we have to distinguish between art and aesthetics: the singularity of the arts is not to be found in how they affect the senses with surprising combinations, but rather in the fact that in creating novel forms of perception, they both inquire into and explicitly thematize their media, practices, and methods, their materials and the conditions of their reception, the places where they take place, the apparatuses of their spatial distribution, the situation of the exhibition, their temporal sequences, and much more. It is this simultaneity of production and reflection that provides the measure for artistic precision. [Z] Artistic precision means that in the end, nothing is random or contingent, nothing is a mere lapse, an imprecision or fault, that, in other words, every element is in its right place, [a] where it has an extraordinary relevance and energy. Every artistic work imbeds itself, inquires itself as art and throws into question its relation to authorship, to the other, to the beholder and his or her relation to perception, to different modes of seeing and hearing and their intensities and so on. [b] Each inquires into its position in public space, its forms of exhibition or presentation, the ways in which it stages or documents something, and into the intervention of the real, its intangibility, and its latent violence. To put it differently: the "wisdom of art" and its modes of knowledge constitute first and foremost a "knowledge of itself" and of its own conditions and possibilities. It constitutes a "knowledge of knowledge" that shifts the position of art and its historical settings as much as it, again with Heidegger, abruptly moves us to another place. Art *that is truly art* "dis-places" the artistic, reformulates it, and thus makes it new. [c] The mode of knowledge production specific to the arts thus consists in inducting reflexivity; it creates a reflexive knowledge, but its implications need a recipient in order to be realized. In other words, art always *evokes something* and

[Y] AA According to my former critique of categorizing perception as medium, and preferring instead to consider it as a variety of action, I would suggest here to reformulate: "work through perception."

 DM Yes, I understand, however this formulation was chosen with regard to Hegel's formulation on dialectics as "work on concepts."

[Z] AA I don't think that "simultaneity" suffices to articulate the relationship of production and reflection in artistic practices. Accepting their reflective character—which I would fundamentally question—I would reformulate using these expressions: "reflection through production," or better, "reflection as production."

 DM For me both are mutually intertwined.

[a] AA I agree but only accepting the contingency of the choice and consequently that "every element is in a right place (and could be in another—right place)."

[b] JH Or at least, we could say that when something is presented as—or taken to be—an artistic work, there is an assumption on the part of the viewer that something else is going on, i.e., that this thing in front of us is more than just a thing (in its own right) but rather also a thing that points toward some other thing to which it has some kind of meaningful relation. But then, by accepting such a relation, does art still not quite escape the problem of abstraction from which (all) language suffers? I.e., by expressing or pointing toward something, it works by association, or categorization. In other words, the artist is saying: this thing that I have experienced (and reproduced, depicted, suggested, etc., here) is something like some other thing that you, the viewer, might have experienced.

 DM However, still the question remains if this thing, presented here, could be also replaced by another thing, or, more precisely, can it be possible that another thing evokes similar effects so that it can simply substitute the thing in the first place? The question which is important here is, what does preciseness and precision mean in art? Since every art-piece is singular, contingency—or the replacement of a thing by another—changes the entire character of an artwork so that, strictly speaking, contingency is absent (although there is a lot of contingency in the production process itself).

[c] AA I agree but: Does it imply "knowledge"?

 DM Yes, in terms of recognition or reflectivity, in terms of revelation or opening up new insights or perspectives …

by doing so, it makes its evocation explicit. It allows us to experience something that only reveals itself outside habitual experience, which in turn enables it to say something about experience as such and thus about our being.

This is why I pointed out, when discussing the experimental nature of artistic work above, that we should not forget that art does more than simply *exposing something*—"ex-perimentally," that is, through the journey itself—by enabling an exceptional perception or an unheard sound; that art does more than just illuminate the "world," "ourselves," our existential condition, our "form of life" or our "sociality" by intervening in it or traversing it. Rather, art is *always also art about art,* which means that by running the artistic process, it cannot but avoid *transforming itself* and the *modes of its reception.* Certainly, art shows something, but by showing it shows itself, points back to itself and shifts itself. Treating art as research then means recognizing that art is always engaged in an ongoing *praxis of self-research.* This brings us back to our initial question: what does research mean in the context of the arts? We can now better grasp the contours of this question by viewing it in the context of the above analysis of artistic thinking, whose definitive characteristics consist in the techniques of composition and "joining," a joining that points beyond itself. This analysis demonstrates that aesthetic, artistic activity constitutes a particular form of thinking and acting that places us in a novel relation to the world, [d] to ourselves, and to others, and that it accomplishes this precisely by revealing and pointing at itself as a unique form of thought and action. The conclusion to be drawn is that there can only be "artistic research" if we radically alter our concept of what research is. At the beginning of this inquiry, I stated that the concept of research cannot be given a single, universally valid, unchanging definition because its meanings are diverse and subject to change. Moreover, I made clear that we cannot simply apply the concept of research used by the sciences to the arts. In the end, we must begin anew if we are to give the concept of

[d] ^^ This seems to me to be a much more accurate formulation than "knowledge production" to describe the results, and even the goals, of artistic
research.

research in the aesthetic field a meaning that is worth anything at all. Thus, if we start by trying to trace the etymological roots of the word "research"—without the intention of uncovering some "original meaning" that would be "more authentic" than the modern usage, but rather to simply discover other connotations—we can see that in German it is rooted in *"finden"* (to find), but in a sense that implies that a specific method or system of searching has not yet been set. But can there be a "finding" without a search, without discipline and methodological norms—a finding that results out of an encounter, unintended and directionless? The English "re-search" is composed of the prefix "re" and the word "search," which more explicitly foregrounds the "searching" aspect of research; indeed, the word connotes a self-verifying search refined by repetition and recurrence. But what would a search that doesn't seek verification and that doesn't first take on its contours through the "re" of reflection look like? [e] A search that remains erratic and without foundations, only held together by the singularity of the process, which can always be *started again?* Such research would be an adventure without a destination, a venture whose journey would transform *everything*—we ourselves, the material used, the setting, the scenario, the spatial constellation and its temporal parameters—until it is all *different* than it was before. Is there a word for this that has not yet been contaminated by the sciences, that, unlike "research," does not immediately stir up associations with the institutional structures of knowledge work and the constancy of progress? [f]

It is revealing that the concept of research hardly played a role in Antique thought on the foundations of science and that it only really came to bear in Antique philosophy. It is also revealing that, when the Ancients spoke of "research," they used *two* different concepts—*ereuna* and *zētēsis*—the latter being seen as the more noble of the two. The first denotes the act of detecting and diagnosing that is performed in medical examinations and pharmacological therapy and that leads to the generation of positive knowledge. [g] In contrast, *zētēsis,* or, in its

[e] | AA The "re" does not necessarily imply the search for verification and the performance of reflection. It means, first of all, simply, "re-petition": to go, or to attack again—to visit again and again the object of research, to "inhabit it" (Victoria Perez Rollo) again and again.

JH In the nationwide UK process of institutional assessment of research quality (REF, Research Excellence Framework), the working definition of research is: "A process of investigation that yields insights, effectively shared." One problem that confronts artistic research in this context is defining precisely what qualifies as insights, especially in a medium as diffuse as music …?

DM The "re" leads in the first place to a refinement, an amelioration. Simply revisiting something, doing it again and again is not enough. Looking twice at something already implies a reflection, a redefinition or reconsideration—but the funny thing here is that the "re" in human practices is so fundamental, that we cannot but define the "re" by constantly repeating it (re-petition, re-finement, re-consideration, re-ferring, re-search, etc.) and referring back to it. Indeed I am constantly struggling here with the question of what cognition, knowledge, insights, etc. mean, for instance, in the realm of music. This is why I strongly distinguish between research in art and scientific research, and the definition we find in National Research Councils or the *Oxford Dictionary* always borrows its paradigm from science. My answer here is, that the knowledge or insights we gain—when for instance it comes to music—pertain to fundamental existential parameters: it changes our entire way and understanding of living. Art is showing us something which science does not even touch. In other words: art is a fundamental human practice which confronts us with existential or social and cultural constraints, distortions, paradoxes or contradictions, etc.—quite similar to philosophy. And what philosophers do I also call research and what they gain I also consider as knowledge, insight or: wisdom. This kind of knowledge or wisdom we cannot compare with scientific knowledge. Maybe—and sometimes I use this notion also—we should speak about artistic wisdom (rather than knowledge), a wisdom which leads us into the abysses of life, technology, politics or communication, etc., in order to provoke transformation.

[f] | AA The question is absolutely relevant but, in my opinion, incomplete. It needs an addition, a subordinated sentence, initiated by "but," that expresses at least one constitutive trait of research or better, of artistic research. I propose this continuation: "… but expresses the power of transforming fundamentally our concepts and the practices that substantiate them?"

DM Maybe, but I prefer to leave it open to the reader …

[g] AA "Positive knowledge" or, according again to your laconic definition of knowledge in section 2, simply, "knowledge."

verb form, *zetomai,* comes from the tradition of skeptical philosophy, or, more precisely, Pyrrhonic skepticism. It denotes a mode of critique that is always already self-critique. *Zētēsis* can be traced back to the root *zē* or Proto-Indo-European *dja,* which means something like "to strive" or "to acquire." *Zētein* or *zēteō* denote the act of carefully weighing or examining, an act that has no definable goal and that privileges the process of searching over the result of the search.[6] In drawing on Antique practices in order to found his "aesthetics of existence" in the "care of the self" [h] *(epimelesthai),* Michel Foucault is saying something very similar, and the practice of *zētēsis* is part of such care of the self. It serves to foster one's further development and is rooted in a search without destination, an ongoing self-inquiry [i] that begins with perception, seeing and hearing and, moving *through* perception and its media, ultimately encompasses the entire phenomenal sphere. *Zētēsis* thus does not constitute research in the scientific sense. Rather, *zētēsis* is a *passion.* This also means that *research in the sense of zētēsis* only takes place within the horizon of ongoing self-inquiry, doubt, and *despair of oneself.* The final claim is thus: if there is artistic research, a research *in, with* and *through* the arts, then it can only be as *zētēsis,* as a constant, but never concludable *work on itself.* [j]

[h] AA Maybe this can be considered to be the goal of this kind of (re)search. A general goal specified every time in and with the moment in which the (re)search takes place.

[i] AA The term "self-inquiry" is problematic here because it can be easily understood as "introspection." On the contrary, I understand its meaning here as a first-person inquiry whose object is, necessarily, the relation between the inquiring self and its environment.

[j] JH This concluding idea also reminds me of the recent enactive definition of perception put forward by philosophers and embodied cognitive scientists such as Alva Noë, and Evan Thompson. Perception in these terms is also always a process of research, an open-ended exploration of the world without a preconceived notion of what will be encountered. An accurate or viable grasp of a perceived object emerges from a sense of how its appearance changes with respect to the movement of the observer. This idea suggests that perception is fundamentally a dynamic and ongoing process, the object cannot therefore be grasped (and is never definitively grasped) from any one individual (static) viewpoint. Every experience is therefore a learning experience, however similar it might first appear to a previous experience.

   DM I agree on both sides.

[FULL TEXT]

ME At one point, the text sums up the formal structure of a scientific endeavor in terms of "A is B." On this formal level, the text itself remains scientific, since it presents artistic research as *zētēsis*. Unlike many scientific texts that are content with securing a position, this rich text makes me think further. If "self" is a feeling of existence then artistic research as *zētēsis* would be work on existence. How should we understand "work" here?

DM Exactly, *zētēsis* means a work on existence, and work here is an ongoing process without any end or goal. There are works of art as singular paradigms for research or the attempt to give an answer to our existential situation. But every work of art, in this sense, is just a passage—therefore James Joyce once said that he wrote so much because he couldn't complete writing or struggling with expression. Every attempt remains incomplete or includes failure. Art as research is similar to this unfinishable process, the art-work as research is just an intersection, a state or temporary model for it.

[FULL TEXT]

GV In the first section, Dieter Mersch's "Artistic Composition as Research" establishes a very useful cartography in six concepts of the uses of the locution "artistic research."

Section 4 examines the case of Alvin Lucier's 1965 piece *Music for Solo Performer,* a very real case of the hybrid of art and natural sciences. Although they are not common, there are other notable cases, for example some of the compositions by John Luther Adams. With his continuous sound-light installation, *The Place Where You Go to Listen* (2005)—a place on the Arctic coast—Adams offered his most intriguing realization of "sonic geography" to date. This sonic and visual environment, permanently installed at the Museum of the North in Fairbanks since the spring equinox of 2006, reflects the geography of interior Alaska. It makes audible in real time this region's cycles of daylight and nighttime; phases of the moon; meteorological, seismic, and geomagnetic activities; and the aurora borealis. Adams' *Place* draws on real-time digital data streams (numerical maps) of this region's geophysical forces, which are continuously fed into a computer and "orchestrated" with electronic sounds. This enterprise required the collaboration of meteorologists, seismologists, scientists, physicist John Olson, mathematicians, and computer programmers. [See Bernd Herzogenrath ed., The Farthest Place: The Music of John Luther Adams, Boston: Northeastern University Press, 2012.]

Sections 5 and 6 are really philosophical pieces. The most interesting question Dieter Mersch poses is that "we should not ask 'what is research,' but rather 'what is thinking,' or, more precisely: What are the specific features of aesthetic or artistic thinking?". Mersch considers that the right answer presupposes that aesthetic thinking is a form of knowledge. It is necessary to stress that artistic research produces several kinds of knowledge, among them aesthetic, autonomous knowledge (different from scientific or philosophical), which is only one of these multiple kinds. A dialogue with Christopher Cox, "Sonic Thought" [Bernd Herzogenrath ed., Sonic Thinking: A Media Philosophical Approach, London and New York: Bloomsbury Academic, 2017] would be of maximum interest.

1 For a survey of the concept of research in the arts see Mersch, Epistemologies of Aesthetics.
2 Lucier, Music 109, 51 ff.
3 Kahn, "Alvin Lucier," 213 ff.
4 Lucier, Reflections, 36.
5 Hegel, Hegel's Aesthetics, 10.
6 Vorländer, Geschichte der Philosophie, 152, 153.

References:

Hegel, Georg Wilhelm Friedrich. Hegel's Aesthetics: Lectures on Fine Art. Translated by T. M. Knox, Vol. 1. Oxford: Oxford University Press, 1975.

Kahn, Douglas. "Alvin Lucier, Edmond Dewan and Music for Solo Performer." In Klangmaschinen zwischen Experiment und Medientechnik, edited by Daniel Gethmann. Bielefeld: transcript, 2010.

Lucier, Alvin. Reflections: Interviews, Scores, Writings 1965–1994. Cologne: MusikTexte, 2005.

Lucier, Alvin. Music 109: Notes on Experimental Music. Middletown CT: Wesleyan University Press, 2012.

Mersch, Dieter. Epistemologies of Aesthetics. Zurich: Diaphanes, 2015.

Vorländer, Karl. Geschichte der Philosophie 1: Philosophie des Altertums. Reinbek bei Hamburg: Rowohlt, 1973.

Aesthetics and Aesthetic Research

Gerard Vilar

Are "aesthetic" and "artistic" synonymous terms? What is the relationship between aesthetic and artistic objects and their relative experiences? This old philosophical problem about the relationship of art and aesthetics is now being renewed and reaffirmed in the field of so-called practice-based research or artistic research. Most art researchers use the expressions just mentioned, but others prefer the phrase "aesthetic research." The question posed by this terminological plurality can be formulated as follows: Is it possible to distinguish aesthetic research from artistic research or are they synonymous expressions? Are they different types of research or are both essentially referring to the same concept (or perhaps family of concepts)? Of course, providing an answer to these questions means having a certain position on the nature of aesthetics, on the definitions of art and artistic research. [A]

 Artistic research seems to grant little place to aesthetics. With few exceptions,[1] the word "aesthetics" is mentioned in discussions

[A] | ^{LG} This also means that artistic and aesthetic research is not just applied research or research by practice or by design; rather, it requires a systematic framework. In this sense, there is no aesthetic research without investigation into aesthetics, perception, and sensibility. The systematic relation between theory and practice aims not only to substantiate the practical framework but also to extend theoretical reflection to the constitution of perception—for instance with respect to an aesthetics that can overcome naturalism. A systematic foundation also implies a new reading of German classical philosophy in order to reactualize—and thus also to extend—Kant's reflection on aesthetics for a theory of embodiment.

^{GV} I agree with you, but it seems to me that today it is impossible to avoid some weak version of naturalism in the theory of perception, like the enactivist proposal of Alva Noë, for example.

about the problems that plague artistic research practices. It seems as if these practices did not have that dimension, or it had little or no importance, and that, therefore, should be placed next to those post-conceptual practices that, according to Peter Osborne, are "beyond aesthetics."[2] [B] However, in the synthesis accounts about the nature of artistic research and the type of knowledge it generates, references to philosophical aesthetics and in particular to the cognitivist tradition recur, starting with the first founder of the discipline, Alexander Baumgarten.[3] On the other hand, the tendency of many exhibitions of artistic research projects to present a text [C] that describes the process and the provisional results of the research with little or no sensitive, visual, sound or other accompaniment, as is usually the case in the "exhibitions" of the *Journal of Artistic Research,* [D] invite an attempt at a clarification, as far as possible, of the relations of aesthetics with artistic research practices. I will begin with a brief explanation of the meanings of the aesthetic term and I will continue with the question of the relationship between art and aesthetics. Next, I will approach the notion of aesthetic research as a generator of spaces of intelligibility, and I will conclude with some examples that help illustrate the positions defended.

1. AESTHETICS

The term aesthetics has several fundamental meanings. In the first place, it refers to a sensitive dimension of all things and phenomena, from a stone to a mathematical demonstration, from a flower to the knob of a door, from a cave painting to a pop concert. All objects and phenomena have a series of properties or qualities by which the individuals of our species can feel attracted, repelled or indifferent. The aesthetic sense or aesthetic consciousness defines us as a species as much as, or more than, moral sense or conscience. The empirical sciences have been trying for some time to explain the nature of the aesthetic consciousness that lies at the root of our aesthetic

[B] ^{DM} One reason for the confusion about art and aesthetics, especially pertaining to avant-garde and post-avant-garde art, I assume, is the philosophical ambiguity of the term "aesthetics" as such, as it is mentioned in the first paragraph of the following considerations.

> ^{GV} Right. And perhaps that is an insurmountable problem because of the very nature of aesthetics and of art, concepts which are not reducible to closed categories as is usual in our culture. In that sense, some thinkers such as T. W. Adorno or Christoph Menke are right in affirming that aesthetics represents a polymorphic negativity.

[C] ^{LG} It is crucial to develop a new criticism regarding the function of the text simply as clarification and not as aesthetic production. There is thus a merely "instrumental" use of the medium of text for disclosing artworks in a descriptive sense. But there is also an internal, "performative" use of the text as a medial dimension that is an essential—not accidental—part of the work. Is it possible to improve this second use of the text as an aesthetic internal practice?

> ^{GV} Answering your question: I am sure that yes. A good example of this seems to me to be Mika Elo's project *What Calls for Thinking?* exposed in the Research Catalogue.

[D] ^{AA} Although the balance between text and non-text and the relationships between these two kinds of components is a constant topic of debate in the editorial board of the *Journal for Artistic Research,* the idea of creating a new platform—the *Research Catalogue*—in order to publish artistic research in *JAR* aimed at enabling and encouraging the "exposition" of this kind of research in multiple media.

> ^{GV} Sure!

conducts—ornamentation, embellishment, evaluation, art. Some of these behaviors may be related to reproduction strategies and sex, [E] that had already emerged in nature amongst countless animal and plant species, before evolution led to the emergence of homo sapiens. At least in part, aesthetics has already invented nature, as we see in the classic examples of turkeys and flowers, even as something totally separate from its functionality.[4] On the other hand, our ability to have aesthetic preferences and to make evaluations, and especially to create art, does not mean that these preferences can merely be naturalized because they have to do with our capacity for symbolization, of which language is perhaps the main manifestation. [F] The shaman of 40,000 years ago preferred to cover his head with a wolf skin because the aesthetic properties of that skin symbolized the strength, the intelligence, the ferocity of the powers of nature or the spirits of the clan, and, therefore, its own power. Nature endowed us with the capacity for aesthetic behavior, produced the appropriate neural connections to elaborate symbols, but the wolf's skin as a shamanic symbol, like the papal miter, is a product of culture, not of nature. This is more evident in the case of the arts. Nature also gave us the capacity for language, but the English tragedy *Romeo and Juliet* is not a product of nature. Art is also a matter of construction of symbolic forms, but in certain ways that, unlike others, allow us to self-define and self-modify as they are devices for reflection.[5] [G] Aesthetic or artistic experience in this reflective sense has less to do with the satisfaction of our preferences than with the destabilization of our preferences and expectations. As Alva Noë has put it: "art is disruptive and destabilizing … it is a mode of investigation, a form of research aiming at transformation and reorganization."[6] So, basic aesthetic experience and art experience are not the same. [H] Here we have, then, to distinguish between *the liminal or basic sense* of aesthetics as that dimension that has every natural or cultural phenomenon or object and that we are capable of appreciating thanks to our aesthetic sense, and aesthetics *in*

[E] DM I would like to claim here, that in biological or evolutionary aesthetics the concept of aesthetics is misused. The examples mentioned there—the courtship behavior in animals or decoration in appealing strategies are nothing but a human projection, an absolutized anthropomorphism. I consider the aesthetic (and also art) as a fundamental human practice, related not to biology but to the human other, the social, the symbolic, as Vilar rightly points out later.

> GV Sure, but as in ethics there are some natural behaviors which make possible later in history the emancipation of the social and cultural behaviors.

[F] AA This assertion is based on a categorical differentiation between nature and culture that I do not share. From a enactivist point of view, which is shared by other approaches in the framework of the embodied and situated cognition theories, culture is not outside of nature but part of it. Accordingly "symbolization" or "language" are natural phenomena performed by a specific form of organized organic matter: humans.

> GV This is a complicated issue. I am in agreement with you in the continuity of nature and culture. I defend a weak naturalism. All our abilities have a natural basis, but not all can be deduced from it. Nature has endowed you with the capacity for language. But, for example, we cannot deduce from this the English of Shakespeare.

[G] AA Arguing again for the continuity between nature and culture—and beyond: the absence of categorical differentiation between both fields, taking culture to be a set of natural developments—I would postulate that "self-definition" and "self-modification" are expressions of the form of organization that define fundamentally living beings: autopoiesis, or, in more general terms, autonomy.

> GV You defend a strong form of naturalism. Since no other form of life—except, perhaps, our Neanderthal cousins—has this form of "self-modification" that we call art, I think it is sensible to make a difference within the eventual continuity of the phenomenon of autopoiesis.

[H] AA Is your argument here, according to your categorical distinction between nature and culture, that "aesthetics" belongs to the first and art to the second?

> GV Yes.

a strong or reflective sense as a way of thinking—aesthetic thinking—[7] and, eventually, of knowing or understanding that we find in art and whose aim is "the disclosure of ourselves to ourselves and so it aims at giving us opportunities to catch ourselves in the act of achieving consciousness—including aesthetic consciousness—of the world around us."[8][I] The naturalization of aesthetics in the liminal sense is plausible to a certain extent; that of the second sense is impossible without breaking the nature-culture continuum and defending some kind of concept of extended mind. There are philosophical strategies to elaborate a good account of this notion of aesthetics, while avoiding the traditional problems of naturalism. The most promising program in that sense is the enactivism defended by Alva Noë or Alex Arteaga.[9][J].

Second, the term aesthetics refers to a regime of existence of aesthetic objects and phenomena, such as art, which emerged progressively in the eighteenth century in Europe and has generated a differentiated cultural sphere—in Max Weber's sense of the term—that interacts with other cultural spheres such as science, money, or the normative sphere that includes politics, law and morals. This sense has been defended fundamentally by Jacques Rancière since 2000,[10] although it is an idea that can be traced back to Kant. Unlike the previous regimes, which Rancière refers to as the ethical regime and the mimetic or representational regime, the aesthetic regime is a regime of identification of art characterized by the autonomy of the work, the creator and the public, that is, the relative freedom for the artistic creation, for the judgment of a universal audience, and for the artwork itself. This autonomy allows the emergence of both the art market and museums, so that old artifacts of religious or representational art can become goods in a market and artworks that hang on the walls of a museum disconnected from their traditional functions, which are now perceived as "art." By definition, the aesthetic regime is not defined once and for all, so that changing itself in a permanent way changes the very concept of all the institutions and practices that it encompasses, starting

[I] LG The distinction between these two levels of aesthetics seems to be problematic because the second sense of aesthetics as reflection is the condition of possibility of the former, which is "basic," but as constituted and not provided.

AA I don't see clearly the distinction between art and aesthetics you are proposing here. Actually what I see is the distinction between two concepts of aesthetics and the outline of art as a set of practices anchored in and/or unfolding or realizing the "strong" sense of aesthetics.

GV You both are right.

[J] LG To go beyond naturalism we need enactivism, of course, but also a reactualization of the notion of a systematic aesthetics founded on a transcendental theory of sensible cognition that is not merely empirical but rather transcendental, in order to explain a common framework by articulating meaning—also from a phenomenological perspective.

GV Of course, but I do not have a very clear idea what "transcendental" means in this context.

with the very concepts of art and artist. Artistic research practices and the artist as a researcher are only contemporary transformations produced within the aesthetic regime now dominant globally, except perhaps in North Korea.

Third, aesthetics means that philosophical reflection initiated in the Enlightenment about the phenomena referred to by the first two meanings of the word. But aesthetics in this latter sense has never agreed on its object in a way that differs from disagreements in theoretical and practical philosophy. Philosophical aesthetics was engendered by Baumgarten as *gnoseologia inferior,* the science that deals with sensory knowledge and theory of fine arts that reaches the apprehension of the beautiful and expresses itself in the images of art, as opposed to logic as the science of conceptual knowledge. Beating the twice-born Dionysus, however, the aesthetic was re-established twice more. Once by Kant as domain indeterminate but differentiated of the cognitive theoretical sphere and the practical normative sphere, in which art was only one of its subdomains. In its last reincarnation, aesthetics was conceived by Hegel as a philosophy of art, where the very aesthetics was defined as a product of art. Thus, one of the central philosophical problems of philosophical aesthetics since its foundation has been how to establish the relationship between aesthetic objects, artistic objects and their relative experiences. [K] This can be seen in discussions about the aesthetics of nature, in the disputes over the relationship of art to nature generated by some of the fundamental artistic practices of the twentieth century that called into question the assumption that every work of art was aesthetic. In all of them we can see that philosophical aesthetics is not simply about the usual intra-philosophical dilemmas between positions, such as between realism and anti-realism or between universalism and relativism, but it is about the impossibility of disciplining, through philosophical reflection, objects and phenomena that resist this type of reflection and point to a critique of it. In this sense, philosophical aesthetics is both a critique

[K]   LG And to consider art as something that is not just a subdomain of cognition.

GV   Right! Of cognition, of religion, of politics, ethics …

of philosophy and a critique of the history of art and of the other social sciences that investigate art. [L] The undisciplined nature of aesthetics with respect to theoretical philosophy and practical philosophy—and science—is what characterizes and defines it, not as a philosophical discipline but as a kind of reflection that permanently puts the rest of philosophy into question.[11] [M] [N]

2. ART AND AESTHETICS

The field of aesthetics is much broader than the field of art. [O] In fact, everything has an aesthetic, or rather we, as human beings, have the universal ability to appreciate the aesthetic qualities of any natural object or cultural artifact. That is a liminal or basic sense of "aesthetics" that presupposes something like an aesthetic sense. There is no art without aesthetics in this first sense. [P] Then there is a second sense of aesthetics that refers to the reflective uses of our aesthetic capabilities. Thus, we could agree that art has been the province par excellence of aesthetics in the second sense, but we must also admit that aesthetics in the first sense is in contemporary art not as important as it was in the past. There are even some types of works of art in which the meaning does not include its aesthetic dimension in a traditional sense, as is the case in a significant number of conceptual works and artistic projects. From the Duchamp *Fountain* to Robert Barry's *All the things I know,* the Art & Language or On Kawara projects, we can mention many famous works that do not "have" or "present" traditional aesthetic qualities to be experienced and appreciated, all works of the so-called "non-perceptual art." [Q] [R] The extension of some arguments of the old Arthur Danto are, here, of last importance. Danto defended the thesis that among the properties of a work of art some of them belong to its meaning, to its definition, and others do not.[12] Thus, for example, usually the weight of a painting does not belong to its meaning. In contrast, size, color and drawing define elements of its meaning. How many kilos weigh the large canvases of Delacroix is something that

[L] AA And, I would like to add, a definition and critique of a particular variety of experience of and relation to the world.

GV Of course.

[M] DM The same holds, by the way, for art as a practice that in itself is already a kind of
theoria (in the Greek sense)—thus, a theory practice that reaches beyond conceptual
limitations, that tears apart what is taken for granted, that practically throws into
question our certainties in perception, in social relationship, in normative orders
and the like. I therefore consider art as another philosophy in terms of a practice of
criticism that not only destabilizes traditional philosophy but the political as well as
science and, last but not least, art itself. There is a certain homology between the
constant self-questioning history of philosophy and the permanent *autodafé* and
iconoclasm in the history of art.

[N] LG This is a crucial point: aesthetics has a critical value. On the one hand, it extends
philosophical reflection to new realms; on the other, more radical hand it represents
a revision, a critical approach to the central questions and assumptions of philosophy. Reflecting on art and analyzing Descartes' concept of vision, Merleau-Ponty
tries to develop an aesthetic phenomenology that is first and foremost a new criticism of theoretical philosophy and scientific knowledge.

GV Completely agree.

[O] LG For me it is the theory of sensibility that extends and expands the border
of the "artistic field".

[P] DM Against Osborne's notion "beyond aesthetics," there is, therefore, no escape
from aesthetics, no outside. Aesthetics indeed, in the first place, is a universal term.
Even in concept-art we have to discern and to discover the concept aesthetically.

GV Totally agree.

[Q] DM Arthur Danto made this point specific with respect to Warhol's *Brillo Boxes:* That
the difference between the everyday Brillo box you find in supermarkets, and Warhol's artwork cannot be perceived; it is not a matter of aesthetics but of concept.
However here we have to keep in mind, that the duplication—the fact that both are
identical—has to be perceived as well—and you can only claim the similarity or indif-
ference on the basic of perception. Moreover: Warhol's idea was not to deconstruct
the close relation between art and aesthetics but to show the strange aesthetics of
advertisement and its design—the strange use of aesthetics in capitalistic economy.

GV Of course. In fact, "non-perceptual" art is an expression that should not
be understood literally because art is always perceptual. By the way, if you
have seen some time a *Brillo Box* by Warhol you will have seen immediately
an enormous perceptual difference with the real Brillo boxes. The supposed
"indiscernibility" has been always an argumentative trick.

[R] AA I think that this passage, or better, the traditionally accepted positions it expresses
are fundamentally problematic. The main reason is that perception is not relevant
for these works. It is the perceptual presence of the pissoir in the museum that
enables Duchamp's *Fountain* as much as the perceptual tension between presence
and absence that is at the basis of Barry's *All the things I know*. Conceptual art does
not exclude perception as a basic form of action but it resituates it in relation to other
forms of intentionality.

GV Conceptual art does not exclude perception, of course, because it is art.
Otherwise it would be philosophy or another form of theory. But this type of
art is based precisely on the fact that the relationship between the sensitive
support and the meaning or concept is different than in the art that Duchamp
called "retinal." The distinction between "internal" and "external" aesthetics
is only one way, perhaps not sufficiently successful, to explain this difference.

only interests carriers when they must move them to exhibit them in other museums or exhibition centers different from those that usually host them. Following, then, the distinction of Danto, there are works of art whose liminal aesthetics are internal, which means that they belong to his concept, and other works whose liminal aesthetics are external, as is the case with the Duchamp urinal, whose qualities such as beauty, proportion and symmetry, as well as its weight, do not belong to its meaning. [S] And just this questioning of the importance of aesthetics in works of art, is what makes Duchamp's works, as works of art, more interesting and pioneering, something that is now commonplace in postconceptual art, an "art beyond aesthetics." [T] But the experience of Duchamp's works, like those of all anti-aesthetic artists,[13] like that of all art that deserves that name, is *negatively aesthetic* in the internal sense, [U] in the reflective sense, because it aims to destabilize the ordinary view, the assumptions about the perception of art, questioning prejudices, breaking intelligibility and, in short, disrupting our habitual ways of seeing. The aesthetic of Duchamp's urinal pertains negatively to the definition of this artwork, like the absence of music pertains to the concept of *4'33"* by Cage. [V] And that negativity is what enables new forms of intelligence, the emergence of new intelligibility by breaking the old one, and so we can transform or "reorganize" ourselves, as Alva Noë maintains.

It is true that since the 1980s, anti-aesthetic art has become an important and very practiced program. Anti-aesthetic art is de-aestheticized art, in the sense that the aesthetic dimension does not matter much to the artist and that it is considered as something secondary, inessential. These works do not usually appear to be works of art, neither traditional nor modernist, given that their typical formats are documentations, archives, video interviews, and theoretical discourses. [W] In this sense, they therefore constitute de-artificated art. [X] However, first, this does not mean that these works do not have an "aesthetic." All of them have an aesthetic. [Y] But in a sense, the aim of

[S] | AA There is a basic aspect of this passage that seems to me to be problematic: it assumes that an art work has a "concept" which constitutes the space that delimits the difference between its "inside" and its "outside." I don't think that this is the case. Nevertheless I would accept the debate about the situation or relevance of perception—in the production and in the reception of the art work, using traditional terms—for the aesthetic experience enabled by it.

GV It would be necessary to distinguish types of aesthetic experience according to the centrality of what I call liminal aesthetics. We cannot use the same concept for the paintings by Robert Ryman and for the works of On Kawara.

[T] DM Osborne's notion "beyond aesthetics," however, uses "aesthetics" in a narrow sense.

[U] LG The notion of negativity can also be related to the general question of the definition of the mediality of art—also with reference to works of art with an external aesthetics: what is their own mediality? Or, in the sense of Dieter Mersch's negative mediality, how can we explain the media constitution of a work of art without speaking about internal aesthetics and the transition from one medium to another—for instance from a discursive medium to an iconic one?

[V] AA And furthermore to the definition of art and of artistic and/of aesthetic experience …

[W] DM However, all these formats, even theoretical discourses, require their aesthetic appearance, their aesthetic "Da-sein." Therefore I strongly support Vilar's objection that in art one cannot neglect the aesthetic dimension (in a broad sense). The entire post-aesthetic discourse exposes itself as misleading. In order to make its point it forgot the true meaning of aesthetics, it even no longer understands the notion as an undeniable term. The preciseness of an artwork, its well-defined impact on the beholder is related to its aesthetic dimension so that any change of the format implies a change in meaning.

[X] LG Related to materiality and its transformation, could we say "without media consciousness"?

[Y] | AA In my opinion the term "an aesthetic" introduces a third concept of the term aesthetics which differs from aesthetics in its liminal or strong sense—although it might be closer to the first. "An aesthetic" means how something—the thing that "has an aesthetic"—looks categorically, i.e. looks like (other things or in relation to other things).

GV I don't see the difference between the first and a third concept of aesthetics. We should elaborate this point.

these works seems to be like a scientific theory: [2] it does not matter if they are written on a chalkboard with chalk or are printed on paper in Arial font—they are always the same theory. This analogy, however, is misguided. In art, the aesthetic dimension is never negligible. The format, for example, of a work of documentation can always be done in different ways, and different formats can determine experiences of the work distinctly to a much greater degree than is the case with painting or sculptures, always conditioned mainly by the power of place. Second, it is also untrue that all works that have an anti-aesthetic tendency are de-aestheticized works. The works of some artists have a marked aesthetic component as primary dimension. This was the case with the work of Barbara Kruger, who was paradigmatic with this tendency in the 1980s and 1990s. The works of Kruger used the resources of billboards and advertisements in general so as to recode or redefine in the normally used formats, alter their meaning in order to transmit politically critical messages regarding the state of women or of the ruling powers. Some of the great artists in political art in the last 30 years, such as Hans Haacke, Martha Rosler, or Raymond Pettibon, have used this type of strategy to break down the cultural codes of the masses to use them critically against power.

On the other hand, the fields of aesthetics are now wider than ever. To the field of aesthetics of natural objects such as flowers, birds and landscapes, we must add fashion, advertising, design, decoration, styling, gastronomy, plastic surgery and, probably, others. Certainly, all these fields share a blurred border with art, but, with few exceptions, they are not art. They relate to liminal aesthetics, but little to reflective aesthetics. The clothes designed by important designers like Armani or Jean-Paul Gaultier, have been the object of great exhibitions in important museums, but this does not imply that all these aesthetic objects are art. An Armani suit can be art if it is used as the central element of an artistic project, of course, but in its normal use it is simply a product of fashion. The case of Jean-Paul Gaultier, on the other hand, is

[Z] ^{LG} Is it perhaps better to say that the language at this point is merely used instrumentally?

      ^{GV} That would be a way of saying it.

different. His costumes for Madonna and other pieces truly worked as art, bringing aesthetic disorder to the prevailing order in several of his senses. Also fantastic Harley-Davidson or Vespa motorcycles have been exhibited in the Guggenheim museums of New York and Bilbao, but I do not know that anyone has ever claimed that they are art in a strong sense, that is, that they are devices for aesthetic reflection.

3. ARTISTIC RESEARCH AND AESTHETIC RESEARCH

So, are these general distinctions made for the relations of art and aesthetics also appropriate for the relations between artistic research and aesthetics? And what would an aesthetic investigation be? We can start with some examples. There is a significant number of artistic research projects where the aesthetic dimension does not matter at all because it is not included in the definition of the project. We can start with some examples. In the autumn of 2015, the Reina Sofía National Art Center Museum of Madrid inaugurated an important retrospective of Hito Steyerl, an ascending German artist in contemporary art who stands out for her politically critical research projects around the mass media, the image and other aspects of life in present-day societies. The exhibition bore the title *Duty-Free Art,* which was one of the projects included in the retrospective and, in fact, at that time the most recent of them all. This project is defined as an investigation into freeport art storage, the important deposits of works of art found in off-shore territories—or free zones—within some international airports, such as the airports of Geneva or Singapore. Collectors, dealers, traffickers, investors, corporations and other people and institutions from all over the planet deposit works of art in these free zones—for example, there are thousands of Picassos stored in such places—for which their owners do not want to pay customs taxes or because of the patrimony tax rates. This type of extra-national space is creating new "no-man's lands of luxury," new "secret museums," which in reality, are part of this extensive network of new tax havens, deep internet,

etc., which are reconfiguring spaces of sovereignty throughout the world. This project of denunciation by Hito Steyerl consists of an article, originally published in the digital magazine e-*flux,* also reproduced in Spanish in the catalog of the retrospective,[14] where these facts are explained and, importantly, are framed within a broader reflection on how contemporary art reveals the transformations of space and time in a globalized world. This text is not merely accessory, but it is the one that articulates the meaning of Steyerl's artistic project, a project that has another part, say visual, that consists of an installation formed by some screens in which videos are seen, singularly of Steyerl herself explaining aspects of the project and its process, as well as a couple of "tables" with scale models and some signs. This visual, aesthetic part is not especially attractive or seductive, and, of course, nothing is understood without reading the article or a summary of its content. By the way, the projects of Hito Steyerl usually have a remarkable or even great aesthetic force, beyond their theoretical and informative dimension. Suffice it to recall her project on Adorno of 2012 *(Adorno's Grey)* or her project for the 2015 Venice Biennale *(The Factory of the Sun),* an authentic visual joy as well as a relentless critique of the use of the image in the contemporary world. However, *Duty-Free Art* is one of those types of artistic research projects whose exposition easily leads many to ask the fatal question: but where is the art? This question arises because the liminal aesthetic does not seem to be part of the concept of this artistic project, something that is infrequent in Steyerl's career.

Let me pose a second example. This is the artistic research project proposed by the German artist Maria Eichhorn in the Documenta 14 of the year 2017, a project that bears the name of *Rose Valland Institute.*[15] The *Rose Valland Institute* is an independent interdisciplinary artistic project. It investigates and documents the expropriation of the properties of the Jewish population of Europe and the permanent impact of these apprehensions. The Institute is named after art historian

Rose Valland, who secretly recorded details of Nazi looting during the German occupation of Paris. After the war, she worked for the Commission de Récupération Artistique (Commission for the Recovery of Works of Art) and was instrumental in restoring artworks stolen by the Nazis. Based on the knowledge obtained from the previous exhibition projects of Maria Eichhorn, *Restitutionspolitik / Politics of Restitution* (2003) and *In den Zelten ...* (2015), the *Rose Valland Institute* is dedicated to the issue of unresolved properties and property relations from 1933 to the present. The Institute investigates fundamental questions about the ownership of works of art, land, real estate, financial assets, businesses, objects and mobile devices, libraries, academic works and patents that were stolen from their Jewish owners in Germany and in the territories occupied during the Nazi era and that, to this day, have not been returned. The *Rose Valland Institute* was presented publicly in March 2017 with a call for papers focusing on the issue of ownership of orphans in Europe. With the open call on the issue of illegal property in Germany, the Institute continues its activities. The *Rose Valland Institute* appeals to the public to investigate the Nazi booty that may exist in inherited properties and send the findings to the Institute. The Institute was founded on the occasion of Documenta 14 and was based at the Neue Galerie in Kassel between June 10 and September 17, 2017. It was situated in a room where the public could contemplate books and documents. In a similar way to the well-known projects of the *Forensic Architecture* collective, this Institute gathers information, generates knowledge about facts that can then be used before courts in processes of restitution of legitimate property. Not only is it a device for reflection, but it also generates corroborative knowledge with pretension of validity before the courts. However, the *Rose Valland Institute* is one of those types of artistic research projects whose exposition easily leads many to ask the fatal question: but where is the art?[16] This question arises because the liminal aesthetic does not seem to be a substantive part of this artistic project, or in the

terminology inspired by Danto, Maria Eichhorn's project does not have an internal aesthetic.

Thus, although research projects have without exception a liminal, external aesthetic, they do not always have an internal aesthetic, as is the case in general for all sorts of artworks. If this is the case, is there a possibility to distinguish aesthetic research from artistic research? I believe that such a possibility exists, if the expression "aesthetic research" is used as the name for a special type of artistic research project that focuses only on research in the field in which the aesthetic dimension becomes crucial for the generation of intelligibility, of meaning or sense. In any case, finally, aesthetic research is always a variety of many types of artistic research. [a] There are examples of this type of research in projects on perception of space and (or) time. My favorite example is *Architecture of Embodiment,* a project by the German Catalan artist Alex Arteaga, an aesthetic research about the ways in which sound interacts with architectural space and bodies to generate meaning.[17] This project has been developed since 2013 in several subprojects or research cells and combines always different media as sound installations, videos, photos, and literary and theoretical texts. But before considering Arteaga's project, I would like to provide some reflections on the art in artistic research projects—and aesthetic ones.

4. INTELLIGIBILITY: IDEAS AND PERCEPTS

Frequently, visiting artistic research exhibitions, or seeing exhibitions in the *Journal of Artistic Research,* one ends up wondering where art is in those projects, since perhaps they could have been undertaken by historians, anthropologists or media experts and their results exhibited in a history or ethnology museum, or a cultural center, or whatever, rather than in an artistic center. No doubt, they usually represent true research, but where is the art? A satisfactory answer to the problem of where art is in artistic research is to be found in the difference

[a] AA This proposition raises for me certain questions. The first refers to the general outline of artistic research. Clearly the goal of this text is not to define artistic research but to differentiate between two forms of research: aesthetic and artistic research. The first move towards this differentiation is to postulate that the first is a subgroup of the second. Consequently, it is not necessary to define any of these varieties of research but to identify the distinctive traits of each. Nevertheless, it seems to me that there is in this text an implicit, general outline of what artistic research might be: any kind of process and/or project realized by artists and accepted as art in the art system, that contributes to "generate knowledge," meaning, according to both described examples, to provide new information about a subject matter. This way of defining artistic research seems to me to be plausible but too vague. It is something like defining bread as what is done by bakers and sold in bakeries … My second question refers to the specific meaning of the formulation "focus only on research in the field in which the aesthetic dimension becomes crucial for the generation of intelligibility, of meaning or sense"—actuality, the criteria of differentiation between aesthetic and artistic research. Does this mean that aesthetic research is basically defined by having aesthetics, epistemologically defined, as object of research? In other words: is aesthetic research research on aesthetics? Is the differentiation between artistic and aesthetic research based on a difference of subject matter?

DM Although I fully understand the argument—and also its direction—I have some doubts. Since the *Rose Valland Institute* was founded on an exhibition and since curation was an important part of its public presentation I consider the aesthetic part as essential for the entire project. Also the way of presentation plays an important part in the argumentation of the Institute—and the same holds, in my view, for *Forensic Architecture.* So, at least in my view, there is no artistic research project without an aesthetic research part. For this reason I would prefer to put the relationship between both the other way round: there is research in general, and different subclasses of it are, among others, scientific and aesthetic research, while a subclass of the latter is artistic research. One of the major features of artistic research then is—according to the argumentation above, especially pertaining to concept art—its aesthetic methodology. Even, one can say, aesthetics is the medium of artistic research in general, because you investigate and present your investigation to the public through aesthetic practices such as a certain space-time-based exhibition, a certain kind of curating, the use of peculiar materials etc. Aesthetic practices include also design, such as arranging things or playing with technological devices aesthetically. So aesthetics always is a condition for the possibility of artistic research which argues close to philosophical reflection.

LG Is aesthetic research just a type of artistic research or a category covering many types of artistic research? If aesthetic research is just a type of artistic research, then it is a kind of subdomain. But if aesthetic research is a category covering many types of artistic research, then the former has a more comprehensive function. This means that aesthetic research does not simply extend the types of artistic research but reveals the necessity of revising its borders. Does aesthetic research put artistic research into question?

GV Well, that's right. I do not try to give a definition of what artistic research is. In fact, I think we can only give pedagogical or open definitions (like the one you sketch or Borgdorff's) because, by its very nature, research based on practice cannot be defined once and for all. Its difference from scientific practices lies in the impossibility of reducing it to a single unified conception and to the same type of practice. As Adorno said about art in general, artistic practices resist the principle of identity. My interest is to try to distinguish aesthetic research as a subclass of artistic research that is distinguished by inquiring into the basic modes in which intelligibility is created, as in your project *Architecture of Embodiment.* In this sense, yes, I think the difference is more in the object of investigation.

between an informative presentation or display and an authentic device for reflection. Social scientists produce theory, information, and factual knowledge. <u>Usually artists do not produce knowledge primarily, but rather create devices for the generation of knowledge.</u> [b] <u>If this distinction is completely erased, the risk is to have bad science and/or bad art, or even to have neither. So, artistic research projects whose aesthetic is external, secondary and absent from the definition of the very project, are often artistic research without art, even if they are very good research.</u> [c] These are the cases of Hito Steyerl's and Maria Eichhorn's projects, mentioned above. <u>In order to produce authentic artistic research, aesthetics must be internal.</u> [d]

To build a philosophical argument appropriate to the intuition that we have just formulated, it is possible to have recourse to Deleuze's thesis about *percepts* as the kind of ideas that artists create, unlike the scientists who create functions and the philosophers who create concepts. The first part of the argument is that works of art, although they may contain information to one degree or another, do not make a cognitive statement, do not propose a thesis with a claim that it is true, as is the case in the sciences, but are devices for reflection, apparatuses for a thinking that cannot be summed up in a certain thesis. The contemporary sciences affirm theses of the following tenor: "In the center of the Milky Way there is a black hole," or "The FoxP2 gene is fundamental for the linguistic capacity of human beings." <u>However, for an artistic research project, even containing this type of information, to be "artistic," it must work as a device for reflection;</u> [e] for example, a multimedia installation about our place in the cosmos or about the natural foundations of the language that we usually ignore. And what is a device for reflection? Well, I think the first one who defined it was the old Königsberg philosopher, Immanuel Kant, in his *Critique of the Faculty of Judgment,* in which he wrote that true works of art are those that expose an aesthetic idea, and that an aesthetic idea, unlike other kinds of ideas, including scientific and philosophical, has a

[b] AA Spontaneously I would tend to agree with this assertion. But reflecting on this differentiation a problem arises. Accepting that scientists also create devices—and I'm not only referring to experimental settings but also to books or papers—and the difference between scientific and artistic research refers to "devices," my conclusion is that the scientific devices tend to be equated to knowledge—the book is the knowledge, or at least contains it—whereas the artistic devices are not knowledge but enable its generation. Is this really the case? I tend to think that a scientific book or a paper are or can be as much devices for the emergence of knowledge as a video installation or even a painting. The difference is that they "do it" in different ways.

GV I think I agree.

[c] LG Or is the risk perhaps the possibility of having artistic research without its own internal mediality? In this case, communication depends on the media that explain and communicate the "sense" of the work without establishing a performative use of the work in order to constitute a new sense.

[d] AA Is a conclusion of this argumentation that only aesthetic research is "authentic artistic research"?

LG If in order to produce authentic artistic research aesthetics must be internal, and if aesthetic research is—as you write further—a reflection on aesthetics, then it seems to me that aesthetic research is not a subdomain but the missing dimension of artistic research.

GV This is a very interesting question: whether there is a normativity in the field of artistic research. I think that's the way it is. Perhaps the term "authentic" is not the most accurate because it implies that there is inauthentic artistic research. It remembers Adorno too much and his disqualification of art with links in the market, like Stravinski's and Gershwin's music. The examples that I put of Hito Steyerl and Maria Eichhorn are not inauthentic artistic research, but are deficient in their artistic dimension, even if they are good research. In this sense they are bad artistic research because its aesthetics is not "internal."

[e] AA Every time that this argument appears I cannot help missing, for my understanding, a constitutive addition: "… a device for reflection 'with aesthetic means'" or shorter: "… a device for 'aesthetic' reflection." According to the critique of the term "reflection" I will present in my comments to your conclusions, I would reformulate in the following way: "… a device of aesthetic thinking."

GV It is an accurate precision. I take note of it.

peculiarity: *"unter einer ästhetischen Idee aber verstehe ich diejenige Vorstellung der Einbildungskraft, die viel zu denken veranlasst, ohne dass ihr doch irgend ein bestimmter Gedanke, d. i. Begriff adäquat sein kann, die folglich keine Sprache völlig erreicht und verständlich machen kann."* "By an aesthetic idea, however, I mean that representation of the imagination that occasions much thinking though without it being possible for any determinate thought, i.e., concept, to be adequate to it, which, consequently, no language fully attains or can make intelligible."[18] That is, we can see an aesthetic idea, hear it, feel it through all our senses, but it does not let itself be enclosed in a concept, that is why it leads us to think indefinitely and always makes a promise of sense without a final accomplishment. [f] This is what we usually find in an artistic installation that may contain information in the form of videos and texts, but whose meaning must be elaborated by each recipient who visits it. [g]

Exactly two hundred years after Kant, the French philosopher Gilles Deleuze, in the final stretch of his life, wondering about the differences between art, science and philosophy, and about the nature of each of these practices, embraced the concept of *percept,* which, although Deleuze did not explicitly state it, is a reconceptualization of the Kantian notion of aesthetic idea. His thesis was that the three practices mentioned above create or invent ideas. Thus, for example, Deleuze called scientific ideas "functions," while he called philosophical ideas "concepts." Scientists invent functions such as the equations of the general theory of relativity or the theory of evolution as a function of adaptability. Philosophers, on the other hand, create concepts. He himself contributed to philosophy by having created concepts such as "body without organs," "fold," "rhizome" and "image-movement." Finally, artists are those who create percepts. Percepts are "sets of perceptions, of sensations that survive those who experience them." [h] The pictorial percepts, for example, invented by the impressionists or by Francis Bacon, are torn from the perceptions, which twist to become

[f] DM I like very much this interpretation which differs from the most common analytical re-readings of Kant. Crucial is indeed that an aesthetic idea produces other ideas in term of determining thoughts without a definite meaning. Therefore it cannot be captured by concepts—and the essential point in Kant here is negativity: The "cannot be captured by." Aesthetic ideas withdraw themselves with respect to proposition or language, but draw on creating thoughts which can be perceived.

[g] LG Is this question of what could count as a device of reflection not only a reference to Kant's concept of an aesthetic idea but also a kind of extension of it through the sensible constitution of the idea? This is an aspect that Kant also mentions with respect to "schematism without concept" but does not relate to the matter of cognition and artistic production. This kind of schematism is the main source of Deleuze's reflection on Kant's view of genesis.

GV Yes it's correct. The notions of schematism without a concept and aesthetic idea belong to the same family, although I am not sure that they are twins.

[h] LG Deleuze refers at this point to the notion of "composition," and Dieter Mersch also uses it systematically in his text. How would you define the notion of composition?

GV I understand "composition" in the plain sense of putting together or arranging.

something lasting, something independent of the subjectivity of the perceiver. Deleuze's universal thesis is that the percepts are no longer perceptions, they are independent, and they exceed any experience. [i] Thus, each work of art embodies a percept that is offered to the thought of the receiver to make his experience, but when it has already occurred, the perception remains there, indefinitely open to new experiences. Art, unlike philosophy, thinks through percepts, that is, art is a way of thinking with the senses, thinking with the hands, thinking with the eyes, thinking with the ears, thinking with the body. Although we cannot elaborate here on this Deleuzian notion, I believe that it is enough to outline the argumentative line I am proposing. What makes an artistic research project more successful, less successful or unsuccessful depends on whether it is able to embody a percept (an aesthetic idea, as Kant would have put it). [j] [k] I think that the normativity of the artistic is unavoidable. Percepts, when they occur, do so with a certain aesthetic force, that is, with a capacity of attraction on our sensorial attention that awakens our thinking, our reflection on the meaning and sense of what we perceive. The latter is valid for art in general, but in artistic research projects aesthetic force is combined with cognitive force, [l] since the meaning of artistic research is the generation of new knowledge.[19]

5. ALEX ARTEAGA: GENERATING INTELLIGIBILITY

This project was developed between November 2013 and November 2016 in several subprojects or research cells and combines different media such as sound, videos, photographs and literary and theoretical texts. The project as a whole aims to show how architecture works as a condition for the emergence of meaning. In this sense, it is not a project about the perception of architecture, but about the cognitive function of architecture. Of the various subprojects of which the global project consists, *transient senses* stands out, a research cell carried out in Barcelona in 2015 in the Mies van der Rohe

[i]   DM I always considered the distinction between percepts and concepts in Deleuze to be a bit too simple, although there is a lot which seems to support this idea (and also: I sometimes use the concept of "percept" in my work). Working with concepts rhetorically or in different design settings in order to reveal certain associations between them, also in order to multiply their connotations and the like, means to use them aesthetically without necessarily referring to percepts. Also the other way round: percepts, used as formula, in a conceptual way such as knots in a complex graphical network of relationships—for instance in diagrams—implies to use them as a distinct order equal to concepts (or almost-concepts), so that there is no clear distinction between them. Sometimes they merge, because concept is no clear conception, as percept is not necessarily something that addresses our perception.

[j]   LG To my mind, the percept cannot be assimilated to Kant's conception of the aesthetic idea. Rather, the percept represents a necessary revision of Kant's aesthetics and stresses the systematic value of Deleuze's reading of Kant.

   GV I agree that Deleuze's conception is a revision of Kantian aesthetics.

[k]   AA Is the question here about the level of success or about being or not being artistic research at all—or as you expressed it before "authentic artistic research"?

   GV It is about whether a work is achieved or not.

[l]   AA As I will describe in one of my comments to your conclusions, I disagree with this duality. My take is to consider "aesthetic" the mobilization of the inherent cognitive power of the sensuous.

Pavilion, in the Fundació Tàpies and at the Goethe Institut. *Transient senses* is a project that revolves around architecture, understood in its most basic terms, structure, form and materiality. It was a reflection on how the interior and exterior space conditions the perception and flow between one and the other. The philosophy of the project is based on the works of Francisco Varela, Evan Thompson and Eleanor Rosch, developed, among other theorists, by Shaun Gallagher, Ezequiel Di Paolo, Thomas Fuchs, and Dan Zahavi. The project questions whether architecture can be a condition in the appearance of meaning. From this question, the artists reflect on the "immediate, sensual, pre-aesthetic interaction between human bodies and their built environment, and lay the foundations to understand the aesthetic experience of architecture and open ways of participation through art." Through different artistic languages, in this project architects collaborate with doctoral students of the school of dramatic art of the Berlin University of the Arts and students of the Master's Degree in Research in Art and Design of Eina and the Autonomous University of Barcelona.[20] This broad project is very enriching because it connects artists, thinkers, researchers and students from different universities and schools working with architecture and design, space and sound. In the case of the intervention in the Mies van der Rohe Pavilion, four Bloomline Omniwave loudspeakers were installed, capable of producing a diffuse sound. Located inside the pavilion, the speakers were connected with four pairs of microphones located on the outdoors. The movement of sounds from the outside to the inside, subjected to digital processing in real time, produced an increase in auditory transparency and a dynamic alteration of the sound inside the pavilion, as if the walls faded and the space became a continuous flow. This aesthetic game pointed to the experience of how architecture conditions the emergence of the sense of the inside and the outside, questioning, or destabilizing the habitual senses that we take for granted.

Alex Arteaga says often that he prefers the expression *aesthetic research* to define his research. In the recent book on *transient senses,* he offers two reasons for his preference. First, to avoid the normativity implicit in the term "artistic" and thus the implicit inclusion of this kind of research in art's system. Second, to stress the function of "aesthetics"—the sensorimotor activity of a body coupled with its surroundings in an unmediated and constitutive manner—as the roots of the research process. So, the denomination "aesthetic" is justified precisely by the primacy of aesthetic practices in the process of inquiry, that is, their fundamental function in the research methodology. [m] The pieces of his investigation, the research cells, as he calls them, for example, *transient senses,* are to be understood as aesthetic devices, apparatuses to reflect, in this case (on) architecture.[21] Ultimately, Arteaga defends the notion that aesthetic research should be differentiated from artistic research and should establish another domain. Right in the introduction to the book, he states that "[s]ense arises in an aesthetic cognitive sphere … Consequently, only through research practices performed on the same cognitive area, that is, activating the immanent epistemic potentialities of aesthetic action, is it possible to access sense as sense. The research of aesthetics must be based on aesthetic research."[22] More recently, Arteaga has argued that aesthetic research exceeds the limits of the art system and is not constrained by its normativity. He argues that he understands "artistic research, or better, *aesthetic research,* as a line of inquiry whose methodology is based on—but not necessarily limited to—a mobilization of the cognitive power of aesthetic conduct through the organization of this variety of actions in *practices.* Therefore, aesthetic research is a field of practice whose social usefulness—its *raison d'être*—is rooted in and corresponds to the cognitive function of aesthetic conduct. Consequently, taking on my characterization of this function, "aesthetic research does not produce knowledge but contributes to it—or to be more precise, to the configuration of *radically new* knowledge—by

[m]   DM The preference for aesthetic research rather than artistic in Arteaga is also due to his phenomenological approach—which uses the aesthetic approach in the broadest sense (in contrast to the narrow usage of the term in the "artistic-research debate").

facilitating the emergence of its most fundamental conditions of possibility through destabilization."23 [n]

This proposal is very interesting, but I think we have to clarify this argument. I cannot help but have the strong impression that Alex Arteaga's projects are artistic and that he is an artist. *Transient senses* was a complex project, consisting of a sound installation, a sound essay, a videographic essay, two texts, some photographs, a research seminar and, finally, a book. All that was an artistic project. I think the Arteaga project is an artistic research project, focused on a subdomain that we can call aesthetic research, but a subdomain, not an alternative domain. [o] This subdomain is characterized because artistic research projects focus on investigating the ways in which the most fundamental aesthetic experiences generate intelligibility. [p] [q]

Now, having said that, I have to agree with Arteaga on the importance of distinguishing aesthetic research from broad sets of artistic research practices. Aesthetic research, even though it is a mode of artistic research, is distinguished from most of others by its fundamental, original character. [r] Any artistic research project on any question of historical memory or on feminist themes has its center shifted towards ethical, political or factual issues in such a way that aesthetics is only a way of external access to them. In these cases, the aesthetic experience is secondary, because what matters is ethics, politics, memory. The aesthetic experience has to do with the opening of an intelligibility that formulates a promise of meaning that then never has been satisfactorily fulfilled. Aesthetic research deals specifically with how these spaces of intelligibility are generated and, therefore, it is fair to distinguish it from other forms of artistic research. That is, aesthetic research is research into the aesthetic. [s]

6. WHEN IS AESTHETIC RESEARCH?

I would like to end my reflections with another example of an artistic project focused on the interaction of sound and architecture, but that

[n] LG To this end, the notions of sensibility, embodiment and enactivism are needed. Can we define a more fundamental level of destabilization as an empirical practice of emergence? Is the emergence simply the result of an empirical constitution, or is it founded in the systematic framework of a transcendental aesthetics? Arteaga's definition of aesthetic conduct also seems to be fundamentally connected to the idea of emergence.

[o] LG The question if aesthetic research is a subdomain of artistic research, as you propose here, can be debated. My position is that only if artistic research is based on aesthetic conduct and aesthetic practices is it worthy to define and practice this kind of research as different from the research in the humanities and social and natural sciences. In other words: only research carried out through aesthetic means—and my use of the term "aesthetics" is close to (although critical of) your term "strong and reflexive" aesthetics—justifies qualifying research as "aesthetic" or "artistic."

[p] LG How would you relate this notion of intelligibility to internal aesthetics?

[q] AA I basically agree with this reflection on my work but I would like to offer a different relationship between its components. First: yes, I consider myself as an artist but in the context of the current development of art and artistic research, I prefer to define myself as an artist researcher. Second: yes, I consider my work—or at least a big part of it—and specifically *transient senses* as art, but I prefer to specify it as projects and/or apparatuses of aesthetic research. Third: I consider the research cell *transient senses* to be "aesthetic research" not because I researched in its framework on aesthetics but because I do it through aesthetics—i.e., through an organization and realization of the cognitive power of what I call "aesthetic conduct" through practices, linked to one another methodically.

[r] DM Again, here I would like to argue that the artistic research is necessarily a subclass of aesthetic research—understood from a phenomenological point of view, that is search through—or by means of—the sense, using perception as its leading medium. Whatever is meant by artistic research it primarily has to conduct its passage of investigation through the senses.

[s] DM I think this passage shows exemplarily the commonalities and differences between our concepts of "aesthetic research." I will summarize them as follows. I absolutely agree with the function and/or goals of aesthetic research you express in the first sentence. I basically agree with your second sentence but would introduce two modifications: first, I would not say that aesthetic research "deals specifically with how these spaces of intelligibility ..." but instead that aesthetic research opens or discloses these spaces. And third, I would come to a different conclusion: aesthetic research is research "through" aesthetic practices.

is not an example of aesthetic research despite appearing to be. At the 53rd Venice Biennale in 2013, Mexico had in its pavilion, located in the ancient Church of San Lorenzo, an installation of sound machines, *Cordiox,* by Ariel Guzik, curated by Itala Schmelz. It was an artwork that had an excellent reception, and much international criticism considered it as a must, one of the works that no one should miss if visiting the Biennale. Ariel Guzik can be referred to as a Renaissance man: his work combines over 25 years of research in biology, mathematics, physics and music. Each of his works is planned and carefully prepared, it can take decades to finish a single one, and they are intended as actions that could contribute to the enchantment of the world. In the catalogue, we can read about *Cordiox:* "After 28 years of being closed, in 2012 the former San Lorenzo Church became the venue of the Mexican Pavilion. The former church of San Lorenzo is an imposing ruin twenty meters high with several sculptures still standing on an abandoned altar. This fact demands that the artistic proposal that takes place there should act with and *in* favour of the space. *Cordiox* is a four-meter-high machine that describes space and the environment through sound, creating an exceptional listening experience. Vivaldi used to rehearse in this church because of its excellent acoustics, and in 1984 the avant-garde composer Luigi Nono presented his opera *Prometeo* here. Guzik's work continues in this tradition, allowing us to undertake an audial journey within the space which, due to its deterioration, cannot be transited."[24] There is no doubt that this art project is the result of high-level artistic research. Its design has behind it three decades of research and study, so it is not a mere representation, but the product of a laboratory, with the strength of extensive experimentation. The center is a fine quartz cylinder, unique in the world (45 cm diameter and 180 cm height) expressly manufactured in Germany by a specialized company. The instrument consists of long and taut strings similar to those found on a musical instrument. All kinds of vibrations and energies of the

environment can be captured by its subtle mechanism that converts invisible entropy in a harmonic order. Now, if we ask: besides the obvious *research for the production* of this work, which is always necessary in an artistic creation, is this work an artistic or aesthetic research project? Does this work produce some form of knowledge? Is the sonic experience that the public makes in itself knowledge? I think the answer is obvious: no. At best it is a starting point for the knowledge that should result from a conceptual work to be done on it. [t] The machine spreads clear tonal cadences, subtle and expansive, but they do not destabilize our perceptual routines, do not create a new space of intelligibility, they are not a new form of knowledge. [u] The machine transforms entropic sounds in harmonies. Only when we throw our concepts on them and we understand them in terms of harmony, resonance, and other properties and parameters of acoustic phenomena, only when we link all this with Vivaldi, with the music of Luigi Nono and the history of the church of San Lorenzo, only when we carry out this *Arbeit des Begriffs,* to say it with Hegel, then perhaps we have some knowledge. Meanwhile, we just have a way to think space aurally, we have only a fuzzy meaning embodied in a sophisticated machine that produces sound waves, but we do not know for sure what this meaning is about. To become knowledge, sensible thought has to become propositional language. [v] But all this practically has nothing to do with research. To sum up, *Cordiox* embodies an aesthetic idea, a percept, certainly, but without research. It is art, not artistic research. It is a device for reflection, a *machine à penser,* so to speak, [w] but it is not a project or aesthetic research. When is aesthetic research then? A necessary condition is to be a project of artistic research, to be a device for reflection that generates some kind of new knowledge. But this is not a sufficient condition. To be specifically aesthetic research it must be research of the aesthetic, of this way of thinking with the senses different from the theoretical modes of thinking. [x]

[t]   ^{DM} Of course, this statement depends on the meaning and understanding of the term "knowledge." Knowledge can be used in the sense of that which is expressible in a proposition, which can be judged as true or false. But maybe there is also a usage of knowledge in a broad sense: as an opening, related to evidence rather than judgment. Evidence requires not only subjective understanding—a sudden *eureka*—but also acknowledgement; and here we should not forget that there is a certain etymological overlapping between knowledge and acknowledgement. The same holds true for testimony, the importance of which for the constitution was traditionally underestimated by emphasizing solely the truth-production of proposition and reasoning. The transformation from entropic to tropic and hence harmonic sounds is linked to this: a testimony that opens up a new and surprising experience and hence addresses its truth in the meaning of disclosure directly to the senses.

[u]   ^{AA} You point here to three different possible results of an artistic project: to "destabilize our perceptual routines," to "create new spaces of intelligibility" and to "be (or produce) knowledge." I think that the first two can be easily linked to one another: a destabilization of perceptual routines—or furthermore, of all kinds of constituted phenomena or states of affairs—can lead to disclose new fields of intelligibility. The third one can obviously be linked to these first ones but has a different nature: it is productive, it relates to constitution instead of to destabilization, disclosure, opening. I see the first two options as genuine results of aesthetic research but not the third one. Nevertheless I propose a link between both. Aesthetic research seeks to destabilize established phenomena or states of affairs and consequently to disclose new fields of intelligibility which should be possible to be inhabited by other research practices aiming at the production of knowledge. (I'm using the term "knowledge" in the way Dieter outlined it in his text in this book which coincides with your formulation in the next sentences in relation to "propositional language").

[v]   ^{DM} I am terribly sorry, but here I disagree with full emphasis.
      ^{GV} Do not be sorry, you're absolutely right. I was using here a too narrow, Kantian concept of knowledge that since many years I don't use anymore. I took a fragment of an old manuscript without noticing this mistaken phrase.

[w]   ^{DM} And here, I fully agree.

[x]   ^{LG} In this sense I think that a transcendental reflection on sensibility is the grounding field of embodiment and aesthetic production both in perception and in art.

Finally, I will conclude by recapitulating my main theses:

1. I started with a distinction between liminal and reflective aesthetics. Reflective aesthetics is a way of thinking with senses.

2. I stated that every artwork has both aesthetic dimensions, liminal and reflective.

3. What makes an artwork art is owning a reflective aesthetic.

4. Later I introduced a distinction between internal and external aesthetics in artworks.

5. Artworks embody an aesthetic idea (Kant) or a percept (Deleuze), they make always a promise of sense.

6. To be artistic, a research project has to embody a percept or aesthetic idea, otherwise it is merely research, even when it is good research.

7. Aesthetic research is a kind of artistic research focused on inquiry into the aesthetic, the specific mode generates intelligibility, the peculiarities of aesthetic experience and thinking.

AA This text is an important contribution to the specification of a distinction between art and aesthetics and to the clarification of the possible relationships between these terms and the concept of research. I basically agree with the approach with which these distinctions are formulated here but I disagree in some specific aspects. I summarize then along your synopsis:

— I think it is necessary to establish a distinction betwen different uses of the senses. I would restrict the term "aesthetics" to what you term here "reflective aesthetics."

— I tend to think that "reflection" is not a genuine trait of the specific and inherent epistemic power of aesthetics. Consequently I would not use this term to characterize the variety of sensuous activity I would term as aesthetic.

— Based on this concept of aesthetics I would suggest to vary the formulation of your definitional criteria for a work to be art. I tend to think that a work can be considered an artwork when it is realized through aesthetic practices.

— Also on this basis, that is, on a clear definition of the aesthetics as a variety of mobilization of the intrinsic epistemic power of the sensuous and of the art work as a work realized based on this kind of action I don't think that the distinction between "internal" and "external" is necessary.

— Finally, I disagree, partially, with your last conclusion. Instead of understanding aesthetic research as a subsystem of artistic research I would rather posit that aesthetic research is research through aesthetic practices despite the object of research to which they refer. Nevertheless I agree that the goal of this variety of research is to disclose new fields of intelligibility.

ME The text asks "where is the art?" and, at least indirectly, "where is the research?", but would the question "where is the knowledge?" be a relevant question within this setting?

1 An exception is Henk Slager, The Pleasure of Research (Otsfildern: Hatje Cantz, 2015). See also Henk Slager, ed., Experimental Aesthetics (Utrecht: Metropolis M, 2015).

2 Peter Osborne, "Art Beyond Aesthetics: Philosophical Criticism, Art History and Contemporary Art," Art History 27 (2004): 651–670.

3 See, for example, Henk Borgdorff, "The Production of Knowledge in Artistic Research," in The Routledge Companion to Research in the Arts, ed. Michael Biggs and Henrik Karlsson (London: Routledge, 2011), 44–63. See also Jens Badura, "Erkenntnis (Sinnliche)," in Künstlerische Forschung. Ein Handbuch, ed. Jens Badura et al. (Zurich: Diaphanes, 2015), 43–48.

4 A great essay in this direction on the complex world of birds is by Richard O. Prum, The Evolution of Beauty: How Darwin's Forgotten Theory of Mate Choice Shapes the Animal World—and Us (New York: Random House, 2017).

5 Here I subscribe to the thesis of so many authors of the tradition from Kant and Hegel who have affirmed that art is fundamental for our self-knowledge and self-determination. My most recent references, however, are Alva Noë, Strange Tools. Art and Human Nature (New York: Hill and Wang, 2015), and Georg Bertram, Kunst als menschliche Praxis (Berlin: Suhrkamp, 2014).

6 Alva Noë, Strange Tools, 73.

7 See Dieter Mersch, Epistemologies of Aesthetics (Zurich: Diaphanes, 2015).

8 Alva Noë, Strange Tools, 71.

9 See Alva Noë, Strange Tools. Interesting is also Lambros Malafouris, How Things Shape the Mind. A Theory of Material Engagement (Cambridge MA: MIT Press, 2013). A synthesis of this account is found in Alex Arteaga, "Embodied and Situated Aesthetics: An enactivist Approach to a Cognitive Notion of Aesthetics," Artnodes 20 (2017): 20–27, http://dx.doi.org/10.7238/a.v0i20.3156 [accessed Jan 20, 2018].

10 See Jacques Rancière, The Politics of Aesthetics: The Distribution of the Sensible (London: Continuum, 2004); Jacques Rancière, Malaise dans l'esthétique (Paris: Galilée, 2004); and Jacques Rancière, Aisthesis: Scenes from the Aesthetic Regime of Art (London: Verso Books, 2013).

11 Christoph Menke argued this idea with some detail in Christoph Menke "Die Dialektik der Ästhetik: Der neue Streit zwischen Kunst und Philosophie," in Ästhetik Erfahrung. Interventionen 13, ed. Jörg Huber (Vienna and New York: Springer, 2004), 21–39; and in Christoph Menke, Kraft. Ein Grundbegriff ästhetischer Anthropologie (Frankfurt am Main: Suhrkamp, 2008), chapter V.

12 Arthur C. Danto, The Abuse of Beauty (Chicago: Open Court, 2003). See also Diarmuid Costello, "On Late Style: Arthur Danto's The Abuse of Beauty," The British Journal of Aesthetics 44 (2004): 424–439, https://doi.org/10.1093/bjaesthetics/44.4.424 [accessed Dec 10, 2017].

13 See Gerard Vilar, "De-Aestheticization: The Dialectics of the Aesthetic and Anti-Aesthetic in Contemporary Art," in Art and the Challenge of Markets, ed. Victoria D. Alexander and Erkki Sevänen (London: Palgrave Macmillan, 2018), vol. 2, 213–233.

14 Hito Steyerl, Duty-Free Art 64 (2015), http://www.e-flux.com/journal/63/60894/duty-free-art/ [accessed Dec 10, 2017]. Also in: Duty-Free Art, Exhibition catalogue (Madrid: MNCARS, 2015). Reprinted in Hito Steyerl, Duty Free Art. Art in the Age of Planetary Civil War (London: Verso, 2017), 75–99.

15 http://www.rosevallandinstitut.org/ [accessed Mar 18, 2018].

16 See Gerard Vilar, "¿Dónde está el arte en la investigación artística?, " ANIAV, Revista de Investigación en artes visuales 1 (2017): 1–8, https://polipapers.upv.es/index.php/aniav/article/view/7817 [accessed Jan 20, 2018].

17 See http://www.architecture-embodiment.org/. Some texts around this project are: Alex Arteaga, Boris Hassenstein and Gunnar Green, eds., Klangumwelt. Ernst Reuter-Platz. A Project of the Auditory Architecture Research Unit (Berlin: Errant Bodies Press, 2016); Alex Arteaga, transient senses (Barcelona: RM, 2016); Alex Arteaga and Raquel Rivera, eds., Aurality and Environment (Madrid: Ministerio de Educación, Cultura y Deporte, 2017).

18 Immanuel Kant, Critique of the Power of Judgment (Cambridge: Cambridge University Press, 2000), 192, § 49.

19 See Gerard Vilar, "El valor cognitivo del arte," in El valor del arte, ed. Pérez Carreño (Madrid: Machado, 2017).

20 https://www.eina.cat/en/postgraus/master-oficial-eees-master-universitari-de-recerca-en-art-i-disseny [accessed Dec 10, 2017].

21 Alex Arteaga, transient senses, 12–13.

22 Ibid., 13.

23 Alex Arteaga, "Embodied and Situated Aesthetics."

24 Ariel Guzik, Cordiox (Barcelona: RM, 2013), 107.

Stuff Framed:
Moving Boxes, Vitrines and a Lot of Words

Mika Elo

One has to start somewhere, turn a specific situation into a starting point. This implies departing from a familiar place. [A] In this essay, I will develop some thoughts about exhibiting. I will also touch on some connections between exhibitions and changing one's residence, which involves literally boxing up a place called home. This connection makes me especially interested in thinking about exhibition as a place. What kind of place is an exhibition?

Unlike home, an exhibition is a temporary place. [B] It is a place where things and materials from different contexts are put together on display for a limited period of time. Visitors come to the exhibition from circumstances that do not necessarily relate to each other in any other ways than through the fact that all these people happen to be visiting the same exhibition. This implies that an exhibition is a place where something new emerges; it is a place where new connections and new associations, quite literally, take place.

[A] ᴬᴬ Or to turn a space into a familiar place …

[B] ᴬᴬ "Home" can also be "temporary." The sense of a space to be "home" does not necessarily depend on length. For those that move houses often, specially if this happens through different cities and countries, the coalescence of temporary and home—even the senses of a nomadic home not necessarily based on space but on objects, habits or rituals—takes place. According to the traveling exhibitions you present in the following lines "home" can be traveling too.

ᴹᴱ Yes, many people need to be very flexible in terms of working and living conditions. I myself am "based" in Helsinki and Bremen. The contrast I build between "exhibition" and "home" could be supplemented with a distinction between private and public space. "Being based" at home takes place more in the private sphere, whereas exhibition implies some form of publicity.

Exhibitions often travel as well: from town to town, from museum to museum. The modern emblem of this dynamic aspect of exhibiting is the series of world expos designed to showcase the achievements of nations. These world's fairs conceived the whole world as a travelling constellation of displayable objects. The *Great Exhibition* in London in 1851 showcased the whole world condensed in a huge vitrine, the Crystal Palace.

An exhibition, in other words, "takes place" in two senses: Firstly, it occupies a specific space for a period of time. Secondly, an exhibition takes place in the sense that it is something that happens. It is a transient event that has the power to gather people and things in a defined spatio-temporal frame. However, unlike a concert or a performance, an exhibition is an event that subsists also in the absence of the audience.

There is a nocturnal reverse side to the exhibition: the time and space of things among themselves without humans.[1]

Nowadays, exhibitions often also extend to the internet, and some even take place completely in a virtual space.[2] Further, a series of exhibitions can be connected to each other through curatorial gestures. Curation can be supplemented with other types of mediation and algorithmic connections, thus opening up a horizon of "systemics," where things are connected as part of a wider and more complex system.[3] Within this horizon, curating turns into a practice of programming that has its counterpart in computer programming, tagging, and the management of metadata.

An exhibition is a place that has a meaningful order. It is arranged with regard to signification. In this respect, exhibition practices are deeply rooted in our everyday life. Indeed, this might even hold from a phylogenetic perspective, as prehistoric humans, too, had the tendency to arrange things in their living environments and thus make sense of a situation by sorting out its parts.[4]

The German word *Stellenwert* ("place value," "standing status") gives us a hint of the intimate relation between place [C] *(Stelle)* and

[C] AA I'm not sure that *Stelle* should be translated here as "place." I understand it rather as "position." Consequently I tend to understand *Stellenwert* as the value something acquires by virtue of the position it takes. This interpretation does not invalidate your use of this term here.

ME I see the point. Further discussion here should include a differentiation between space, position and place. Part of the problem is certainly the quite complicated "fate of place" in western thinking.

value *(Wert)*. Moving from one flat to another is one of those moments when we concretely face the fact that spatial order and meaningfulness are intimately connected: squeezed into a moving van, our precious objects start to feel like stuff that just takes up space instead of constituting a place. A successful move has to be methodically executed. Boxes need to be packed according to some clear categories, [D] and it is good to have the boxes labeled as if they were vitrines that are temporarily not on display. Boxes stuffed with diverse things in a hurry often remain unpacked for a long time after the move. Do we touch here upon something like the domestic form of the material logic of all history?

An exhibition never consists of just "stuff," since the act of exhibiting endows all odds and ends with a potential meaning. An exhibition is a place of transformation: it transforms stuff into items. Something that just takes up space turns into something that makes up a place. The disturbing aspect of this process is the fact that in order for something to make up a place, it also has to take up space in a specific place. To make up a place is to take a place somewhere. [E] The container and the contained are intertwined. The spatial paradoxes of the relational character of what we are accustomed to call "form" and "content" are addressed in a playful way in Maija Närhinen's work *Content* (2017)—a wall made of cardboard boxes filled with cardboard boxes.[5]

Even if exhibitions "come and go," as we tend to say of these kind of organized events, they do not take place within an already existing empty time. They do not occur on a preexisting time line, even if the program booklets of museums around the world suggest otherwise.

These program slots are not exhibitions in the strong sense. Strictly speaking, the time of exhibiting emerges only within an exhibition. A set of gestures marking the "taking place" itself is at the core of an exhibition. It is worth noting that gestures, even the ambiguous and ambivalent ones, are necessarily finite: a gesture is a gesture *towards* something, and it always excludes something else.

[D] AGV What is a "clear category" in an exhibition? Categorizing is a question of placing, of setting things next to each other, as in the well-known example of the animal classification in Borges' *The analytical language of John Wilkins.* I wonder if it is possible to evaluate or specify more that kind of placing, that categorizing. In the natural sciences there are criteria for this (completeness, mutual exclusivity, etc.). How could this placing in an exhibit be further differentiated? And, more importantly, how would this placing or categorizing be connected to those "forces of differing and gathering" (below), those forces of emplacement, that are pondered in an exhibition?

> ME In my view the exhibiting gesture implies a thematisation of some kind of figure/background relation which in turn has to do with categorising. Of course this gesture can remain suspended, as is often the case in art exhibitions. Then the emerging categories are obviously not clear.

[E] AA I wonder if the introduction of a second term like "space" would help to formulate the transformations you are describing. Similarly to the relationships between *Umgebung* and *Umwelt* by Uexkül (see Lidia's text) which I translated respectively as "surroundings" and "environment", "space" could designate the topographical entity which will turn into a place through the operations of exhibiting. A weakness of this strategy is that there is no topographical unit that in touch with an observer does not become, more or less immediately, significant to the observer. That is, it becomes an environment, and consequently the existence of a "neutral", non-connotated, non-significant topology—a surroundings, a space—is merely speculative.

> ME Here we touch upon the fate of place again. My choice is to stick with everyday language as a way of asking whether our meaningful surroundings can be penetrated by a clear spatial scheme or does meaningfulness imply messy paradoxes.

Exhibitions thus have implicit and explicit rules. Visitors are instructed how to behave, how to view, how to walk, how to touch or not to touch, and how to speak during and after the visit. Various "metadata" help communicate these instructions: wall texts, handouts, catalogues, image captions, and work titles. Another name for these rules could be "techniques of aesthetic detachment." [F] These techniques involve a certain habituation of the viewer's body, as Mireia Saladrigures' work *A Specific Representation* compellingly suggests.[6] It is, at the same time, also a question of mental habituation, as the *Humanoid Hypothesis* by the Other Spaces live arts collective convincingly demonstrates.[7]

An exhibition in the strict sense is an uncanny place where the accustomed sense-order is, at least temporarily, displaced. [G] With reference to the peculiar etymology of the Finnish word for place, *paikka,* I would say that an exhibition is the "place of a place," *paikan paikka.* I am not making this detour to etymology in order to establish more solid conceptual proof. Instead, I want to highlight (in a Benjaminian vein) the fact that language is a rich and multi-layered archive of displaced similarities and connections that contribute to the sense-order we tend to take for granted.[8] The Finnish word *paikka* has its equivalents in many related languages.[9] Together they show multiple connections between conceptions of place, patch, filling, spot, and target. The pattern that can be discerned from these etymological connections shows that the notion of place, in the Finnish language, is characterized by a tension between showing and covering differences in relations of juxtaposition. On the one hand, *paikka* is a "clearly discernible spot." On the other hand, it is something that mends disruptions, fills in, and seals gaps. In a word, place is a relational setting traversed by the forces of differing and gathering. An exhibition in the strong sense offers a place for these forces. To make an exhibition is to work out an articulation of a sense-order that invites people to ponder these forces of emplacement. [H]

[F]   AA Why "detachment"? I understand that taking distance from what is not the exhibition, from what is or remains outside of it, can be a condition of possibility for experiencing the exhibition, but I think that you are referring rather to the contrary move: the actions that seek to establish a strong connection with the exhibition.

[G]   AA And, furthermore, a place that aims at displacing or destabilizing established senses—of course in saying that I'm referring implicitly to exhibition of contemporary art and/or artistic research.

[H]   AGV In my view, it would be illuminating to elaborate further on how that kind of pondering takes place and its relation to some of the questions opened up in other chapters, as in the case of the ideas of aesthetic understanding and/or aesthetic knowledge.

   ME Definitely, I hope I will have the chance to do so in the near future.

Here, my choice of the word "emplacement" is motivated by Samuel Weber's translation of Heidegger's *Gestell*.[10] In Heidegger's vocabulary, *Gestell* is an epochal configuration of technics that formats our sense of time and space. In modernity (since the Renaissance), its mode is representative: it tends to render the whole world as an image.[11] In more concrete terms, emplacement is the operative aspect of an apparatus that prepares, delimits, and formats the configuration of meaningful discourses, practices and techniques, as the related terms of Foucault's *dispositif* and Agamben's *dispositivo* (in English "apparatus") reveal.[12]

These philosophical references hint at the ways in which an exhibition that invites visitors to ponder the forces of differing and gathering also operates on an ontological level.[13]

An exhibition is necessarily enmeshed in the power relations prevailing in a specific historical context. Otherwise it would not function as an exhibition; its gestures of exhibiting would not be recognizable as such. This implies that the exhibition as an articulation of sense-order is fragile; it takes place in a contested space of discourses, practices, and technical arrangements. This is particularly true of art exhibitions, since in art contexts, the exhibition as an apparatus is an "open machine."[14] It is not sealed, so to say, to serve predetermined functions only; its elements can be "re-functioned" through the very gestures of exhibiting.

Contemporary art exhibitions confront us with two compelling issues[15]: 1) Multi-dimensionality of sense, which implies that sense cannot be reduced to meaning. Neither the artist's or curator's explicit intentions nor discursively established interpretations can serve as ultimate points of reference. All facts are made; they are factishes that imply selection and reduction in regard to the excess of sense. 2) Non-human agencies: Artistic gestures do not take place only on the level of (verbal) communication or thematic content, and they cannot necessarily be traced back to the author. Material circumstances

interfere in the hermeneutic horizon. Artworks have an agency of their own, or perhaps more precisely: *on* their own, independent of particular human settings. [I] This means that artworks have real effects independent of their interpretation. [J] Guan Xiao's work *David* (2013), which was exhibited at the Venice Biennale in 2017, demonstrates this in a rich way by focusing on various appropriations of and cultural phenomena related to Michaelagelo's *David.*[16]

An art exhibition is an exhibition *par excellence.* An art exhibition is not just a display. It is not just a means of representation. It is not a closed machine, at least when it is not fully immersed in the mechanisms of the art market. That which is shown in an art exhibition is shown through a set of gestures that are part of the setting. In other words, one could say that an art exhibition makes it impossible to completely bracket various parergonal elements.[17] This implies that it has aesthetic stakes. It engages with the tension between the overwhelming richness of sense experience and the unifying tendency of conceptual thinking. When visiting or experiencing an exhibition, the focus of attention can be set either on topical issues or on framing conditions. But it is important to note that the very gesture of setting the focus is an aesthetic issue, since appropriate focusing can emerge only in accordance with the aforementioned tension (the tension between sensing and conceptualizing), which is, necessarily, something felt. [K]

This implies that an exhibition in the strict sense is an *aesthetic apparatus.* Exhibition practices that incorporate the questioning of their aesthetic conditions into their gestures of showing can be considered aesthetic research. But how does this relate to art? Is there a difference between aesthetic research and artistic research? In order to unfold these questions a bit further, we need to consider more closely the concept of "apparatus."

Here, my main point of reference is Giorgio Agamben's expansion of the Foucauldian notion of *dispositif.*[18] For Agamben, an apparatus *(dispositivo)* is "literally anything that has in some way the capacity

[I] AGV In principle, I would agree with that position, but how is that idea of agency of artworks characterized? Do artworks actually act and do things? If so, how do their actions, independent from their author's intentions and from the interpretations they might originate, relate to human actions? Can they be completely isolated from each other (if not, what does "independent" here mean)? Also, is there any kind of intentionality in this non-human agency?

[J] AA Yes, "on their own" but not "independently of a particular human setting." I absolutely agree with the idea of the autonomous agency of artworks—and furthermore of architectural and non-architectural components of the space of exhibition and its surroundings—but they unfold their respective agency in a system of relationships, that is as contingent agents (see Ana's text). Accordingly, I agree that "artworks have real effects" but not that they are independent of interpretation. On the one hand because these effects can only be identified as part of interpretations—understanding "interpretation" here in a broad and fundamental sense as "constitution of significance"—and on the other hand because the "real" emerges out of the interaction between different "effects": among others, the ones caused by the agency of the artworks and the ones caused by human agency, including "interpretation."

ME In another vocabulary we could speak of "affordance." Artworks suggest various connections and perspectives as much as they tease out certain kinds of reactions and interpretations. I am less thinking of intentionality here. But of course the matter is more complicated than this. We should specify, for example, "real" effects in relation to "potential," "virtual" and "actual" effects.

[K] AA This dense formulation seems to me to be problematic. Probably the basis of the problem begins a few sentences before. It is not clear to me if both "the overwhelming richness of sense experience" and "the unifying tendency of conceptual thinking" belong constitutively to aesthetics or if this is the case only in reference to the first term. If the second option is the right one, I would not agree with your affirmation that "setting the focus is an aesthetic issue," since setting a focus reduces necessarily the richness of sense experience. And although the tension between both terms is, as you write, "something felt," this would not be a necessary and sufficient reason to consider it to be aesthetic. It could be simply a case of "liminal" use of the senses (see Gerard's text).

ME Well, I am referring to the Kantian primal scene of aesthetics and its relation to schematism. To argue this through philosophically would require quite some work and open a whole new chapter.

to capture, orient, determine, intercept, model, control, or secure the gestures, behaviours, opinions, or discourses of living beings."[19] For him, the key issues at stake in such apparatuses are "processes of sub-jectification," "humanization," and "the possibility of knowing the being as such," that is, the construction of a world.[20] In short, an apparatus is an assemblage of material circumstances and technical arrangements that determines—as the etymology of "apparatus," *apparare,* "make ready for," suggests—the phenomenal horizon of experience. Agam-ben, in other words, expands the notion of apparatus beyond the his-torical specificity of Foucauldian knowledge/power settings to include all kinds of cultural techniques and their ontological effects.

Agamben's account highlights the relevance and historical vari-ability of the sense-making processes operative in exhibition appara-tuses. It is important to note that Agamben insists on the multiplicity of apparatuses. As medial settings of sense they never appear alone, but are always embedded in one another's co-appearance; they inter-sect and intermingle in multiple ways. The intersemiotic encounters between different modes of articulation in an exhibition constitute mo-ments of reconfiguration through relations of exteriority, both material and expressive in kind.

As a sense-making apparatus, an exhibition is an assemblage of relations between the languages or modes of articulation that it brings together in a space. Instead of speaking *of* things, an exhibition speaks *on the same level* as the things it brings together. An exhibition takes place *in medias res;* it participates in the world of things. [L] This comes close to what Deleuze and Guattari call an "abstract machine." [M] In their account, language is an abstract machine that does not appeal to any extrinsic factor. When conceived in terms abstract enough, a lan-guage machine is no longer just a matter of verbal language; it appears as the machinic aspect of the collective assemblage of acts, state-ments, and incorporeal transformations attributed to bodies.[21] An exhi-bition (as an assemblage) is the place—the force-field of differing and

[L] | AGV What consequences does this in medias res situatedness of an exhibition have for the kind of research that it can carry out?

ME In order to go with this question it would be helpful to delve into the discussions concerning "expositionality" (Schwab) in artistic research. The key issue here is the impotence of a search for any convincing meta-perspective. The research gestures take place, so to speak, "in medias res," without the back-up of an "extrinsic factor."

[M] | LG The "abstract machine" is defined by Foucault as a diagram, and Deleuze also interprets this term in relation to Francis Bacon's painting practice. A diagram, in Peirce's theory, is constituted by relations and should not be equated with an iconic image. Applied to exhibition, could we say that exhibition is a medium of relations that, like the diagram, generates new possibilities of sense? Does place in this sense become a diagrammatic dispositif of the constitution of meaning?

ME Yes, exhibition is a "medium of relations," but perhaps in the sense that the relations first emerge in and through this medium.

gathering—where techniques, practices, and discourses *entangle and emerge* as distinct aspects of sense-making.

During the past few years, "artistic research" has gained the status of an overarching label for various research activities within the arts and art universities. In its broadest sense, "artistic research" refers to a wide range of research activities and approaches, for which the arts do not constitute the object of study but rather the practical and methodological terrain of research. In a narrower sense preferred by some authors, the term refers to a specific methodology or a field of research. In both cases, the question of its status as a discipline arises.[22]

I think the focus should be shifted away from questions of discipline towards dispositions that move beyond the logic of representation. Viewed through the lens of assemblage theory discussed above, the apparatus of artistic research appears as a distributive unity of processes, technics, arrangements, material circumstances, regulations, and articulations that format the experiential horizon of artistic inquiry.

Thus, one of the key challenges of theoretical discussions on artistic research is to grasp this set of loosely related arrangements and agencies in terms of its capacity to generate sense. Attention has to be paid to the consistency of distributed processes instead of to the proprieties of a conceptually or institutionally delimited field of research. This implies considering artistic research as a frame that transposes various elements rather than as a discipline.

Here, a shift in the vocabulary is needed, since "artistic research" is a problematic notion. The problem lies in the qualifier "artistic" and its implied counterparts "scientific" and "academic." The key issue is not whether particular research is "artistic" enough to qualify as *artistic* research or "academic" or "scientific" enough to count as artistic *research.* Supporters of this kind of view end up reproducing normative conceptions of art and of research. The real question is how to conceive of a framework in which multiple forms of inventive processes fostered in the arts can be critically discussed and developed

further in terms of research relevant for artist-researchers. We need to divert our reading of the term from its disciplinary connections to the sphere of its dispositional surplus: the commitment to transform "knowledge production" into a "space of thinking," as Michael Schwab puts it.[23] Leaving open the question as to what extent this space is also the space of aesthetic thinking, I think it is important to assert that discussions on artistic research have to grapple with the question of *multiple* forms of research, not only because there are multiple arts, and not because different artistic research projects might have a vast range of motivations, but due to the dynamic character of the whole constellation within which a distinction between "artistic research" and "aesthetic research" can be worked out.

Pondering the differences between "artistic research" and "aesthetic research" is one way of working against the disciplinary closure of artistic research. I hope that the thoughts concerning exhibitions as aesthetic apparatuses developed in this essay will prove themselves helpful in this delaying battle.

GV I have two main comments to the text *Stuff Framed* by Mika Elo on exhibition spaces as apparatuses.

1. He takes for granted that exhibition spaces are very special spaces. Unlike home, an exhibition, to mention only some of the features listed by the author, is a temporary place, it is a place of transformation because it transforms stuff into items ordered in a significant form. It is an opening or disclosing place, strange and disturbing; it is a space of thinking and it is an apparatus, or open machine, organized in such a way that an exhibition can be considered a practice form of aesthetic research. Elo, then, subscribes to the thesis that exhibitions are an *Espèces d'espaces,* to use the title of an inspiring book by French writer Georges Perec (Species of Spaces and Other Pieces, London: Penguin, 1997) which is completely different from everyday spaces. Everyday places are not evident, but blindness and anesthetic *("car ce que nous appelons quotidienneté n'est pas évidence, mais opacité : une forme de cécité, une manière d'anesthésie");* i. e., the opposite of exhibition spaces.

Such a thesis, however, is not completely evident, because the quality of everydayness is relative. For professionals of art theory, art criticism, curators or artists, students and teachers in the field of art, exhibition spaces can be as familiar as the living rooms of their homes. However, what home is for one depends on the kind of person one is. For some people home is a space of self-creation, of permanent change and transformation, with movable furnishings and decoration.

Consequently, the radical opposition between exhibition and ordinary space must be, at least, tempered.

2. Furthermore, I find that Elo's list of features misses a practical and pragmatic effect of the kind of space that an exhibition is: it is also a space of power. The placement of a place is also the institution of a space of power relations, because someone selects some work(s), some artist(s), some discourses instead of others. This is especially the case when institutional curators establish programs reflecting strong ideas about what should and should not be exhibited.

ME These two comments indicate the fact that exhibition, obviously, needs to be characterized as a public space as well. This might even be the most decisive aspect of an art exhibition as a place. In order to address this, I would discuss curating as *"paikkaaminen,"* as preparing a place, which, as the Finnish word *"paikka"* suggests, involves gestures of "patching" and "mending" that direct the attention to certain issues while downplaying others.

1   In popular culture, the nocturnal life of the exhibits has fed the imagination in ways that speak to wide audiences. The American fantasy-comedy *Night at the Museum* (2006), for example, was a great box office success.

2   For example, Google Art and Culture project is a massive attempt to translate physical exhibitions into virtual ones. In her artistic research work, Mireia Saladrigues thematises this kind of virtual extension of exhibitions https://virtualpresenttour.com/ [accessed Dec 17, 2017].

3   Joasia Krysa, "Introduction: Systemics of Systemics," in Systemics (or, Exhibition as Series): Index of Exhibition and Related Materials, 2013–14, ed. Joasia Krysa (Berlin: Sternberg Press, 2017), 7–14.

4   This has been pointed out for example by André Leroi-Gourhan. "[T] the prime originality of Leroi-Gourhan as a prehistorian was his realization that spatial relationships – from cave drawings to objects in a habitation – was the key to an understanding of what remains of systems of thought and the daily life of prehistoric peoples." (François Valla et al., "From foraging to farming. The contribution of the Mallaha (Eynan) excavations 1996–2011," Bulletin du CRFJ no. 10 (Spring 2002): 73). Mary Douglas has thematised questions of dirt and purity in a similar vein: dirt is matter out of place. See Mary Douglas, Purity and Danger: An Analysis of Concepts of Pollution and Taboo (London: Routledge and Keegan Paul, 1966).

5   http://www.maijanarhinen.fi/works/content/ [accessed Dec 17, 2017].

6   http://www.mireiasaladrigues.com/w/specific-representation [accessed Dec 17, 2017].

7   The performance starts with a "humanoid training," a bodily exercise which prepares the participants for a humanoid mode of perception. The participants trained as humanoids will then accomplish a 45 minute long expedition in the urban surroundings, or, in one variant of the performance, in an art exhibition. http://toisissatiloissa.net/humanoid-hypothesis/ and http://kiasma.fi/nayttelyt-ja- ohjelmisto/kiasma-teatteri/toisissa- tiloissa-maan-ulkopuolinen-taide- humanoidihypoteesi-2/ [accessed Dec 17, 2017].

8   This mimetic dimension of language plays an important role in Benjamin's philosophy of language. See for example Walter Benjamin, "On the Mimetic Faculty," in Selected Writings, ed. Michael W. Jennings et al., vol 2. part 2 (Cambridge MA: Harvard University Press, 2005), 722.

9   Kaisa Häkkinen, Nykysuomen etymologinen sanakirja (Helsinki: WSOY, 2004), 854.

10 See for example Samuel Weber, Massmediauras. Form, Technics, Media (Palo Alto CA: Stanford University Press, 1996).

11 See for example Martin Heidegger, "Die Zeit des Weltbildes," in Gesamtausgabe. I. Abteilung: Veröffentliche Schriften 1914–1970, Band 5. Holzwege (Frankfurt am Main: Vittorio Klostermann, 1977).

12 On relations bewteen *Gestell, dispositif* and *dispositivo* see for example Susanna Lindberg, Le mode defait. L'être su monde aujourd'hui (Paris: Hermann Éditeurs, 2016).

13 In his Artwork-essay, Benjamin presents a multifaceted analysis of the ways in which an artwork incorporates in its very structure key elements of the framing conditions of its display. He thematises this in terms of Aura, Zerstreuung and Sammlung (Mika Elo, Valokuvan medium, 69).

14 For the implications of this Simondonian term, see for example Erich Hörl, "A Thousand Ecologies: The Process of Cyberneticization and General Ecology," in The Whole Earth. California and the Disappearance of the Outside, ed. Diedrich Diederichsen and Anselm Franke (Berlin: Sternberg Press, 2013), 121–130, 123.

15 Mika Elo, "Ineffable Dispositions."

16 https://www.youtube.com/watch?v=c3Y7UpGPZXg [accessed Apr 29, 2018].

17 See for example Jacques Derrida, Truth in Painting (Chicago: University of Chicago Press, 1987).

18 I have presented the following argument earlier in Mika Elo, "Ineffable Dispositions."

19 Giorgio Agamben, What is an Apparatus? and Other Essays (Palo Alto, CA: Stanford University Press, 2009), 14.

20 Ibid, 12–14.

21 Gilles Deleuze and Félix Guattari, A Thousand Plateaus: Capitalism and Schizophrenia (Minneapolis: Minnesota University Press, 2014), 87–91.

22 For a useful terminological mapping see Vytautas Michelkevicius, Mapping Artistic Research. Towards Diagrammatic Knowing (Vilnius: Vilnius Academy of Arts Press, 2018).

23 Michael Schwab, "Between a Rock and a Hard Place," in Intellectual Birdhouse: Artistic Practice as Research, ed. Florian Dombois, Ute Meta Bauer, Claudia Mareis, and Michael Schwab (London: Koenig Books, 2012), 229–247, 243. See also Mika Elo "Ineffable Dispositions," 290.

The Ends of Design

Susanne Hauser

Some twenty years ago I analyzed two landscape designs. At that time
I was not mainly interested in concepts of designs or designing but in
questions of how former industrial wastelands were reinterpreted and
turned into sites for new activities. But my focus of interest changed
during the analysis as I became more and more fascinated by the designs as outcomes of a process.[1] Both designs implied answers to
a variety of heterogeneous questions, among them decisions about
materials to be used, about structures to be built, but also answers to
such fundamental questions as how to define and present the relations of "man" and "nature." [A] I realized how many different aspects
had been dealt with in the design processes while the results, the
finished and finally realized designs, were undeniably entities in their
own right. I began thinking about the process of designing as an operation dealing with heterogeneous aspects leading to a synthesis and
about the practice of designing as a cultural technique.[2] This paper

[A]   ᴬᴬ Basically, this is the question that Boris and I were addressing, when we wrote the sentence you quote at the end of this text.

suggests several approaches to the interpretation of designs as single and complex entities.

Environmental models: In a first and tentative approach I proposed to read the two inspiring landscape designs as "environmental models" *(Umweltmodelle).* The intention was to indicate the wide scope of their topics and their potential impact. I coined the expression in reference to Jacob von Uexküll's semiotic concept of the *"Umwelt."*[3] Uexküll's description of sign-processes as the bonds of any living being and, for this being, the relevant traits of its surroundings seemed to offer a promising approach to the understanding of the manifold aspects of our permanent individual, collective and societal exchange with our environment. The concept of environment as a sign-based relation implied the idea that designs were readable as complex offers of sensations, communications, and activities: as new proposals of environmental models. I liked the metaphor and the assumption of a multifaceted relatedness of single designs. I assumed that this perspective provided an adequate approach to the further analysis of the manifold aspects of architecture and landscape architecture.

Crystallization foci: A second helpful reference for the understanding of designs was due to the observation that we tend to talk about designs as single entities emerging in a process: this process starts with a first idea, a first sketch pointing to a future result meeting the aims or the initial intentions of the design.[4] In the course of the process a variety of decisions about future sensations, communications and exchanges will be molded into one single result finally called "the design." This observation led me to Ernst Cassirer's suggestive metaphor of the "crystallization foci." This is how he understands, in his *Philosophy of Symbolic Forms,* the origins of conceptual formations, the beginnings of the separation and organization of an unorganized field into meaningful structures and thus the beginning of language.[5] His vision of a slowly stabilized core and its characteristic structure born out of a non-ordered potentiality provided a useful image for the

understanding of the emergence of designs in architecture or land-scape architecture, even if this image did not reflect the complexity of the knowledge and of the methods involved.

Completeness: At the beginning of a design process, architects or designers do not know in detail how to get to what final result.[6] Design processes start with incomplete knowledge and, at least in principle, questionable methods. [B] Without the intention of change, of challenging rules and routines, there is no need for a process whose most important quality is its capacity to produce new results. Doing a design may imply revisions of established knowledge, the questioning of trusted rules and regulations and the necessity to go beyond common or familiar methodological approaches. Research is required and an expected part of the process. The idea of completeness in the acquisition of useful or necessary knowledge for a design, however, is specific and in so far of interest: any research will be done to exactly the extent that allows for the continuation of the design process. Not each and every aspect of a design has to be tackled with the same curiosity or intensity. Completeness in the sense of doing an exhaustive research on decisive issues is not necessary. The only criterion for its completion is whether the required answers to the open questions are found according to the unfolding aims of the unfolding design process.

Synthesis: The relevant issues in architectural designs are manifold. They include, for example, the necessity of satisfying basic needs such as shelter from weather and climatic conditions; the spatial organization of social processes; mechanic and constructive questions; aesthetic qualities and choices of materials; functional options such as the adaptability to specific social situations; sustainability; ecological consequences and their monitoring or measuring; financial outcomes of investments. There are many more issues at stake. The aspects or layers deemed relevant for a design follow different types of logic. They do not belong to or refer to just one societal subsystem systems theory could identify. This means that their expressions in designs cannot be

[B] | AA I guess this is always the case for any kind of process we could consider to be "creative": by addressing, somehow, the unknown. This is not the case, for example, in the crafts or in automatized processes of mass production. But this is for sure the case in any process related to thinking, by any kind of practices, the environment, that is, the relationships between the thinker or thinkers—the practitioners—and their surroundings. On this basis, this is maybe an acceptable minimal definition of creativity: at the beginning we don't know.

JH Even in a craft process there is also an interesting degree of uncertainty about the exact nature of the outcome, some kind of unpredictability about how the particular piece of material being worked will turn out. One could therefore perhaps also think of designing as a craft process in its own right. Given the nature of the various tools and media that designers have to work with (and through) in order to realize a design—there may be some kind of preconceived image in the designer's mind about what they think they are trying to design, but still some degree of surprise about what appears on the paper (or screen) in front of them. I also discuss this in my own paper, with reference to Merleau-Ponty's understanding of the kind of creativity inherent in the use of language—how our own words often surprise us, and teach us our thoughts.

> SH I understand design/the practice of designing basically as a cultural technique. This includes the idea of renewal that happens in any productive process. In this respect my approach expresses about the same intention as Jonathan's reference to "craft." But reflecting on the concept of craft I have the idea of a well defined process that can be learned in a training led by a master and without the intention of redefining the conditions of the work. Learning to face not defined issues and tasks is not often involved in the practice of any craft or at least much less expected as in architecture, in *Gestaltung,* or as in the arts. I'm sure that many people who design or write or practice a certain craft on a masterly level know the surprise about their own results as they may surmount their own expectations. This is what we may call "creativity" and is certainly related to the idea of change and renewal.

evaluated according to the same rules although all these aspects are involved in the definition of one single design. The key qualification in architectural design may be described as the ability to synthesize [C] heterogeneous issues, different kinds of knowledge including practices, skills and aptitudes and to turn them into one single option.

Universality: This requires a highly qualified and yet non-specialized approach also implying decisions on sensual matters as designs propose visual, tactile, and auditory sensations. I assume that the generalist and universal approach and the close affinity of design processes to sensual options are responsible for the unclear status of architecture and architectural knowledge in academic institutions such as universities, colleges, art schools, and academies. Schools of architecture are found within all these institutions and they all seem to be exceptional compared to the neighboring faculties. Architecture is too artistic to be seen as an obviously serious engineering discipline in technical universities; architecture offers too many pragmatic or profitable solutions for pragmatic problems to be fully accepted as art in art schools; it is too much involved with and dependent on engineering concepts and approaches to impress the humanities still surviving in classic universities. And colleges providing merely practice-oriented courses are observed suspiciously by architects from other schools as they may support less ambitious and more opportunistic habits in building processes. This position of architecture schools among, above, and between other disciplines and practices is a challenge and a special condition resisting specialization in methodology as well as in knowledge. [D] This position is due to the non-restricted approach necessarily implied in seriously innovative work.

Holism: In 2006 Ivar Holm described the striving for "holism" as a guiding principle in so far as it functioned as a regulative idea in architectural education. Used in this context, holism tends to imply "an all-inclusive design perspective which is often regarded as somewhat exclusive to the two design professions" (architecture and industrial

[C] | AA Is it really a "synthesis"? Or better: is it always a synthesis? Could it be possible here to make use of Dieter's concept of "constellation"? (By the way, for architectural designs as well as for this text!). This would be coherent with the idea of a crystal: materialized relationships. Another possible formulation: coherent coexistence.

> SH This question opens up an interesting perspective on the diversity of issues and questions addressed, tamed and finally delivered as a "single option," a single architectural design. Tying together sites, materials, ecological issues, expected affordances etc., means creating constellations—it also means relating all these issues in a way that they cannot be taken out of the "single option" as they have been adapted to each other and tied together in a unique way in the course of the design process. Changing a certain trait may thus result in further changes and even question the design in general. This is the aspect I want to stress in this paragraph. But the comment makes me think about different degrees of integration—there may be aspects in "coherent coexistence" too.

[D] | JH In the UK context, many of the so-called "new" (post-1992) universities have architecture departments within an art school setting, i.e., within schools or faculties of art and design, and these programs have traditionally focused on creative exploration through hands-on making and conceptual, formal and material exploration. In older, more traditional, universities (many of which still have no architecture programs), when they exist, architecture departments tend to sit either within faculties of engineering, where they often take on a strong focus on technology, or faculties of social science, where they may have little synergy or meaningful contact with their neighbor departments, such as geography, sociology, law, education and business. In the latter case they may have more autonomy, but sometimes struggle to establish a distinctive identity, oscillating between the three poles (art, humanities, and technology) that you outline here.

> SH Yes, there are many interesting traditions, a variety of new inventions in architecture programs and different ways of organizing the institutional environment for architectural education. Some traditions go back to schools of national importance, others have developed from aesthetic and/or conceptual innovations. The identity of architecture is indeed a contested question anyway. Still, I cannot see any other reasonable basic concept other than the "universal" idea of architecture including the three poles. Giving up this idea results in an even more specialized and technical approach to building in general and possibly rules out architectural design as an (among other qualities) aesthetic and in this respect critical and "creative" approach to the environment.

design) distinguishing them from other professions involved in design projects.[7] According to Holm, architectural students and students of industrial design are trained to develop "a" design as a single whole, as a project encompassing all possible traits, and understand these traits as necessarily linked. [E] They also learn to see themselves as the "natural person to be in charge of the design process,"[8] a definition of the architect's position seriously challenged through economic, technological and conceptual developments since the 1980s.[9] Holm contrasts this attitude with the usual approach to education in the engineering disciplines. According to his observations, young engineers learn how to solve single problems on a functional basis and are not expected to deal with the general, the "holistic" perspective.[10]

"Holism" may also find a different interpretation stressing the idea of a perfect control of designs. The necessary precondition is, as Holm realizes, the identification of all possible questions, aspects, and relations of a certain design or of designing in general. [F] Holm quotes Harold G. Nelson and Erik Stoltermann who indeed come to this conclusion.[11] This "holistic" approach needs a complete set of tools or at least a complete set of criteria and standards only a complete and final "system" can provide. Its ideal expression would be a single tool defining the ends and means of the process of designing. [G] This option challenges the idea of the architect's professional role as well as the idea of designing as a cultural technique with the unique potential to question even its own methodology.[12]

Inconsistencies: [H] Sometimes, inconsistencies happen to disturb design processes. It is instructive to read Jan Turnovsky's observations on what he called the moment of resistance or inertia of empirical matter *(Widerstandsmoment des empirischen Materials),* the experience of the physicality, the syntactical and the pragmatic necessities of architecture *(die physisch-materiellen, die syntaktischen und die pragmatischen Unabdingbarkeiten der Architektur).*[13] These are possible sources of inconsistencies coming into play when design

[E] | AA Yes, I agree that this is the common way to understand it. But a reinterpretation of the article "a"—precisely by virtue of being an indefinite or undetermined article—can open other possible understandings. "A" here means "one": a singular design. In this sense "a" loses its indeterminacy and actually means "the" or even "this" (design). But rescuing "a" from this surreptitious attempt to fix its undetermined character, "a" can be taken as meaning "a possible" (design): only one possibility among infinite others. This interpretation liberates "a design" to be "the solution" of all problems, but simply one of the possibilities of approaching them. Accepting this alternative interpretation, architectural design comes closer to the arts, which produce artifacts that, on the one hand, are absolutely determined—enclosing a big indeterminacy—and, on the other hand, are only one possibility among many others.

> SH Here I have to defend Holm as he just gives an account of common beliefs without adopting them. Neither would I adopt the idea of "holism". But you are right: This approach implies the definition of architectural design as "the" or "a" "solution" to a "problem." This is not adequate as "problems" may add to the motivations of designs but cannot explain the process or the results.—And yes, architecture is close to art, also in the sense that most designs still happen to be created for just one occasion, a single site, one realization—although traditional copying, modernist seriality and, most recently, mass customization blur this image of architecture. (In the arts these practices are common too—but then not as an economic but as an artistic strategy. This is an important difference.) A more reliable difference between the arts and architecture are the pragmatic aims that have to be considered in architectural designs: They draw a fragile but in many cases quite reliable line between art and *Gestaltung*.

[F] | AA Would it be possible to depart from Holm's concept of holism but substituting "control" with "awareness"? The architect has to (try to) be aware of all aspects but not (necessarily) in order to control them.

> SH This is a great idea—the change of just one word could turn Nelson's and Stoltermann's "fundamental" and controlling concepts into an open approach.

[G] | JH It is also interesting to expand both the process and the product of design to consider what happens before the design, in terms of the design brief (and what goes into it) and after, i.e., the life of the building once realized, and what happens to it during its ongoing occupation. Both ends of the design process struggle to deal with the open-ended and indeterminate nature of these two conditions, which I think is what makes Holm's suggstion of a truly holistic design process quite problematic.

> SH Definitely—the idea of a "holistic design" is problematic and Holm knows quite well that it does not work. There are open ends of course. I think designs begin already with somebody's intention to change something (see above, the paragraph on "completeness") and this is way before there is a brief. I also like the idea that buildings come to their completion through their uses and their users—even if this paper ends with some short remarks on the effects of the realization of a design.

LG A holistic approach to identifying and controlling each and every aspect of a design becomes a normative theory when the conditions we define relate to empirical semantics—in this case, we define the design content, and that means, as you say, full control and a static view of design "creativity." But is it not possible to define a different form of holism as the heuristic description of the possible conditions that allow for architectural design as spatial constitution? In this holistic sense, the architectural process deals with the realm of its possibilities, for instance with respect to its realization through media and aesthetic practices.

> SH I agree, the normative and controlling approach is not productive. Saving the idea (or the term?) of "holism" in the proposed way is definitely an interesting option yet to be explored.

[H] | AA This section reinforces the option (which I favor) of considering architecture as art. Vagueness, indeterminacy, ungraspability, "inconsistencies" are at the core of architectural and artistic practices but not as a problem—not as something to be fought and eliminated or at least reduced—but, on the contrary, as conditions of possibility for these practices to be performed.

> SH I agree in so far as architecture is an art and in this I refer to my answer to one of your former comments. I do hope that architects do not forget to insist on the options opened through this categorization for their work—at least in principle and wherever they find a way to contribute to innovative environments.

principles are on the verge of being defined. [I] Constructive needs and options may have created an order, and this order may produce conflicts, e.g., with an ideal or abstract concept of a design. The disturbing effect does not necessarily depend on missing knowledge or on wrong assumptions. Conflicting principles may lead to unconvincing solutions and even to insurmountable paradoxes, as Turnovsky states[14] referring to Wittgenstein's problems with the positioning of a window in his famous design for his sister's house in Vienna. The window Wittgenstein wanted to place in vain precisely in the middle of an inner side of the wall and also precisely in the middle of its outer side is a monument to the problems of synthesis of different principles, rules, or layers in designs. Designers are not always able to follow all possible and attractive maxims concerning all questions they decide to tackle. The ability to tame inconsistencies, however, seems to belong to the required skills in design processes as well as, sometimes, the sovereignty to accept them. [J]

Coherence: [K] There are several and different criteria for the judgment of architectural designs. Among the desired qualities are what we may call "fitness," in the sense of fitting into a certain condition or in the sense of making a certain condition fit the new design, "suitability," or "coherence" of a design for the buildings, urban structures or open spaces at stake. These criteria may be assumed for any artistic endeavor and so there is some use in consulting theories of art such as Richard Wollheim's reflection on *Art and its Objects.* Wollheim begins his discussion of coherence with reference to incoherencies emerging over time and observes that in the case of works of art no rule applies to gain a generalized view on these phenomena: "it is evident that, though works of art can become incoherent, it is impossible to construct a set of rules or a theory by reference to which this could be exhibited."[15] Even if works of art cannot be judged with respect to their consistency according to defined rules, there is a historically situated knowledge and sensibility, a changing way of identifying the loss

[I] JH But also, I would want to argue (as I did before) that this happens also during the design process, depending on the various material media employed by the designer.

SH Definitely, and I should add that the principles and rules finally organizing a design tend to be defined through all available means suitable as media. When I speak of (the definition of) "principles" I do not refer to "mental" operations but to manifestations depending on media and materials—also, e.g., in the very corporeal sense of working with clay, wax or other materials suitable for modeling.

[J] LG Design is defined by Wittgenstein as a gesture: "You design a door and look at it and say: 'Higher, higher, higher … oh, all right.' "Gesture" What is this? Is it an expression of content? Perhaps the most important thing in connection with aesthetics is what may be called "aesthetic reactions" (Ludwig Wittgenstein, Lectures and Conversations on Aesthetics, II, § 10). Design of course also deals with inconsistency, but to my mind this is not the contrary of consistency but rather a different level on which design constitutes space.

SH I prefer the idea that Wittgenstein demonstrates what design does through the description of a gesture indicating the height of a door. The interesting result is that we, as observers, are able to show "aesthetic reactions"—and accept a certain position of the hand as "oh, all right." The inconsistency Turnovsky discusses and Wittgenstein observes is a different case. Probably it is so annoying as no gesture and no aesthetic approach will solve the basically geometrical problem.

[K] AA What about considering "coherence" in architecture according to a possible general goal or even function of architectural design: to enable different forms of relationship with the environment (as suggested by Boris and I in the final quotation of this text)? Taking this as a basis, the terms to be coherent to one another can be neither exclusively nor primarily intrinsic elements of the architectural design. Instead, the most relevant manifestation of coherence should not be included in the design but refer to the design as enabling condition for the emergence of alternative environments.

SH Wollheim's idea of coherence depends on a traditional idea of "the work of art," and I agree, it does not reflect environments. But he refers to changing concepts of order and to effects of time in general. Thus he questions the "autonomy" and the "timelessness" of "works of art"—an important contribution to the discussion of art in the 1960s and still of interest.

of coherence. The suggestion that there is "a concept for characteriz-
ing deviation"[16] is not a promising approach, although there are hints
and relations to ideas of order or systems to be found even if they do
not match:

> The appeal of the suggestion lies in the idea that we can
> straightforwardly equate the coherence demanded of
> works of art with some clear-cut concept of order as this
> has been systematically developed in some adjacent the-
> ory: for instance, with mathematical concepts of symme-
> try or ratio, alternatively with the concept of *gestalt* as this
> occurs in experimental psychology. The trouble, however,
> is that any such equation yields us at best a characteriza-
> tion of certain versions, or historical variants, of the coher-
> ence demand: it does not give us a universal account: It
> allows for instance for the Renaissance notion of *concin-
> nitas,* [L] which was, significantly enough, developed with
> a mathematical model explicitly in mind: It will not, how-
> ever, allow for the types of order that we find exemplified
> in many of the great Romanesque sculptural ensembles
> or, again, in the work of late Monet or Pollock.[17]

Wollheim assumes changes in the idea of consistency and thus
asserts the historicity in the understanding of what a single "work" may
be. And he insists on the observation that even if rules, models of order
such as systems can be identified behind an assumed inconsistency,
there have never been rules defining the object or work of art in its
totality.

Integration: Nelson Goodman introduced the notion of the "fit"
or "fitness" as an ultimate criterion for a critique of a work of art.[18] This
state of "fitting" and the "concrete technical object" in the sense of
Gilbert Simondon's term are related concepts in so far as both mark
the end of a productive process. Simondon's essay in the philosophy
of technology was an innovative contribution to the long European

[L] | JH But also, according to Marco Frascari, etymologically linked to cooking, meaning the "balance of flavors," referencing a practice that likewise embodies an interesting relationship between rule-based procedures and individual (bodily) skills and sensibilities.

> SH I remember a great exhibition in Berlin's Pfefferberg in the early 1990s *We cook architecture.* Its location was the huge kitchen of the old brewery and the cooks were young and inventive architects. The exploration of "balance" is possibly one of the interesting doorways to the (aesthetic?) core of convincing designs. ("Balance" is possibly akin to the idea of fit, etc., discussed later on in this text.)

history of philosophical thought about concepts of wholeness and unity.[19] According to Simondon, the concrete technical object is completed when the manifold aspects it reflects and the different "forces" it contains are brought together in such a way that the involved powers and functions do not disturb each other, but result in a new arrangement merging the synergies of all implied elements and functions in a harmonious way.[20] This seems to be a useful description of designs too. It is interesting to note that Gilbert Simondon and Nelson Goodman do not attempt to fully explain what their respective ideal integrations in a work of technology or in a work of art may mean. Neither do they assume that anyone, including the designers themselves, is able to understand the complexity involved. Simondon's "concrete object" is not completely analyzable by its makers, and the same applies for the works of art and architecture Nelson Goodman and Catherine Z. Elgin discuss.[21] In this respect the philosopher of technology and the philosophers of signs and representations agree.

Results: [M] There is no rule explaining how and when designs are finished, and they tend to be revised again when it comes to building. In any case it is by decisions that design processes come to their end. The diagnosis that a certain design is finished, at least for the moment, is backed through different reasons and arguments. As designs include answers to many and heterogeneous questions it is not surprising that the criteria for these decisions are manifold. Some of the many criteria refer to norms, to usual practices of crafts and engineering and to other trusted disciplines such as mathematics or biology. These criteria seem to be the least problematic, especially if they are based on practices usually seen as reliable, such as measuring or calculating. Functional qualities, the conviction that pragmatic aims are met and that usability will be achieved with a design are also important. Then there is the evaluation of designs according to less well-defined aesthetic criteria as a certain degree of suitability, unity, and coherence has to be acquired to create sensual satisfaction.[22] The

[M] AA According to my comment on "coherence," I suggest that a fundamental criteria to accept a design to be "finished" is its efficacy in relation to its main goal: to make possible specific relationships that enable the emergence of alternative environments.

SH Question: What defines efficacy and how is it related to aesthetic concepts?

results of design processes have to be seen as aesthetic accomplish-
ments, they have to show an aesthetic necessity, and these criteria are
not easily explained through well defined, explicable and generally accepted standards. Designers and trained critics, however, seem to be
able to agree on the answer to the question whether a design shows
these qualities of suitability, coherence, or fitness and is worth being
accepted as completed in this respect too—even if their evaluations
may differ in other aspects.

   Realizations: Whenever designs are translated into a built structure, they impose their program on the respective situation. They reorganize its material, functional, social, and economic context and
develop manifold relationships reprogramming the broader environment. [N] Usually built structures are intended to serve certain individuals or groups as users.[23] All designs, however, redefine the conditions on a certain spot not just for the expected and intended users
but also for everybody else who enters the sphere of impact of a
proposed building or landscaped site. The visual or climatic effects
of architectural designs, to single out just two possible kinds of effects, are important for the intended users of a certain structure and
for passers-by too. Lengthy discussions on the architecture of public
buildings and especially on designs for public open space are proof
of this wide-reaching effect of building and buildings in general and
are rarely solved with grace and sovereignty. The fact that designs are
never reflected in all their possible traits and aspects and presumably
include some inconsistencies does not prevent designs from implying
decisions on all aspects involved. Some of these decisions are taken
with consideration. But there will also be decisions taken without any
reflection or intention. Even if architects do not reflect on ecology, their
design implies a certain effect on the ecological situation of the environment; even if they try not to dwell on aesthetics, the building will
provide sensations for all senses for all living beings passing or entering the building or site. And even if designs ignore their neighborhood,

[N]   ^AA This formulation, I think, comes close to what I mean by architecture being a condition for the emergence of environments.

the neighborhood's future development will be affected through the newly implemented and thus realized design.

Finis: Designs are powerful entities, unfortunately even if they are done without any ambition. [O] Designing implies an ever-provisional process of synthesizing heterogeneous aspects and relations. The prototypical beginning of a design process in architecture or landscape architecture is the beginning of an exploratory endeavor motivated and regulated through aims, ideas or questions. Designing is not problem-solving. [P] The production of "a design" requires research and a multi-layered analysis of heterogeneous moments involved while their kind and their scope depend on the aims of the project. These become more and more explicit and may even change in the course of the design process. As long as architecture is understood "as an aesthetics-based network of practices of environmental transformation,"[24] the idea of a final definition of design will not be the final idea in designing and the creation of models for new and enriching environments.

^{JH} And, I would add, become meaningful (through use) even if they are made without any intention to be so—to express an idea, to communicate with an audience, or to engage in political dialogue, etc., etc.

 ^{SH} Yes, these are some of the open ends, usually coming up when the designs are realized and the architects have left the scene …

^{AA} That's why design can be considered to be a variety of thinking: because thinking is fundamentally not problem-solving but, as architectural design, an intervention in the common processes of sense-making.

^{ME} This text is designed to reflect the different aspects of design, and it is carefully structured in accordance with the demands of developing a discourse on design processes in terms of the multiple heterogeneous moments involved. The setting is compelling. Therefore, my comment can only be an unnecessary addition, a secondary twist that tries to indicate a speculative space that could open up possibilities for gaining critical distance from the ways in which designs "impose their program" in specific situations. I do this by adding the notion of incongruence to the list of aspects or layers of design processes already addressed in this rich text.

As a left-handed person I am painfully aware of the way in which Fiskars scissors, an internationally known product of Finnish design, impose their program on my body (https://www.fiskars.com/en-us/crafting-and-sewing/products/scissors-and-shears) [accessed Dec 17, 2017]. The configuration of the grip strongly suggests a choice between left and right. I am supposed to use the ones fitted to left hands, not the normal ones. I am faced with two problems: firstly, left-handed scissors are often not available in my working environment, since being right-handed is the norm; secondly, the blades of the left-handed scissors are set the wrong way around for me, since I am used to cut with "normal" scissors. Only, Fiskars makes this painful, with the red-handed grip cutting into the flesh of my left thumb. I am living in a space where a layer of designed functionality is, in many cases, incongruent with my body image.

This seemingly banal example of incongruence hints at the fact that spatial arrangements—and I dare to generalize: arrangements through which sense emerges—involve "total parts," regions full of sense that can never be fully fitted together, since they are not parts of the same map, even if they are intimately related with each other. This might be one reason for the "unclear status of architecture and architectural knowledge." If there is no total map of "sensual options," why, then, would architecture be more encompassing in terms of design processes involved than, for example, graphic design? Euclidian space is often used as the starting point for enumeration of dimensions of sense, but imagination and desire introduce many kinds of twists into this setting, where the ideal of total design is still kept up, too often.

 ^{SH} Thank you all for the rich, suggestive, critical, and challenging comments to my text!

1 Susanne Hauser, "Environmental Models – Landscape Planning and New Descriptions of Nature," in Eco-Semiotics, ed. Hess-Lüttich and Ernest W. B. (Tübingen, Basel: Francke, 2006), 95–104.

2 See e.g. Susanne Hauser, "Verfahren des Überschreitens. Entwerfen als Kulturtechnik," in Wissenschaft Entwerfen. Vom forschenden Entwerfen zur Entwurfsforschung der Architektur, ed. Sabine Ammon and Eva Maria Froschauer (Munich: Fink, 2013), 363–381.

3 Jakob von Uexküll, "Bedeutungslehre," in Streifzüge durch die Umwelten von Tieren und Menschen/Bedeutungslehre, ed. Jakob von Uexküll and Georg Kriszat (Reinbek bei Hamburg: Rowohlt, 1956), 103–159.

4 See Nigel Cross, "Expertise in design: an overview," Design Studies 25 (2004): 427–441. Cross argues that experienced architects and designers tend to solve and analyze the "problems" (of a certain design) at the same time and produce ideas and concepts already at a very early stage of their acquaintance with a certain project.

5 Ernst Cassirer, Philosophie der symbolischen Formen, Dritter Teil, "Phänomenologie der Erkenntnis." (Darmstadt: Wissenschaftliche Buchgemeinschaft, 1990), 135.

6 Even the number of aspects to be explored and their relations cannot be listed conclusively. An enumeration of tasks and aspects would reduce any analytical approach to the processing of a checklist and also neglect the possible relations of different issues. If we understand designing as an exploratory activity with the potential to create new options, it is quite clear that the checking of checklists is not the defining aspect of this activity.

7 Ivar Holm, Ideas and beliefs in architecture: How attitudes, orientations, and underlying assumptions shape the built environment (Oslo: Oslo School of Architecture and Design, 2006), 173.

8 Ibid., 174. Holm links this observation to the question of possible conflicts in building processes.

9 See e.g. Tim Anstey et al., eds., Architecture and Authorship (London: Black Dog Publishing, 2007).

10 Holm, Ideas and beliefs in architecture, 173.

11 Harold G. Nelson and Erik Stoltermann, The design way: intentional change in an unpredictable world: foundations and fundamentals of design competence (Englewood Cliffs NJ: Educational Technology Publications, 2003).

12 See the introduction in: Daniel Gethmann and Susanne Hauser, eds., Kulturtechnik Entwerfen (Bielefeld: transcript, 2009).

13 Jan Turnovsky, Die Poetik eines Mauervorsprungs. Essay (Braunschweig: Vieweg, 1987), 15.

14 Ibid. Turnovsky's fascinating essay insists on the impossibility of the perfect building and the perfect design as he analyzes a geometrically inevitable paradox and inconsistency. This inconsistency is a perfect example of its kind, as it cannot be solved through any alternative strategy.

15 Richard Wollheim, Art and Its Objects. An Introduction to Aesthetics (New York, Evanston, London: Harper & Row, 1968), 120.

16 Ibid., 121.

17 Ibid., 121 f.

18 Nelson Goodman, Ways of Worldmaking (Hassocks, Sussex: The Harvester Press, 1978), 138; Nelson Goodman, Languages of Art (Hassocks, Sussex: The Harvester Press, 1981), 264.

19 The idea of an inseparable whole, a complex unit, a single integrated object, is of course a traditional subject in reflections on art and aesthetics since the eighteenth century; see e.g.: Lucien Dällenbach and Christiaan L. Hart Nibbrig, eds., Fragment und Totalität (Frankfurt am Main: Suhrkamp, 1984).

20 See the first subsection of the first chapter of Gilbert Simondon, On the Mode of Existence of Technical Objects (Minnesota: Univocal Publishing, 2016).

21 "(…) great works are often full of unintended realizations," (Nelson Goodman and Catherine Z. Elgin, Reconceptions in Philosophy & Other Arts and Sciences (Indianapolis, Cambridge: Hackett Publications, 1988), 44.

22 These criteria may be still summed up in (interpretations of) Vitruv's definition of the key requirements in building: firmitas, utilitas, venustas.

23 A non-exclusive design is rare, very difficult to achieve and, if intended, usually commissioned by public authorities such as municipalities.

24 Alex Arteaga, "Architecture without walls: an introduction," in Architecture without walls, ed. Alex Arteaga and Boris Hassenstein (Berlin: Errant Bodies Press, 2016), 4–12, 8.